LIVING LITURGY™

SUNDAY MISSAL

2015

CELEBRATING THE EUCHARIST

LITURGICAL PRESS
Collegeville, Minnesota

www.litpress.org

Published with the approval of the
Committee on Divine Worship
United States Conference of Catholic Bishops

Nihil Obstat: Reverend Robert C. Harren, *Censor deputatus*

Imprimatur: ✠ Most Reverend Donald J. Kettler, J.C.L., Bishop of St. Cloud,
Minnesota, March 20, 2014

The Engish translation of Psalm Responses, Alleluia Verses, Gospel Verses, Lenten Gospel Acclamations from *Lectionary for Mass* © 1969, 1981, 1997, International Commission on English in the Liturgy Corporation (ICEL); excerpts from the English translation of *Rite of Baptism for Children* © 1969, ICEL; excerpts from the English translation of *Holy Communion & Worship of the Eucharist outside Mass* © 1974, ICEL; excerpts from the English translation of *Rite of Confirmation (Second Edition)* © 1975, ICEL; excerpts from the English translation of *Rite of Christian Initiation of Adults* © 1985, ICEL; excerpts from the English translation of *The Roman Missal* © 2010, ICEL. All rights reserved.

Scripture readings are taken from the *Lectionary for Mass for Use in the Dioceses of the United States of America, second typical edition* Copyright © 1970, 1986, 1997, 1998, 2001 Confraternity of Christian Doctrine, Inc., Washington, D.C. All rights reserved. No part of this book may be reproduced or transmitted in any form or by any means, electronic or mechanical, including photocopying, recording, or by any information storage and retrieval system, without permission in writing from the copyright owner.

Cover design by Ann Blattner. Art by Martin Erspamer, OSB, a monk of St. Meinrad Archabbey, Indiana.

© 2014 by Order of Saint Benedict, Collegeville, Minnesota. All rights reserved. No part of this book may be reproduced in any form, by print, microfilm, microfiche, mechanical recording, photocopying, translation, or by any other means, known or yet unknown, for any purpose except brief quotations in reviews, without the previous written permission of Liturgical Press, Saint John's Abbey, P.O. Box 7500, Collegeville, Minnesota 56321-7500. Printed in the United States of America.

ISSN 1949-1166
ISBN 978-0-8146-3815-6

Contents

	The Order of Mass	1
	Celebration of the Liturgy of the Word [with Holy Communion]	27
November 30	First Sunday of Advent	31
December 7	Second Sunday of Advent	35
December 8	The Immaculate Conception of the Blessed Virgin Mary	40
December 14	Third Sunday of Advent	45
December 21	Fourth Sunday of Advent	50
December 24	The Nativity of the Lord (Christmas)—At the Vigil Mass	55
December 25	The Nativity of the Lord—At the Mass during the Night	61
December 25	The Nativity of the Lord—At the Mass at Dawn	65
December 25	The Nativity of the Lord—At the Mass during the Day	69
December 28	The Holy Family of Jesus, Mary, and Joseph	74
January 1	Solemnity of Mary, the Holy Mother of God	80
January 4	The Epiphany of the Lord—At the Vigil Mass	84
January 5	The Epiphany of the Lord—At the Mass during the Day	85
January 11	The Baptism of the Lord	90
January 18	Second Sunday in Ordinary Time	95
January 25	Third Sunday in Ordinary Time	99
February 1	Fourth Sunday in Ordinary Time	103
February 8	Fifth Sunday in Ordinary Time	108
February 15	Sixth Sunday in Ordinary Time	112
February 18	Ash Wednesday	116
February 22	First Sunday of Lent	122
March 1	Second Sunday of Lent	126
March 8	Third Sunday of Lent	131
March 15	Fourth Sunday of Lent	137
March 22	Fifth Sunday of Lent	142
March 29	Palm Sunday of the Lord's Passion	147
April 2	Thursday of the Lord's Supper (Holy Thursday)—At the Evening Mass	165
April 3	Friday of the Passion of the Lord (Good Friday)	171
April 4	Holy Saturday—The Easter Vigil in the Holy Night	190
April 5	Easter Sunday of the Resurrection of the Lord—At the Mass during the Day	228
April 12	Second Sunday of Easter (or of Divine Mercy)	234
April 19	Third Sunday of Easter	239
April 26	Fourth Sunday of Easter	243
May 3	Fifth Sunday of Easter	247
May 10	Sixth Sunday of Easter	252

May 13 or 16	The Ascension of the Lord—Vigil Mass	256
May 14 or 17	The Ascension of the Lord—Mass During the Day	257
May 17	Seventh Sunday of Easter	263
May 23	Pentecost Sunday—Vigil Mass	268
May 24	Pentecost Sunday—Mass during the Day	272
May 31	The Most Holy Trinity	280
June 7	The Most Holy Body and Blood of Christ	284
June 14	Eleventh Sunday in Ordinary Time	291
June 21	Twelfth Sunday in Ordinary Time	296
June 23	The Nativity of St. John the Baptist—At the Vigil Mass	300
June 24	The Nativity of St. John the Baptist—At the Mass during the Day	305
June 28	Thirteenth Sunday in Ordinary Time	309
July 5	Fourteenth Sunday in Ordinary Time	314
July 12	Fifteenth Sunday in Ordinary Time	319
July 19	Sixteenth Sunday in Ordinary Time	324
July 26	Seventeenth Sunday in Ordinary Time	328
August 2	Eighteenth Sunday in Ordinary Time	333
August 9	Nineteenth Sunday in Ordinary Time	338
August 14	The Assumption of the Blessed Virgin Mary—At the Vigil Mass	343
August 15	The Assumption of the Blessed Virgin Mary—At the Mass during the Day	346
August 16	Twentieth Sunday in Ordinary Time	351
August 23	Twenty-First Sunday in Ordinary Time	356
August 30	Twenty-Second Sunday in Ordinary Time	362
September 6	Twenty-Third Sunday in Ordinary Time	367
September 13	Twenty-Fourth Sunday in Ordinary Time	371
September 20	Twenty-Fifth Sunday in Ordinary Time	376
September 27	Twenty-Sixth Sunday in Ordinary Time	380
October 4	Twenty-Seventh Sunday in Ordinary Time	385
October 11	Twenty-Eighth Sunday in Ordinary Time	390
October 18	Twenty-Ninth Sunday in Ordinary Time	395
October 25	Thirtieth Sunday in Ordinary Time	400
November 1	All Saints	404
November 8	Thirty-Second Sunday in Ordinary Time	409
November 15	Thirty-Third Sunday in Ordinary Time	414
November 22	Our Lord Jesus Christ, King of the Universe	418
	Eucharistic Prayer for Reconciliation I	423
	Personal Prayers	426

The Order of Mass

The Introductory Rites

Entrance Chant STAND

Sign of the Cross
Priest: In the name of the Father, and of the Son, and of the Holy Spirit.
People: Amen.

Greeting

A **Priest:** The grace of our Lord Jesus Christ,
and the love of God,
and the communion of the Holy Spirit
be with you all.
People: And with your spirit.

B **Priest:** Grace to you and peace from God our Father
and the Lord Jesus Christ.
People: And with your spirit.

C **Priest:** The Lord be with you.
People: And with your spirit.

Penitential Act

A **Priest:** Brethren (brothers and sisters), let us acknowledge our sins,
and so prepare ourselves to celebrate the sacred mysteries. (Pause)

All: **I confess to almighty God
and to you, my brothers and sisters,
that I have greatly sinned,
in my thoughts and in my words,
in what I have done and in what I have failed to do,**

And, striking their breast, they say:

**through my fault, through my fault,
through my most grievous fault;**

Then they continue:

**therefore I ask blessed Mary ever-Virgin,
all the Angels and Saints,
and you, my brothers and sisters,
to pray for me to the Lord our God.**

Priest: May almighty God have mercy on us,
forgive us our sins,
and bring us to everlasting life.

People: **Amen.**

B Priest: Brethren (brothers and sisters), let us acknowledge our sins,
and so prepare ourselves to celebrate the sacred mysteries. (Pause)

Priest: Have mercy on us, O Lord.
People: **For we have sinned against you.**

Priest: Show us, O Lord, your mercy.
People: **And grant us your salvation.**

Priest: May almighty God have mercy on us,
forgive us our sins,
and bring us to everlasting life.

People: **Amen.**

C *These or other invocations may be used:*

Priest: Brethren (brothers and sisters), let us acknowledge our sins,
and so prepare ourselves to celebrate the sacred mysteries. (Pause)

Priest (Deacon or another minister):
You were sent to heal the contrite of heart:
Lord, have mercy.   Or: Kyrie, eleison.
People: **Lord, have mercy.   Or: Kyrie, eleison.**

Priest: You came to call sinners:
Christ, have mercy.   Or: Christe, eleison.
People: **Christ, have mercy.   Or: Christe, eleison.**

The Order of Mass 3

Priest: You are seated at the right hand of the Father to
intercede for us:
Lord, have mercy. Or: Kyrie, eleison.
People: **Lord, have mercy.** Or: **Kyrie, eleison.**

Priest: May almighty God have mercy on us,
forgive us our sins,
and bring us to everlasting life.
People: **Amen.**

KYRIE

The Kyrie, eleison (Lord, have mercy) invocations follow, unless they have just occurred in a formula of the Penitential Act.

℣. Lord, have mercy.   ℟. **Lord, have mercy.**
℣. Christ, have mercy.   ℟. **Christ, have mercy.**
℣. Lord, have mercy.   ℟. **Lord, have mercy.**

Or:

℣. Kyrie, eleison.   ℟. **Kyrie, eleison.**
℣. Christe, eleison.   ℟. **Christe, eleison.**
℣. Kyrie, eleison.   ℟. **Kyrie, eleison.**

GLORIA

All: **Glory to God in the highest,
and on earth peace to people of good will.**

**We praise you,
we bless you,
we adore you,
we glorify you,
we give you thanks for your great glory,
Lord God, heavenly King,
O God, almighty Father.**

**Lord Jesus Christ, Only Begotten Son,
Lord God, Lamb of God, Son of the Father,
you take away the sins of the world,
   have mercy on us;
you take away the sins of the world,
   receive our prayer;
you are seated at the right hand of the Father,
   have mercy on us.**

**For you alone are the Holy One,
you alone are the Lord,
you alone are the Most High,
Jesus Christ,
with the Holy Spirit,
in the glory of God the Father.
Amen.**

Collect (Opening Prayer)

Priest: **Let us pray.**

All pray in silence with the Priest for a while.

Then the Priest, with hands extended, says the Collect prayer, at the end of which the people acclaim:

Amen.

The Liturgy of the Word

First Reading   SIT

Then the reader goes to the ambo and reads the First Reading, while all sit and listen.

To indicate the end of the reading, the reader acclaims:

The word of the Lord.

All: **Thanks be to God.**

Responsorial Psalm

The psalmist or cantor sings or says the Psalm, with the people making the response.

Second Reading

After this, if there is to be a Second Reading, a reader reads it from the ambo, as above.

To indicate the end of the reading, the reader acclaims:

The word of the Lord.

All: **Thanks be to God.**

Gospel Acclamation   STAND

There follows the **Alleluia** or another chant laid down by the rubrics, as the liturgical time requires.

Gospel Dialogue

Deacon or Priest: The Lord be with you.
People: **And with your spirit.**
Deacon or Priest: A reading from the holy Gospel according to N.
People: **Glory to you, O Lord.**

Gospel Reading

At the end of the Gospel, the Deacon, or the Priest, acclaims:
The Gospel of the Lord.
All: **Praise to you, Lord Jesus Christ.**

Homily   SIT

Profession of Faith   STAND

All: **I believe in one God,
the Father almighty,
maker of heaven and earth,
of all things visible and invisible.**

**I believe in one Lord Jesus Christ,
the Only Begotten Son of God,
born of the Father before all ages.
God from God, Light from Light,
true God from true God,
begotten, not made, consubstantial with the Father;
through him all things were made.
For us men and for our salvation
he came down from heaven,**

At the words that follow, up to and including **and became man**, all bow.

   **and by the Holy Spirit was incarnate of the Virgin Mary,
   and became man.**

**For our sake he was crucified under Pontius Pilate,
he suffered death and was buried,
and rose again on the third day
in accordance with the Scriptures.**

He ascended into heaven
and is seated at the right hand of the Father.
He will come again in glory
to judge the living and the dead
and his kingdom will have no end.

I believe in the Holy Spirit, the Lord, the giver of life,
who proceeds from the Father and the Son,
who with the Father and the Son is adored and glorified,
who has spoken through the prophets.

I believe in one, holy, catholic and apostolic Church.
I confess one Baptism for the forgiveness of sins
and I look forward to the resurrection of the dead
and the life of the world to come. Amen.

Instead of the Niceno-Constantinopolitan Creed, especially during Lent and Easter Time, the baptismal Symbol of the Roman Church, known as the Apostles' Creed, may be used.

All: **I believe in God,
the Father almighty,
Creator of heaven and earth,
and in Jesus Christ, his only Son, our Lord,**

At the words that follow, up to and including the Virgin Mary, all bow.

**who was conceived by the Holy Spirit,
born of the Virgin Mary,
suffered under Pontius Pilate,
was crucified, died and was buried;
he descended into hell;
on the third day he rose again from the dead;
he ascended into heaven,
and is seated at the right hand of God the Father almighty;
from there he will come to judge the living and the dead.**

**I believe in the Holy Spirit,
the holy catholic Church,
the communion of saints,
the forgiveness of sins,
the resurrection of the body,
and life everlasting. Amen.**

Universal Prayer
(*or* Prayer of the Faithful *or* Bidding Prayers)

The Liturgy of the Eucharist

Presentation and Preparation of the Gifts   SIT
The Priest, standing at the altar, takes the paten with the bread and holds it slightly raised above the altar with both hands, saying in a low voice:

Blessed are you, Lord God of all creation,
for through your goodness we have received
the bread we offer you:
fruit of the earth and work of human hands,
it will become for us the bread of life.

If, however, the Offertory Chant is not sung, the Priest may speak these words aloud; at the end, the people may acclaim:

Blessed be God for ever.

The Deacon, or the Priest, pours wine and a little water into the chalice, saying quietly:

By the mystery of this water and wine
may we come to share in the divinity of Christ
who humbled himself to share in our humanity.

The Priest then takes the chalice and holds it slightly raised above the altar with both hands, saying in a low voice:

Blessed are you, Lord God of all creation,
for through your goodness we have received
the wine we offer you:
fruit of the vine and work of human hands,
it will become our spiritual drink.

If, however, the Offertory Chant is not sung, the Priest may speak these words aloud; at the end, the people may acclaim:

Blessed be God for ever.

After this, the Priest, bowing profoundly, says quietly:

With humble spirit and contrite heart
may we be accepted by you, O Lord,
and may our sacrifice in your sight this day
be pleasing to you, Lord God.

Then the Priest, standing at the side of the altar, washes his hands, saying quietly:

Wash me, O Lord, from my iniquity
and cleanse me from my sin.

Standing at the middle of the altar, facing the people, extending and then joining his hands, he says:

Pray, brethren (brothers and sisters),
that my sacrifice and yours
may be acceptable to God,
the almighty Father.

The people rise and reply: **STAND**

**May the Lord accept the sacrifice at your hands
for the praise and glory of his name,
for our good
and the good of all his holy Church.**

Prayer over the Offerings

Then the Priest, with hands extended, says the Prayer over the Offerings, at the end of which the people acclaim:

Amen.

The Eucharistic Prayer

Priest: The Lord be with you.
People: **And with your spirit.**
Priest: Lift up your hearts.
People: **We lift them up to the Lord.**
Priest: Let us give thanks to the Lord our God.
People: **It is right and just.**

Preface

our weak human nature,
which he had united to himself,
and in communion with those whose memory we venerate,
especially the glorious ever-Virgin Mary,
Mother of our God and Lord, Jesus Christ, †

On Pentecost Sunday
Celebrating the most sacred day of Pentecost,
on which the Holy Spirit
appeared to the Apostles in tongues of fire,
and in communion with those whose memory we venerate,
especially the glorious ever-Virgin Mary,
Mother of our God and Lord, Jesus Christ, †

Therefore, Lord, we pray:
graciously accept this oblation of our service,
that of your whole family;
order our days in your peace,
and command that we be delivered from eternal damnation
and counted among the flock of those you have chosen.
(Through Christ our Lord. Amen.)

From the Mass of the Easter Vigil until the Second Sunday of Easter
Therefore, Lord, we pray:
graciously accept this oblation of our service,
that of your whole family,
which we make to you
also for those to whom you have been pleased to give
the new birth of water and the Holy Spirit,
granting them forgiveness of all their sins:
order our days in your peace,
and command that we be delivered from eternal damnation
and counted among the flock of those you have chosen.
(Through Christ our Lord. Amen.)

Be pleased, O God, we pray,
to bless, acknowledge,
and approve this offering in every respect;
make it spiritual and acceptable,
so that it may become for us
the Body and Blood of your most beloved Son,
our Lord Jesus Christ.

On the day before he was to suffer,
he took bread in his holy and venerable hands,
and with eyes raised to heaven

to you, O God, his almighty Father,
giving you thanks, he said the blessing,
broke the bread
and gave it to his disciples, saying:

**Take this, all of you, and eat of it,
for this is my Body,
which will be given up for you.**

In a similar way, when supper was ended,
he took this precious chalice
in his holy and venerable hands,
and once more giving you thanks, he said the blessing
and gave the chalice to his disciples, saying:

**Take this, all of you, and drink from it,
for this is the chalice of my Blood,
the Blood of the new and eternal covenant,
which will be poured out for you and for many
for the forgiveness of sins.**

Do this in memory of me.

The mystery of faith.

And the people continue, acclaiming:

A We proclaim your Death, O Lord,
and profess your Resurrection
until you come again.

B When we eat this Bread and drink this Cup,
we proclaim your Death, O Lord,
until you come again.

C Save us, Savior of the world,
for by your Cross and Resurrection
you have set us free.

Priest:
Therefore, O Lord,
as we celebrate the memorial of the blessed Passion,
the Resurrection from the dead,
and the glorious Ascension into heaven
of Christ, your Son, our Lord,
we, your servants and your holy people,
offer to your glorious majesty
from the gifts that you have given us,
this pure victim,
this holy victim,

this spotless victim,
the holy Bread of eternal life
and the Chalice of everlasting salvation.

Be pleased to look upon these offerings
with a serene and kindly countenance,
and to accept them,
as once you were pleased to accept
the gifts of your servant Abel the just,
the sacrifice of Abraham, our father in faith,
and the offering of your high priest Melchizedek,
a holy sacrifice, a spotless victim.

In humble prayer we ask you, almighty God:
command that these gifts be borne
by the hands of your holy Angel
to your altar on high
in the sight of your divine majesty,
so that all of us, who through this participation at the altar
receive the most holy Body and Blood of your Son,
may be filled with every grace and heavenly blessing.
(Through Christ our Lord. Amen.)

Commemoration of the Dead

Remember also, Lord, your servants N. and N.,
who have gone before us with the sign of faith
and rest in the sleep of peace.

Grant them, O Lord, we pray,
and all who sleep in Christ,
a place of refreshment, light and peace.
(Through Christ our Lord. Amen.)

To us, also, your servants, who, though sinners,
hope in your abundant mercies,
graciously grant some share
and fellowship with your holy Apostles and Martyrs:
with John the Baptist, Stephen,
Matthias, Barnabas,
(Ignatius, Alexander,
Marcellinus, Peter,
Felicity, Perpetua,
Agatha, Lucy,
Agnes, Cecilia, Anastasia)
and all your Saints;
admit us, we beseech you,
into their company,
not weighing our merits,

but granting us your pardon,
through Christ our Lord.

Through whom
you continue to make all these good things, O Lord;
you sanctify them, fill them with life,
bless them, and bestow them upon us.

Through him, and with him, and in him,
O God, almighty Father,
in the unity of the Holy Spirit,
all glory and honor is yours,
for ever and ever.

People: **Amen.**

Then follows the Communion Rite, p. 23.

Eucharistic Prayer II

Preface
It is truly right and just, our duty and our salvation,
always and everywhere to give you thanks, Father most holy,
through your beloved Son, Jesus Christ,
your Word through whom you made all things,
whom you sent as our Savior and Redeemer,
incarnate by the Holy Spirit and born of the Virgin.

Fulfilling your will and gaining for you a holy people,
he stretched out his hands as he endured his Passion,
so as to break the bonds of death and manifest the resurrection.

And so, with the Angels and all the Saints
we declare your glory,
as with one voice we acclaim:

Holy, Holy, Holy Lord God of hosts.
Heaven and earth are full of your glory.
Hosanna in the highest.
Blessed is he who comes in the name of the Lord.
Hosanna in the highest.

Priest:
You are indeed Holy, O Lord,
the fount of all holiness.
Make holy, therefore, these gifts, we pray,
by sending down your Spirit upon them like the dewfall,
so that they may become for us
the Body and ✠ Blood of our Lord Jesus Christ.

At the time he was betrayed
and entered willingly into his Passion,

he took bread and, giving thanks, broke it,
and gave it to his disciples, saying:

TAKE THIS, ALL OF YOU, AND EAT OF IT,
FOR THIS IS MY BODY,
WHICH WILL BE GIVEN UP FOR YOU.

In a similar way, when supper was ended,
he took the chalice
and, once more giving thanks,
he gave it to his disciples, saying:

TAKE THIS, ALL OF YOU, AND DRINK FROM IT,
FOR THIS IS THE CHALICE OF MY BLOOD,
THE BLOOD OF THE NEW AND ETERNAL COVENANT,
WHICH WILL BE POURED OUT FOR YOU AND FOR MANY
FOR THE FORGIVENESS OF SINS.

DO THIS IN MEMORY OF ME.

The mystery of faith.

People:

A We proclaim your Death, O Lord,
and profess your Resurrection
until you come again.

B When we eat this Bread and drink this Cup,
we proclaim your Death, O Lord,
until you come again.

C Save us, Savior of the world,
for by your Cross and Resurrection
you have set us free.

Priest:
Therefore, as we celebrate
the memorial of his Death and Resurrection,
we offer you, Lord,
the Bread of life and the Chalice of salvation,
giving thanks that you have held us worthy
to be in your presence and minister to you.

Humbly we pray
that, partaking of the Body and Blood of Christ,
we may be gathered into one by the Holy Spirit.

Remember, Lord, your Church,
spread throughout the world,
and bring her to the fullness of charity,

together with N. our Pope and N. our Bishop*
and all the clergy.

> In Masses for the Dead, the following may be added:
> Remember your servant N.,
> whom you have called (today)
> from this world to yourself.
> Grant that he (she) who was united with your Son in a death like his,
> may also be one with him in his Resurrection.

Remember also our brothers and sisters
who have fallen asleep in the hope of the resurrection,
and all who have died in your mercy:
welcome them into the light of your face.
Have mercy on us all, we pray,
that with the Blessed Virgin Mary, Mother of God,
with blessed Joseph, her Spouse,
with the blessed Apostles,
and all the Saints who have pleased you throughout the ages,
we may merit to be coheirs to eternal life,
and may praise and glorify you
through your Son, Jesus Christ.

Through him, and with him, and in him,
O God, almighty Father,
in the unity of the Holy Spirit,
all glory and honor is yours,
for ever and ever.

People: Amen.

Then follows the Communion Rite, p. 23.

EUCHARISTIC PRAYER III
Priest:
You are indeed Holy, O Lord,
and all you have created
rightly gives you praise,
for through your Son our Lord Jesus Christ,
by the power and working of the Holy Spirit,
you give life to all things and make them holy,
and you never cease to gather a people to yourself,
so that from the rising of the sun to its setting
a pure sacrifice may be offered to your name.

---

* Mention may be made here of the Coadjutor Bishop, or Auxiliary Bishops,
as noted in the *General Instruction of the Roman Missal*, no. 149.

Therefore, O Lord, we humbly implore you:
by the same Spirit graciously make holy
these gifts we have brought to you for consecration,
that they may become the Body and ✠ Blood
of your Son our Lord Jesus Christ,
at whose command we celebrate these mysteries.

For on the night he was betrayed
he himself took bread,
and, giving you thanks, he said the blessing,
broke the bread and gave it to his disciples, saying:

Take this, all of you, and eat of it,
for this is my Body,
which will be given up for you.

In a similar way, when supper was ended,
he took the chalice,
and, giving you thanks, he said the blessing,
and gave the chalice to his disciples, saying:

Take this, all of you, and drink from it,
for this is the chalice of my Blood,
the Blood of the new and eternal covenant,
which will be poured out for you and for many
for the forgiveness of sins.

Do this in memory of me.

The mystery of faith.

People:

A We proclaim your Death, O Lord,
and profess your Resurrection
until you come again.

B When we eat this Bread and drink this Cup,
we proclaim your Death, O Lord,
until you come again.

C Save us, Savior of the world,
for by your Cross and Resurrection
you have set us free.

Priest:
Therefore, O Lord, as we celebrate the memorial
of the saving Passion of your Son,
his wondrous Resurrection
and Ascension into heaven,
and as we look forward to his second coming,

we offer you in thanksgiving
this holy and living sacrifice.

Look, we pray, upon the oblation of your Church
and, recognizing the sacrificial Victim by whose death
you willed to reconcile us to yourself,
grant that we, who are nourished
by the Body and Blood of your Son
and filled with his Holy Spirit,
may become one body, one spirit in Christ.

May he make of us
an eternal offering to you,
so that we may obtain an inheritance with your elect,
especially with the most Blessed Virgin Mary, Mother of God,
with blessed Joseph, her Spouse,
with your blessed Apostles and glorious Martyrs
(with Saint N.: the Saint of the day or Patron Saint)
and with all the Saints,
on whose constant intercession in your presence
we rely for unfailing help.

May this Sacrifice of our reconciliation,
we pray, O Lord,
advance the peace and salvation of all the world.
Be pleased to confirm in faith and charity
your pilgrim Church on earth,
with your servant N. our Pope and N. our Bishop,*
the Order of Bishops, all the clergy,
and the entire people you have gained for your own.

Listen graciously to the prayers of this family,
whom you have summoned before you:
in your compassion, O merciful Father,
gather to yourself all your children
scattered throughout the world.

† To our departed brothers and sisters
and to all who were pleasing to you
at their passing from this life,
give kind admittance to your kingdom.
There we hope to enjoy for ever the fullness of your glory
through Christ our Lord,
through whom you bestow on the world all that is good. †

---

*Mention may be made here of the Coadjutor Bishop, or Auxiliary Bishops, as noted in the *General Instruction of the Roman Missal*, no. 149.

The Order of Mass

> When this Eucharistic Prayer is used in Masses for the Dead, the following may be said:
>
> † Remember your servant N.
> whom you have called (today)
> from this world to yourself.
> Grant that he (she) who was united with your Son in a death like his,
> may also be one with him in his Resurrection,
> when from the earth
> he will raise up in the flesh those who have died,
> and transform our lowly body
> after the pattern of his own glorious body.
> To our departed brothers and sisters, too,
> and to all who were pleasing to you
> at their passing from this life,
> give kind admittance to your kingdom.
> There we hope to enjoy for ever the fullness of your glory,
> when you will wipe away every tear from our eyes.
> For seeing you, our God, as you are,
> we shall be like you for all the ages
> and praise you without end,
> through Christ our Lord,
> through whom you bestow on the world all that is good. †

Through him, and with him, and in him,
O God, almighty Father,
in the unity of the Holy Spirit,
all glory and honor is yours,
for ever and ever.

People: **Amen.**

Then follows the Communion Rite, p. 23.

Eucharistic Prayer IV

Preface
It is truly right to give you thanks,
truly just to give you glory, Father most holy,
for you are the one God living and true,
existing before all ages and abiding for all eternity,
dwelling in unapproachable light;
yet you, who alone are good, the source of life,
have made all that is,
so that you might fill your creatures with blessings
and bring joy to many of them by the glory of your light.

And so, in your presence are countless hosts of Angels,
who serve you day and night

and, gazing upon the glory of your face,
glorify you without ceasing.

With them we, too, confess your name in exultation,
giving voice to every creature under heaven,
as we acclaim:

Holy, Holy, Holy Lord God of hosts.
Heaven and earth are full of your glory.
Hosanna in the highest.
Blessed is he who comes in the name of the Lord.
Hosanna in the highest.

Priest:
We give you praise, Father most holy,
for you are great
and you have fashioned all your works
in wisdom and in love.
You formed man in your own image
and entrusted the whole world to his care,
so that in serving you alone, the Creator,
he might have dominion over all creatures.
And when through disobedience he had lost your friendship,
you did not abandon him to the domain of death.
For you came in mercy to the aid of all,
so that those who seek might find you.
Time and again you offered them covenants
and through the prophets
taught them to look forward to salvation.

And you so loved the world, Father most holy,
that in the fullness of time
you sent your Only Begotten Son to be our Savior.
Made incarnate by the Holy Spirit
and born of the Virgin Mary,
he shared our human nature
in all things but sin.
To the poor he proclaimed the good news of salvation,
to prisoners, freedom,
and to the sorrowful of heart, joy.
To accomplish your plan,
he gave himself up to death,
and, rising from the dead,
he destroyed death and restored life.

And that we might live no longer for ourselves
but for him who died and rose again for us,
he sent the Holy Spirit from you, Father,

as the first fruits for those who believe,
so that, bringing to perfection his work in the world,
he might sanctify creation to the full.

Therefore, O Lord, we pray:
may this same Holy Spirit
graciously sanctify these offerings,
that they may become
the Body and ✜ Blood of our Lord Jesus Christ
for the celebration of this great mystery,
which he himself left us
as an eternal covenant.

For when the hour had come
for him to be glorified by you, Father most holy,
having loved his own who were in the world,
he loved them to the end:
and while they were at supper,
he took bread, blessed and broke it,
and gave it to his disciples, saying:

TAKE THIS, ALL OF YOU, AND EAT OF IT,
FOR THIS IS MY BODY,
WHICH WILL BE GIVEN UP FOR YOU.

In a similar way,
taking the chalice filled with the fruit of the vine,
he gave thanks,
and gave the chalice to his disciples, saying:

TAKE THIS, ALL OF YOU, AND DRINK FROM IT,
FOR THIS IS THE CHALICE OF MY BLOOD,
THE BLOOD OF THE NEW AND ETERNAL COVENANT,
WHICH WILL BE POURED OUT FOR YOU AND FOR MANY
FOR THE FORGIVENESS OF SINS.

DO THIS IN MEMORY OF ME.

The mystery of faith.

People:

A **We proclaim your Death, O Lord,**
   and profess your Resurrection
   until you come again.

B **When we eat this Bread and drink this Cup,**
   we proclaim your Death, O Lord,
   until you come again.

22 *The Order of Mass*

C **Save us, Savior of the world,
for by your Cross and Resurrection
you have set us free.**

Priest:
Therefore, O Lord,
as we now celebrate the memorial of our redemption,
we remember Christ's Death
and his descent to the realm of the dead,
we proclaim his Resurrection
and his Ascension to your right hand,
and, as we await his coming in glory,
we offer you his Body and Blood,
the sacrifice acceptable to you
which brings salvation to the whole world.

Look, O Lord, upon the Sacrifice
which you yourself have provided for your Church,
and grant in your loving kindness
to all who partake of this one Bread and one Chalice
that, gathered into one body by the Holy Spirit,
they may truly become a living sacrifice in Christ
to the praise of your glory.

Therefore, Lord, remember now
all for whom we offer this sacrifice:
especially your servant N. our Pope,
N. our Bishop,* and the whole Order of Bishops,
all the clergy,
those who take part in this offering,
those gathered here before you,
your entire people,
and all who seek you with a sincere heart.

Remember also
those who have died in the peace of your Christ
and all the dead,
whose faith you alone have known.

To all of us, your children,
grant, O merciful Father,
that we may enter into a heavenly inheritance
with the Blessed Virgin Mary, Mother of God,
with blessed Joseph, her Spouse,
and with your Apostles and Saints in your kingdom.

---

* Mention may be made here of the Coadjutor Bishop, or Auxiliary Bishops, as noted in the *General Instruction of the Roman Missal*, no. 149.

There, with the whole of creation,
freed from the corruption of sin and death,
may we glorify you through Christ our Lord,
through whom you bestow on the world all that is good.

Through him, and with him, and in him,
O God, almighty Father,
in the unity of the Holy Spirit,
all glory and honor is yours,
for ever and ever.

People: **Amen.**

The Communion Rite   STAND

The Lord's Prayer

Priest: At the Savior's command
and formed by divine teaching,
we dare to say:

All: **Our Father, who art in heaven,
hallowed be thy name;
thy kingdom come,
thy will be done
on earth as it is in heaven.
Give us this day our daily bread,
and forgive us our trespasses,
as we forgive those who trespass against us;
and lead us not into temptation,
but deliver us from evil.**

Priest: Deliver us, Lord, we pray, from every evil,
graciously grant peace in our days,
that, by the help of your mercy,
we may be always free from sin
and safe from all distress,
as we await the blessed hope
and the coming of our Savior, Jesus Christ.

All: **For the kingdom,
the power and the glory are yours
now and for ever.**

Sign of Peace

Priest: Lord Jesus Christ,
who said to your Apostles:
Peace I leave you, my peace I give you,
look not on our sins,
but on the faith of your Church,
and graciously grant her peace and unity
in accordance with your will.
Who live and reign for ever and ever.

People: Amen.

Priest: The peace of the Lord be with you always.

People: And with your spirit.

Then, if appropriate, the Deacon, or the Priest, adds:

Let us offer each other the sign of peace.

Fraction of the Bread

The Priest says quietly:

Priest: May this mingling of the Body and Blood
of our Lord Jesus Christ
bring eternal life to us who receive it.

**All: Lamb of God, you take away the sins of the world,
have mercy on us.
Lamb of God, you take away the sins of the world,
have mercy on us.
Lamb of God, you take away the sins of the world,
grant us peace.**

The Priest says quietly: **KNEEL**

Lord Jesus Christ, Son of the living God,
who, by the will of the Father
and the work of the Holy Spirit,
through your Death gave life to the world,
free me by this, your most holy Body and Blood,
from all my sins and from every evil;
keep me always faithful to your commandments,
and never let me be parted from you.

Or:

The Order of Mass 25

May the receiving of your Body and Blood,
Lord Jesus Christ,
not bring me to judgment and condemnation,
but through your loving mercy
be for me protection in mind and body
and a healing remedy.

INVITATION TO COMMUNION

Priest: Behold the Lamb of God,
behold him who takes away the sins of the world.
Blessed are those called to the supper of the Lamb.

All: **Lord, I am not worthy
that you should enter under my roof,
but only say the word
and my soul shall be healed.**

COMMUNION

The Priest says quietly: May the Body of Christ
keep me safe for eternal life.

The Priest says quietly: May the Blood of Christ
keep me safe for eternal life.   **STAND**

The Priest says to each of the communicants: The Body of Christ.
The communicant replies: **Amen.**

Priest says quietly: What has passed our lips as food, O Lord,
may we possess in purity of heart,
that what has been given to us in time
may be our healing for eternity.

PRAYER AFTER COMMUNION   **STAND**
The Priest says: Let us pray.
At the end the people acclaim: **Amen.**

THE CONCLUDING RITES

FINAL BLESSING
Priest: The Lord be with you.
People: **And with your spirit.**

Priest: May almighty God bless you,
the Father, and the Son, ✠ and the Holy Spirit.

People: Amen.

Dismissal

The Deacon, or the Priest himself:

Go forth, the Mass is ended.

Or:

Go and announce the Gospel of the Lord.

Or:

Go in peace, glorifying the Lord by your life.

Or:

Go in peace.

People: Thanks be to God.

Celebration of the Liturgy of the Word
[With Holy Communion]

Introductory Rites

Introduction
Deacon or lay leader:
We gather here to celebrate the Lord's Day.
Sunday has been called the Lord's Day because
    it was on this day
that Jesus conquered sin and death and rose to new life.
Unfortunately, we are not able to celebrate the Mass today
because we do not have a Priest.
Let us be united in the spirit of Christ with
    the Church around the world
and celebrate our redemption in Christ's suffering,
    Death and Resurrection.

Sign of the Cross   **STAND**
Deacon or lay leader:
In the name of the Father, and of the Son, and of the Holy Spirit.
All respond: **Amen.**

Greeting
Deacon or lay leader:
Grace to you and peace from God our Father
and the Lord Jesus Christ.
Blessed be God for ever.
All: **Blessed be God for ever.**

Collect

Liturgy of the Word   **SIT**

First Reading

Responsorial Psalm

Celebration of the Liturgy of the Word

SECOND READING

GOSPEL ACCLAMATION   STAND

GOSPEL

HOMILY OR REFLECTION ON THE READINGS   SIT

PERIOD OF SILENCE

PROFESSION OF FAITH   STAND
[The Nicene Creed can be found on page 5]

Apostles' Creed

**I believe in God,
the Father almighty,
Creator of heaven and earth,
and in Jesus Christ, his only Son, our Lord,**

> At the words that follow, up to and including the Virgin Mary, all bow.

**who was conceived by the Holy Spirit,
born of the Virgin Mary,
suffered under Pontius Pilate,
was crucified, died and was buried;
he descended into hell;
on the third day he rose again from the dead;
he ascended into heaven,
and is seated at the right hand of God the Father
    almighty;
from there he will come to judge the living and the
    dead.**

**I believe in the Holy Spirit,
the holy catholic Church,
the communion of saints,
the forgiveness of sins,
the resurrection of the body,
and life everlasting. Amen.**

PRAYER OF THE FAITHFUL

Celebration of the Liturgy of the Word

Communion Rite

Lord's Prayer
Deacon or lay leader:
The Father provides us with food
for eternal life.
Let us pray for nourishment
and strength.

All say:
**Our Father, who art in heaven,
hallowed be thy name;
thy kingdom come,
thy will be done
on earth as it is in heaven.
Give us this day our daily bread,
and forgive us our trespasses,
as we forgive those who trespass against us;
and lead us not into temptation,
but deliver us from evil.
Amen.**

Invitation to Communion   **KNEEL**
Deacon or lay leader:
Behold the Lamb of God,
behold him who takes away the sins of the world.
Blessed are those called to the supper of the Lamb.

All say:
**Lord, I am not worthy
that you should enter under my roof,
but only say the word
and my soul shall be healed.**

Communion

Act of Thanksgiving   **STAND**

Concluding Rites

Invitation to Pray for Vocations to the Priesthood
Deacon or lay leader:

Mindful of the Lord's word, "Ask the Master of the harvest to send out laborers for the harvest," let us pray for an increase of vocations to the Priesthood. May our prayer hasten the day when we will be able to take part in the celebration of the Holy Eucharist every Sunday.

Blessing

Sign of Peace

First Sunday of Advent

November 30, 2014

Reflection on the Gospel

Four times in this gospel Christ commands us, "Be watchful!" or "Watch!" Being watchful and alert for the Second Coming is not enough; we must consciously seek to identify Christ already present now. *If we are proactively watching for everyday encounters with Christ, he will surely not find us "sleeping," neither now nor when he returns. The Second Coming becomes real for us in our encounters with Christ in the here and now.*

- *I am watchful for Christ's coming when I . . .*

—Living Liturgy™, *First Sunday of Advent 2014*

Entrance Antiphon (Cf. Psalm 25[24]:1-3)

To you, I lift up my soul, O my God.
In you, I have trusted; let me not be put to shame.
Nor let my enemies exult over me;
and let none who hope in you be put to shame.

Collect

Grant your faithful, we pray, almighty God,
the resolve to run forth to meet your Christ
with righteous deeds at his coming,
so that, gathered at his right hand,
they may be worthy to possess the heavenly Kingdom.
Through our Lord Jesus Christ, your Son,
who lives and reigns with you in the unity of the Holy Spirit,
one God, for ever and ever. All: **Amen.**

Reading I (L 2) (Isaiah 63:16b-17, 19b; 64:2-7)

A reading from the Book of the Prophet Isaiah

Oh, that you would rend the heavens and come down!

**You, Lord, are our father,
   our redeemer you are named forever.**

Why do you let us wander, O Lord, from your ways,
    and harden our hearts so that we fear you not?
Return for the sake of your servants,
    the tribes of your heritage.
Oh, that you would rend the heavens and come down,
    with the mountains quaking before you,
while you wrought awesome deeds we could not hope for,
    such as they had not heard of from of old.
No ear has ever heard, no eye ever seen, any God but you
    doing such deeds for those who wait for him.
Would that you might meet us doing right,
    that we were mindful of you in our ways!
Behold, you are angry, and we are sinful;
    all of us have become like unclean people,
    all our good deeds are like polluted rags;
we have all withered like leaves,
    and our guilt carries us away like the wind.
There is none who calls upon your name,
    who rouses himself to cling to you;
for you have hidden your face from us
    and have delivered us up to our guilt.
Yet, O Lord, you are our father;
    we are the clay and you the potter:
    we are all the work of your hands.

The word of the Lord. All: Thanks be to God.

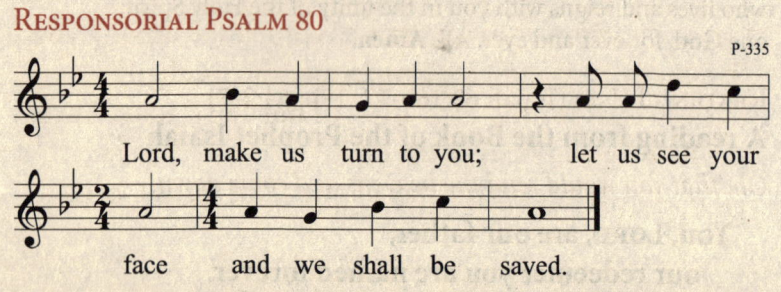

Responsorial Psalm 80

Lord, make us turn to you; let us see your face and we shall be saved.

Music: Jay F. Hunstiger, ©1993, administered by Liturgical Press. All rights reserved.

Psalm 80:2-3, 15-16, 18-19

℟. (4) **Lord, make us turn to you; let us see your face and we shall be saved.**

O shepherd of Israel, hearken,
  from your throne upon the cherubim, shine forth.
Rouse your power,
  and come to save us. ℟.

Once again, O L<small>ORD</small> of hosts,
  look down from heaven, and see;
take care of this vine,
    and protect what your right hand has planted,
    the son of man whom you yourself made strong. ℟.

May your help be with the man of your right hand,
  with the son of man whom you yourself made strong.
Then we will no more withdraw from you;
  give us new life, and we will call upon your name. ℟.

R<small>EADING</small> II (1 Corinthians 1:3-9)

A reading from the first Letter of Saint Paul to the Corinthians

We wait for the revelation of our Lord Jesus Christ.

Brothers and sisters:
Grace to you and peace from God our Father
  and the Lord Jesus Christ.

I give thanks to my God always on your account
  for the grace of God bestowed on you in Christ Jesus,
  that in him you were enriched in every way,
  with all discourse and all knowledge,
  as the testimony to Christ was confirmed among you,
  so that you are not lacking in any spiritual gift
  as you wait for the revelation of our Lord Jesus Christ.
He will keep you firm to the end,
  irreproachable on the day of our Lord Jesus Christ.

God is faithful,
>   **and by him you were called to fellowship with his Son,
>   Jesus Christ our Lord.**

The word of the Lord. All: **Thanks be to God.**

Gospel (Mark 13:33-37)
Alleluia (Psalm 85:8)
℣. Alleluia, alleluia. ℟. **Alleluia, alleluia.**
℣. Show us Lord, your love;
>   and grant us your salvation. ℟.

✠ **A reading from the holy Gospel according to Mark**

All: **Glory to you, O Lord.**

Be watchful! You do not know when the Lord of the house is coming.

**Jesus said to his disciples:
"Be watchful! Be alert!
You do not know when the time will come.
It is like a man traveling abroad.
He leaves home and places his servants in charge,**
>   **each with his own work,**
>   **and orders the gatekeeper to be on the watch.**

Watch, therefore;
>   **you do not know when the Lord of the house is coming,**
>   **whether in the evening, or at midnight,**
>   **or at cockcrow, or in the morning.**

**May he not come suddenly and find you sleeping.
What I say to you, I say to all: 'Watch!'"**

The Gospel of the Lord. All: **Praise to you, Lord Jesus Christ.**

Prayer over the Offerings
Accept, we pray, O Lord, these offerings we make,
gathered from among your gifts to us,
and may what you grant us to celebrate devoutly here below
gain for us the prize of eternal redemption.
Through Christ our Lord. All: **Amen.**

Communion Antiphon (Psalm 85[84]:13)
The Lord will bestow his bounty, and our earth shall yield
 its increase.

Prayer after Communion
May these mysteries, O Lord,
in which we have participated,
profit us, we pray,
for even now, as we walk amid passing things,
you teach us by them to love the things of heaven
and hold fast to what endures.
Through Christ our Lord. All: **Amen.**

Second Sunday of Advent

December 7, 2014

Reflection on the Gospel

John was a desert ascetic whose mission was to prepare the people for a life-transforming change—the Lord is coming! Who is this Lord? One mightier than John. How so? John announces the nearness of salvation; Jesus is the salvation. John baptizes with water, Jesus with the Holy Spirit. What does this mean? Jesus' baptism instills God's very Life through the power of the Holy Spirit within us. Baptism with the Holy Spirit transforms our preparation into fulfillment—the Lord has come!

- *Who is my Lord? . . .*

—Living Liturgy™, *Second Sunday of Advent 2014*

Entrance Antiphon (Cf. Isaiah 30:19, 30)
O people of Sion, behold,
the Lord will come to save the nations,
and the Lord will make the glory of his voice heard
in the joy of your heart.

December 7

COLLECT

Almighty and merciful God,
may no earthly undertaking hinder those
who set out in haste to meet your Son,
but may our learning of heavenly wisdom
gain us admittance to his company.
Who lives and reigns with you in the unity of the Holy Spirit,
one God, for ever and ever. All: **Amen.**

READING I (L 5) (Isaiah 40:1-5, 9-11)

A reading from the Book of the Prophet Isaiah

Prepare the way of the Lord.

> **Comfort, give comfort to my people,
>   says your God.
> Speak tenderly to Jerusalem, and proclaim to her
>   that her service is at an end,
>   her guilt is expiated;
> indeed, she has received from the hand of the LORD
>   double for all her sins.**
>
>   **A voice cries out:
> In the desert prepare the way of the LORD!
>   Make straight in the wasteland a highway for our
>   God!
> Every valley shall be filled in,
>   every mountain and hill shall be made low;
> the rugged land shall be made a plain,
>   the rough country, a broad valley.
> Then the glory of the LORD shall be revealed,
>   and all people shall see it together;
>   for the mouth of the LORD has spoken.**
>
> **Go up onto a high mountain,
>   Zion, herald of glad tidings;
> cry out at the top of your voice,
>   Jerusalem, herald of good news!
> Fear not to cry out
>   and say to the cities of Judah:
>   Here is your God!**

**Here comes with power
    the Lord God,
    who rules by his strong arm;
here is his reward with him,
    his recompense before him.
Like a shepherd he feeds his flock;
    in his arms he gathers the lambs,
carrying them in his bosom,
    and leading the ewes with care.**

The word of the Lord. All: **Thanks be to God.**

Responsorial Psalm 85

Lord, let us see your kindness, and grant us your salvation.

Music: Jay F. Hunstiger, © 1993, administered by Liturgical Press. All rights reserved.

Psalm 85:9-10, 11-12, 13-14

℟. (8) **Lord, let us see your kindness, and grant us your salvation.**

I will hear what God proclaims;
    the Lord—for he proclaims peace to his people.
Near indeed is his salvation to those who fear him,
    glory dwelling in our land. ℟.

Kindness and truth shall meet;
    justice and peace shall kiss.
Truth shall spring out of the earth,
    and justice shall look down from heaven. ℟.

The Lord himself will give his benefits;
    our land shall yield its increase.
Justice shall walk before him,
    and prepare the way of his steps. ℟.

Reading II (2 Peter 3:8-14)
A reading from the second Letter of Saint Peter

We await new heavens and a new earth.

Do not ignore this one fact, beloved,
> that with the Lord one day is like a thousand years
> and a thousand years like one day.

The Lord does not delay his promise, as some regard "delay,"
> but he is patient with you,
> not wishing that any should perish
> but that all should come to repentance.

But the day of the Lord will come like a thief,
> and then the heavens will pass away with a mighty roar
> and the elements will be dissolved by fire,
> and the earth and everything done on it will be found out.

Since everything is to be dissolved in this way,
> what sort of persons ought you to be,
> conducting yourselves in holiness and devotion,
> waiting for and hastening the coming of the day of God,
> because of which the heavens will be dissolved in flames
> and the elements melted by fire.

But according to his promise
> we await new heavens and a new earth
> in which righteousness dwells.

Therefore, beloved, since you await these things,
> be eager to be found without spot or blemish before him, at peace.

The word of the Lord. All: Thanks be to God.

Gospel (Mark 1:1-8)
Alleluia (Luke 3:4, 6)

℣. Alleluia, alleluia. ℟. **Alleluia, alleluia.**

℣. Prepare the way of the Lord, make straight his paths:
all flesh shall see the salvation of God. ℟.

✣ **A reading from the holy Gospel according to Mark**

All: **Glory to you, O Lord.**

Make straight the paths of the Lord.

The beginning of the gospel of Jesus Christ the Son of God.

As it is written in Isaiah the prophet:
Behold, I am sending my messenger ahead of you;
he will prepare your way.
A voice of one crying out in the desert:
"Prepare the way of the Lord,
make straight his paths."
John the Baptist appeared in the desert
proclaiming a baptism of repentance for the forgiveness of sins.
People of the whole Judean countryside
and all the inhabitants of Jerusalem
were going out to him
and were being baptized by him in the Jordan River
as they acknowledged their sins.
John was clothed in camel's hair,
with a leather belt around his waist.
He fed on locusts and wild honey.
And this is what he proclaimed:
"One mightier than I is coming after me.
I am not worthy to stoop and loosen the thongs of his sandals.
I have baptized you with water;
he will baptize you with the Holy Spirit."

The Gospel of the Lord. All: **Praise to you, Lord Jesus Christ.**

Prayer over the Offerings
Be pleased, O Lord, with our humble prayers and offerings,
and, since we have no merits to plead our cause,
come, we pray, to our rescue
with the protection of your mercy.
Through Christ our Lord. All: **Amen.**

COMMUNION ANTIPHON (Baruch 5:5; 4:36)
Jerusalem, arise and stand upon the heights,
and behold the joy which comes to you from God.

PRAYER AFTER COMMUNION
Replenished by the food of spiritual nourishment,
we humbly beseech you, O Lord,
that, through our partaking in this mystery,
you may teach us to judge wisely the things of earth
and hold firm to the things of heaven.
Through Christ our Lord. All: **Amen.**

The Immaculate Conception of the Blessed Virgin Mary

December 8, 2014

Reflection on the Gospel

Even before assenting to conceiving Jesus by the Holy Spirit, Mary had made "May it be done to me" the abiding habit of her way of relating to God and choosing to do God's will. The relationship between Mary and God had grown all her life to the point where her yes was simply the natural thing for her to do. It didn't take thinking; it was an answer of the heart. So must our yes to God be an answer of the heart.

- *I choose to do the will of God by . . .*

—Living Liturgy™, *Immaculate Conception 2014*

ENTRANCE ANTIPHON (Isaiah 61:10)
I rejoice heartily in the Lord,
in my God is the joy of my soul;
for he has clothed me with a robe of salvation,
and wrapped me in a mantle of justice,
like a bride adorned with her jewels.

Collect

O God, who by the Immaculate Conception of the Blessed Virgin
prepared a worthy dwelling for your Son,
grant, we pray,
that, as you preserved her from every stain
by virtue of the Death of your Son, which you foresaw,
so, through her intercession,
we, too, may be cleansed and admitted to your presence.
Through our Lord Jesus Christ, your Son,
who lives and reigns with you in the unity of the Holy Spirit,
one God, for ever and ever. All: **Amen.**

Reading I (L 689) (Genesis 3:9-15, 20)

A reading from the Book of Genesis

I will put enmity between your offspring and hers.

**After the man, Adam, had eaten of the tree,
the Lord God called to the man and asked him,
"Where are you?"
He answered, "I heard you in the garden;
but I was afraid, because I was naked,
so I hid myself."
Then he asked, "Who told you that you were naked?
You have eaten, then,
from the tree of which I had forbidden you to eat!"
The man replied, "The woman whom you put here
with me—
she gave me fruit from the tree, and so I ate it."
The Lord God then asked the woman,
"Why did you do such a thing?"
The woman answered, "The serpent tricked me into it,
so I ate it."
Then the Lord God said to the serpent:
"Because you have done this, you shall be banned
from all the animals
and from all the wild creatures;
on your belly shall you crawl,
and dirt shall you eat
all the days of your life.**

I will put enmity between you and the woman,
> and between your offspring and hers;
he will strike at your head,
> while you strike at his heel."

The man called his wife Eve,
> because she became the mother of all the living.

The word of the Lord. All: Thanks be to God.

Responsorial Psalm 98

Sing to the Lord a new song, for he has done marv-'lous deeds.

Music: Jay F. Hunstiger, © 1990, administered by Liturgical Press. All rights reserved.

Psalm 98:1, 2-3ab, 3cd-4

℟. (1a) **Sing to the Lord a new song, for he has done marvelous deeds.**

Sing to the Lord a new song,
> for he has done wondrous deeds;
His right hand has won victory for him,
> his holy arm. ℟.

The Lord has made his salvation known:
> in the sight of the nations he has revealed his justice.
He has remembered his kindness and his faithfulness
> toward the house of Israel. ℟.

All the ends of the earth have seen
> the salvation by our God.
Sing joyfully to the Lord, all you lands;
> break into song; sing praise. ℟.

Reading II (Ephesians 1:3-6, 11-12)

A reading from the Letter of Saint Paul to the Ephesians

He chose us in Christ before the foundation of the world.

Brothers and sisters:
Blessed be the God and Father of our Lord Jesus Christ,
   who has blessed us in Christ
   with every spiritual blessing in the heavens,
   as he chose us in him, before the foundation of the
      world,
   to be holy and without blemish before him.
In love he destined us for adoption to himself through
      Jesus Christ,
   in accord with the favor of his will,
   for the praise of the glory of his grace
   that he granted us in the beloved.

In him we were also chosen,
   destined in accord with the purpose of the One
   who accomplishes all things according to the intention
      of his will,
   so that we might exist for the praise of his glory,
   we who first hoped in Christ.

The word of the Lord. All: **Thanks be to God.**

GOSPEL (Luke 1:26-38)
ALLELUIA (See Luke 1:28)
℣. Alleluia, alleluia.   ℟. **Alleluia, alleluia.**
℣. Hail, Mary, full of grace, the Lord is with you;
blessed are you among women. ℟.

✠ **A reading from the holy Gospel according to Luke**

All: **Glory to you, O Lord.**

Hail, full of grace! The Lord is with you.

**The angel Gabriel was sent from God
   to a town of Galilee called Nazareth,
   to a virgin betrothed to a man named Joseph,
   of the house of David,
   and the virgin's name was Mary.
And coming to her, he said,
   "Hail, full of grace! The Lord is with you."**

But she was greatly troubled at what was said
   and pondered what sort of greeting this might be.
Then the angel said to her,
   "Do not be afraid, Mary,
   for you have found favor with God.
Behold, you will conceive in your womb and bear a son,
   and you shall name him Jesus.
He will be great and will be called Son of the Most High,
   and the Lord God will give him the throne of David
      his father,
   and he will rule over the house of Jacob forever,
   and of his Kingdom there will be no end."
But Mary said to the angel,
   "How can this be,
   since I have no relations with a man?"
And the angel said to her in reply,
   "The Holy Spirit will come upon you,
   and the power of the Most High will overshadow you.
Therefore the child to be born
   will be called holy, the Son of God.
And behold, Elizabeth, your relative,
   has also conceived a son in her old age,
   and this is the sixth month for her who was called
      barren;
   for nothing will be impossible for God."
Mary said, "Behold, I am the handmaid of the Lord.
May it be done to me according to your word."
Then the angel departed from her.

The Gospel of the Lord. All: **Praise to you, Lord Jesus Christ.**

Prayer over the Offerings

Graciously accept the saving sacrifice
which we offer you, O Lord,
on the Solemnity of the Immaculate Conception
of the Blessed Virgin Mary,
and grant that, as we profess her,
on account of your prevenient grace,

to be untouched by any stain of sin,
so, through her intercession,
we may be delivered from all our faults.
Through Christ our Lord. All: **Amen.**

Communion Antiphon
Glorious things are spoken of you, O Mary,
for from you arose the sun of justice,
Christ our God.

Prayer after Communion
May the Sacrament we have received,
O Lord our God,
heal in us the wounds of that fault
from which in a singular way
you preserved Blessed Mary in her Immaculate Conception.
Through Christ our Lord. All: **Amen.**

Third Sunday of Advent
December 14, 2014

Reflection on the Gospel

After saying clearly who he is not ("Christ or Elijah or the Prophet"), John does say who he is: "I am the voice of one crying out in the desert." "Voice": the audible revelation of self. "Crying out": testifying to core convictions. "Desert": place of barrenness and desolation as well as a place of testing and growth. So who is John? The one who in his very being recognizes the Christ who has come to lead the people into the fullness of light and Life.

• *I am a voice of one crying in the desert as I . . .*

—Living Liturgy™, *Third Sunday of Advent 2014*

December 14

Entrance Antiphon (Philippians 4:4-5)
Rejoice in the Lord always; again I say, rejoice.
Indeed, the Lord is near.

Collect
O God, who see how your people
faithfully await the feast of the Lord's Nativity,
enable us, we pray,
to attain the joys of so great a salvation
and to celebrate them always
with solemn worship and glad rejoicing.
Through our Lord Jesus Christ, your Son,
who lives and reigns with you in the unity of the Holy Spirit,
one God, for ever and ever. All: **Amen.**

Reading I (L 8) (Isaiah 61:1-2a, 10-11)
A reading from the Book of the Prophet Isaiah

I rejoice heartily in the Lord.

> **The spirit of the Lord God is upon me,**
>   **because the Lord has anointed me;**
> **he has sent me to bring glad tidings to the poor,**
>   **to heal the brokenhearted,**
> **to proclaim liberty to the captives**
>   **and release to the prisoners,**
> **to announce a year of favor from the Lord**
>   **and a day of vindication by our God.**
>
> **I rejoice heartily in the Lord,**
>   **in my God is the joy of my soul;**
> **for he has clothed me with a robe of salvation**
>   **and wrapped me in a mantle of justice,**
> **like a bridegroom adorned with a diadem,**
>   **like a bride bedecked with her jewels.**
> **As the earth brings forth its plants,**
>   **and a garden makes its growth spring up,**
> **so will the Lord God make justice and praise**
>   **spring up before all the nations.**

The word of the Lord. All: **Thanks be to God.**

Responsorial Psalm

My soul rejoices, my soul rejoices in my God.

<small>Music: Jay F. Hunstiger, © 1993, administered by Liturgical Press. All rights reserved.</small>

Luke 1:46-48, 49-50, 53-54

℟. (Isaiah 61:10b) **My soul rejoices in my God.**

My soul proclaims the greatness of the Lord;
> my spirit rejoices in God my Savior,
for he has looked upon his lowly servant.
> From this day all generations will call me blessed: ℟.

The Almighty has done great things for me,
> and holy is his Name.
He has mercy on those who fear him
> in every generation. ℟.

He has filled the hungry with good things,
> and the rich he has sent away empty.
He has come to the help of his servant Israel
> for he has remembered his promise of mercy. ℟.

Reading II (1 Thessalonians 5:16-24)

A reading from the first Letter of Saint Paul to the Thessalonians

May you entirely, spirit, soul, and body, be preserved blameless for the coming of our Lord Jesus Christ.

**Brothers and sisters:
Rejoice always. Pray without ceasing.
In all circumstances give thanks,**
> **for this is the will of God for you in Christ Jesus.**

**Do not quench the Spirit.
Do not despise prophetic utterances.
Test everything; retain what is good.
Refrain from every kind of evil.**

**May the God of peace make you perfectly holy
> and may you entirely, spirit, soul, and body,**

> be preserved blameless for the coming of our Lord
>> Jesus Christ.
> The one who calls you is faithful,
>> and he will also accomplish it.

The word of the Lord. All: Thanks be to God.

GOSPEL (John 1:6-8, 19-28)
ALLELUIA (Isaiah 61:1 (cited in Luke 4:18))

℣. Alleluia, alleluia. ℟. **Alleluia, alleluia.**
℣. The Spirit of the Lord is upon me,
   because he has anointed me
   to bring glad tidings to the poor. ℟.

✠ A reading from the holy Gospel according to John

All: **Glory to you, O Lord.**

There is one among you whom you do not recognize.

A man named John was sent from God.
He came for testimony, to testify to the light,
   so that all might believe through him.
He was not the light,
   but came to testify to the light.

And this is the testimony of John.
When the Jews from Jerusalem sent priests
      and Levites to him
   to ask him, "Who are you?"
   he admitted and did not deny it,
   but admitted, "I am not the Christ."
So they asked him,
   "What are you then? Are you Elijah?"
And he said, "I am not."
"Are you the Prophet?"
He answered, "No."
So they said to him,
      "Who are you, so we can give an answer to those who
         sent us?
What do you have to say for yourself?"

He said:
> "I am *the voice of one crying out in the desert,*
> *make straight the way of the Lord,*
> as Isaiah the prophet said."

Some Pharisees were also sent.
They asked him,
> "Why then do you baptize
> if you are not the Christ or Elijah or the Prophet?"

John answered them,
> "I baptize with water;
> but there is one among you whom you do not recognize,
> the one who is coming after me,
> whose sandal strap I am not worthy to untie."

This happened in Bethany across the Jordan,
> where John was baptizing.

The Gospel of the Lord. All: **Praise to you, Lord Jesus Christ.**

Prayer over the Offerings

May the sacrifice of our worship, Lord, we pray,
be offered to you unceasingly,
to complete what was begun in sacred mystery
and powerfully accomplish for us your saving work.
Through Christ our Lord. All: **Amen.**

Communion Antiphon (Cf. Isaiah 35:4)

Say to the faint of heart: Be strong and do not fear.
Behold, our God will come, and he will save us.

Prayer after Communion

We implore your mercy, Lord,
that this divine sustenance may cleanse us of our faults
and prepare us for the coming feasts.
Through Christ our Lord. All: **Amen.**

Fourth Sunday of Advent

December 21, 2014

Reflection on the Gospel

God's whole plan of salvation is a perpetual annunciation. In this gospel, there are numerous "annunciations" beyond Gabriel's revealing to Mary that she would conceive "the Son of God." Gabriel makes known that Mary is holy; that the child shall be named Jesus; that the kingdom of this Child would have no end; that this Child is "holy, the Son of God"; that Elizabeth has conceived; that "nothing will be impossible for God"; and that Mary is God's faithful and obedient handmaid. Indeed, perpetual annunciation is God's pattern of relating to us.

• I announce the coming of the Lord by . . .

—*Living Liturgy*™, *Fourth Sunday of Advent 2014*

ENTRANCE ANTIPHON (Cf. Isaiah 45:8)

Drop down dew from above, you heavens,
and let the clouds rain down the Just One;
let the earth be opened and bring forth a Savior.

COLLECT

Pour forth, we beseech you, O Lord,
your grace into our hearts,
that we, to whom the Incarnation of Christ your Son
was made known by the message of an Angel,
may by his Passion and Cross
be brought to the glory of his Resurrection.
Who lives and reigns with you in the unity of the Holy Spirit,
one God, for ever and ever. All: **Amen.**

READING I (L 11) (2 Samuel 7:1-5, 8b-12, 14a, 16)

A reading from the second Book of Samuel

The kingdom of David shall endure forever before the Lord.

**When King David was settled in his palace,
and the LORD had given him rest from his enemies on every side,**

he said to Nathan the prophet,
"Here I am living in a house of cedar,
while the ark of God dwells in a tent!"
Nathan answered the king,
"Go, do whatever you have in mind,
for the LORD is with you."
But that night the LORD spoke to Nathan and said:
"Go, tell my servant David, 'Thus says the LORD:
Should you build me a house to dwell in?

"'It was I who took you from the pasture
and from the care of the flock
to be commander of my people Israel.
I have been with you wherever you went,
and I have destroyed all your enemies before you.
And I will make you famous like the great ones of the earth.
I will fix a place for my people Israel;
I will plant them so that they may dwell in their place
without further disturbance.
Neither shall the wicked continue to afflict them as they did of old,
since the time I first appointed judges over my people Israel.
I will give you rest from all your enemies.
The LORD also reveals to you
that he will establish a house for you.
And when your time comes and you rest with your ancestors,
I will raise up your heir after you, sprung from your loins,
and I will make his kingdom firm.
I will be a father to him,
and he shall be a son to me.

Your house and your kingdom shall endure forever
> before me;
> your throne shall stand firm forever.'"

The word of the Lord. All: Thanks be to God.

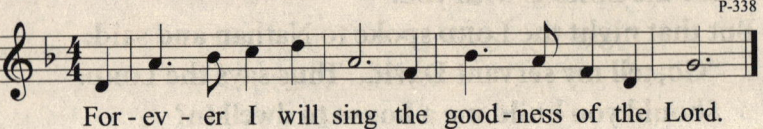

Responsorial Psalm 89

For-ev-er I will sing the good-ness of the Lord.

_{Music: Jay F. Hunstiger, © 1993, administered by Liturgical Press. All rights reserved.}

Psalm 89:2-3, 4-5, 27, 29

℟. (2a) **Forever I will sing the goodness of the Lord.**

The promises of the Lord I will sing forever;
> through all generations my mouth shall proclaim
>> your faithfulness.

For you have said, "My kindness is established forever";
> in heaven you have confirmed your faithfulness. ℟.

"I have made a covenant with my chosen one,
> I have sworn to David my servant:

forever will I confirm your posterity
> and establish your throne for all generations." ℟.

"He shall say of me, 'You are my father,
> my God, the Rock, my savior.'

Forever I will maintain my kindness toward him,
> and my covenant with him stands firm." ℟.

Reading II (Romans 16:25-27)

A reading from the Letter of Saint Paul to the Romans

The mystery kept secret for long ages has now been manifested.

Brothers and sisters:
To him who can strengthen you,
> according to my gospel and the proclamation of Jesus
>> Christ,
> according to the revelation of the mystery kept secret
>> for long ages

but now manifested through the prophetic writings and,
according to the command of the eternal God,
made known to all nations to bring about the obedience of faith,
to the only wise God, through Jesus Christ
be glory forever and ever. Amen.

The word of the Lord. **All:** Thanks be to God.

GOSPEL (Luke 1:26-38)
ALLELUIA (Luke 1:38)

℣. Alleluia, alleluia. ℟. **Alleluia, alleluia.**
℣. Behold, I am the handmaid of the Lord.
May it be done to me according to your word. ℟.

☩ **A reading from the holy Gospel according to Luke**
All: Glory to you, O Lord.

Behold, you will conceive in your womb and bear a son.

The angel Gabriel was sent from God
to a town of Galilee called Nazareth,
to a virgin betrothed to a man named Joseph,
of the house of David,
and the virgin's name was Mary.
And coming to her, he said,
"Hail, full of grace! The Lord is with you."
But she was greatly troubled at what was said
and pondered what sort of greeting this might be.
Then the angel said to her,
"Do not be afraid, Mary,
for you have found favor with God.

"Behold, you will conceive in your womb and bear a son,
and you shall name him Jesus.
He will be great and will be called Son of the Most High,
and the Lord God will give him the throne of David his father,
and he will rule over the house of Jacob forever,
and of his kingdom there will be no end."

But Mary said to the angel,
  "How can this be,
  since I have no relations with a man?"
And the angel said to her in reply,
  "The Holy Spirit will come upon you,
  and the power of the Most High will overshadow you.
Therefore the child to be born
  will be called holy, the Son of God.
And behold, Elizabeth, your relative,
  has also conceived a son in her old age,
    and this is the sixth month for her who was called barren;
  for nothing will be impossible for God."
Mary said, "Behold, I am the handmaid of the Lord.
May it be done to me according to your word."
Then the angel departed from her.

The Gospel of the Lord. All: **Praise to you, Lord Jesus Christ.**

Prayer over the Offerings
May the Holy Spirit, O Lord,
sanctify these gifts laid upon your altar,
just as he filled with his power the womb of the Blessed Virgin Mary.
Through Christ our Lord. All: **Amen.**

Communion Antiphon (Isaiah 7:14)
Behold, a Virgin shall conceive and bear a son;
and his name will be called Emmanuel.

Prayer after Communion
Having received this pledge of eternal redemption,
we pray, almighty God,
that, as the feast day of our salvation draws ever nearer,
so we may press forward all the more eagerly
to the worthy celebration of the mystery of your Son's Nativity.
Who lives and reigns for ever and ever. All: **Amen.**

The Nativity of the Lord (Christmas)

AT THE VIGIL MASS

December 24, 2014

The Mass of the Vigil of Christmas is to be used on Wednesday evening in those places where the Sunday (holy day of) obligation may be fulfilled on Saturday evening.

Reflection on the Gospel

There is perhaps no other gospel story that has been told and retold in so many thousands of ways as this one about the birth of Jesus. The picturesque and memorable details of the story, however, can limit our appreciation for what we really celebrate. Christmas is less about the birth of a baby and far more about the birth of a divine Savior. It is less about glory and joy of long ago and more about an invitation to us today to enter into the saving mystery God revealed so uniquely in Jesus Christ.

- *I experience the birth of the Lord as I . . .*

—Living Liturgy™, *Christmas 2014*

ENTRANCE ANTIPHON (Cf. Exodus 16:6-7)

Today you will know that the Lord will come, and he will save us,
and in the morning you will see his glory.

COLLECT

O God, who gladden us year by year
as we wait in hope for our redemption,
grant that, just as we joyfully welcome
your Only Begotten Son as our Redeemer,
we may also merit to face him confidently
when he comes again as our Judge.
Who lives and reigns with you in the unity of the Holy Spirit,
one God, for ever and ever. All: **Amen.**

Reading I (L 13) (Isaiah 62:1-5)

A reading from the Book of the Prophet Isaiah

The Lord delights in you.

> For Zion's sake I will not be silent,
> for Jerusalem's sake I will not be quiet,
> until her vindication shines forth like the dawn
> and her victory like a burning torch.
>
> Nations shall behold your vindication,
> and all the kings your glory;
> you shall be called by a new name
> pronounced by the mouth of the LORD.
> You shall be a glorious crown in the hand of the LORD,
> a royal diadem held by your God.
> No more shall people call you "Forsaken,"
> or your land "Desolate,"
> but you shall be called "My Delight,"
> and your land "Espoused."
> For the LORD delights in you
> and makes your land his spouse.
> As a young man marries a virgin,
> your Builder shall marry you;
> and as a bridegroom rejoices in his bride
> so shall your God rejoice in you.

The word of the Lord. **All: Thanks be to God.**

Responsorial Psalm 89

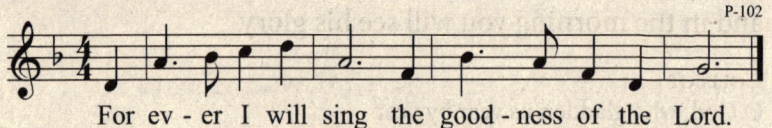

P-102

For ev-er I will sing the good-ness of the Lord.

Music: Jay F. Hunstiger, © 1990, administered by Liturgical Press. All rights reserved.

Psalm 89:4-5, 16-17, 27, 29

℟. (2a) **For ever I will sing the goodness of the Lord.**

> I have made a covenant with my chosen one,
> I have sworn to David my servant:

> forever will I confirm your posterity
> and establish your throne for all generations. ℟.

> Blessed the people who know the joyful shout;
> in the light of your countenance, O Lord, they walk.
> At your name they rejoice all the day,
> and through your justice they are exalted. ℟.

> He shall say of me, "You are my father,
> my God, the Rock, my savior."
> Forever I will maintain my kindness toward him,
> and my covenant with him stands firm. ℟.

Reading II (Acts of the Apostles 13:16-17, 22-25)

A reading from the Acts of the Apostles

Paul bears witness to Christ, the Son of David.

**When Paul reached Antioch in Pisidia and entered the synagogue,
he stood up, motioned with his hand, and said,
"Fellow Israelites and you others who are God-fearing, listen.
The God of this people Israel chose our ancestors
and exalted the people during their sojourn in the land of Egypt.
With uplifted arm he led them out of it.
Then he removed Saul and raised up David as king;
of him he testified,
'I have found David, son of Jesse, a man after my own heart;
he will carry out my every wish.'
From this man's descendants God, according to his promise,
has brought to Israel a savior, Jesus.
John heralded his coming by proclaiming a baptism of repentance
to all the people of Israel;
and as John was completing his course, he would say,
'What do you suppose that I am? I am not he.**

Behold, one is coming after me;
  I am not worthy to unfasten the sandals of his feet.'"

The word of the Lord. All: **Thanks be to God.**

Gospel (Matthew 1:1-25) *or* Shorter Form [ ] (Matthew 1:18-25)
Alleluia
℣. Alleluia, alleluia. ℟. **Alleluia, alleluia.**
℣. Tomorrow the wickedness of the earth will be destroyed: the Savior of the world will reign over us. ℟.

✠ **A reading from the beginning of the holy Gospel according to Matthew**

All: **Glory to you, O Lord.**

The genealogy of Jesus Christ, the Son of David.

The book of the genealogy of Jesus Christ,
  the son of David, the son of Abraham.

Abraham became the father of Isaac,
  Isaac the father of Jacob,
  Jacob the father of Judah and his brothers.
Judah became the father of Perez and Zerah,
  whose mother was Tamar.
Perez became the father of Hezron,
  Hezron the father of Ram,
  Ram the father of Amminadab.
Amminadab became the father of Nahshon,
  Nahshon the father of Salmon,
  Salmon the father of Boaz,
  whose mother was Rahab.
Boaz became the father of Obed,
  whose mother was Ruth.
Obed became the father of Jesse,
  Jesse the father of David the king.

David became the father of Solomon,
  whose mother had been the wife of Uriah.
Solomon became the father of Rehoboam,
  Rehoboam the father of Abijah,
  Abijah the father of Asaph.

Asaph became the father of Jehoshaphat,
    Jehoshaphat the father of Joram,
    Joram the father of Uzziah.
Uzziah became the father of Jotham,
    Jotham the father of Ahaz,
    Ahaz the father of Hezekiah.
Hezekiah became the father of Manasseh,
    Manasseh the father of Amos,
    Amos the father of Josiah.
Josiah became the father of Jechoniah and his brothers
    at the time of the Babylonian exile.

After the Babylonian exile,
    Jechoniah became the father of Shealtiel,
    Shealtiel the father of Zerubbabel,
    Zerubbabel the father of Abiud.
Abiud became the father of Eliakim,
    Eliakim the father of Azor,
    Azor the father of Zadok.
Zadok became the father of Achim,
    Achim the father of Eliud,
    Eliud the father of Eleazar.
Eleazar became the father of Matthan,
    Matthan the father of Jacob,
    Jacob the father of Joseph, the husband of Mary.
Of her was born Jesus who is called the Christ.

Thus the total number of generations
    from Abraham to David
    is fourteen generations;
    from David to the Babylonian exile,
    fourteen generations;
    from the Babylonian exile to the Christ,
    fourteen generations.

[Now this is how the birth of Jesus Christ came about.
When his mother Mary was betrothed to Joseph,
    but before they lived together,
    she was found with child through the Holy Spirit.

Joseph her husband, since he was a righteous man,
> yet unwilling to expose her to shame,
> decided to divorce her quietly.
Such was his intention when, behold,
> the angel of the Lord appeared to him in a dream
> > and said,
> "Joseph, son of David,
> do not be afraid to take Mary your wife into your home.
For it is through the Holy Spirit
> that this child has been conceived in her.
She will bear a son and you are to name him Jesus,
> because he will save his people from their sins."
All this took place to fulfill
> what the Lord had said through the prophet:
> > *Behold, the virgin shall conceive and bear a son,*
> > > *and they shall name him Emmanuel,*
> which means "God is with us."
When Joseph awoke,
> he did as the angel of the Lord had commanded him
> and took his wife into his home.
He had no relations with her until she bore a son,
> and he named him Jesus.]

The Gospel of the Lord. **All: Praise to you, Lord Jesus Christ.**

Prayer over the Offerings
As we look forward, O Lord,
to the coming festivities,
may we serve you all the more eagerly
for knowing that in them
you make manifest the beginnings of our redemption.
Through Christ our Lord. **All: Amen.**

Communion Antiphon (Cf. Isaiah 40:5)
The glory of the Lord will be revealed,
and all flesh will see the salvation of our God.

Prayer after Communion
Grant, O Lord, we pray,
that we may draw new vigor

from celebrating the Nativity of your Only Begotten Son,
by whose heavenly mystery we receive both food and drink.
Who lives and reigns for ever and ever. All: **Amen.**

The Nativity of the Lord

AT THE MASS DURING THE NIGHT

December 25, 2014

ENTRANCE ANTIPHON (Psalm 2:7)
The Lord said to me: You are my Son.
It is I who have begotten you this day.

Or:

Let us all rejoice in the Lord, for our Savior has been born
 in the world.
Today true peace has come down to us from heaven.

COLLECT
O God, who have made this most sacred night
radiant with the splendor of the true light,
grant, we pray, that we, who have known the mysteries of his light on
 earth,
may also delight in his gladness in heaven.
Who lives and reigns with you in the unity of the Holy Spirit,
one God, for ever and ever. All: **Amen.**

READING I (L 14) (Isaiah 9:1-6)
A reading from the Book of the Prophet Isaiah

A son is given us.

> The people who walked in darkness
> have seen a great light;
> upon those who dwelt in the land of gloom
> a light has shone.

**You have brought them abundant joy
    and great rejoicing,
as they rejoice before you as at the harvest,
    as people make merry when dividing spoils.
For the yoke that burdened them,
    the pole on their shoulder,
and the rod of their taskmaster
    you have smashed, as on the day of Midian.
For every boot that tramped in battle,
    every cloak rolled in blood,
    will be burned as fuel for flames.
For a child is born to us, a son is given us;
    upon his shoulder dominion rests.
They name him Wonder-Counselor, God-Hero,
    Father-Forever, Prince of Peace.
His dominion is vast
    and forever peaceful,
from David's throne, and over his kingdom,
    which he confirms and sustains
by judgment and justice,
    both now and forever.
The zeal of the LORD of hosts will do this!**

The word of the Lord. All: **Thanks be to God.**

RESPONSORIAL PSALM 96

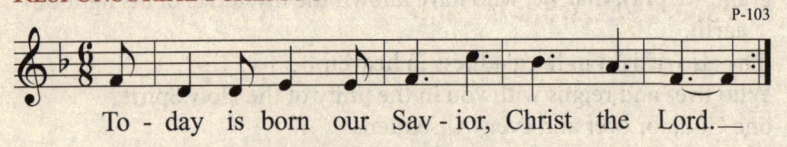

P-103

To - day is born our Sav - ior, Christ the Lord.

Music: Jay F. Hunstiger, © 1990, administered by Liturgical Press. All rights reserved.

Psalm 96:1-2, 2-3, 11-12, 13

℟. (Luke 2:11) **Today is born our Savior, Christ the Lord.**

Sing to the LORD a new song;
    sing to the LORD, all you lands.
Sing to the LORD; bless his name. ℟.

Announce his salvation, day after day.
> Tell his glory among the nations;
> among all peoples, his wondrous deeds. ℟.

Let the heavens be glad and the earth rejoice;
> let the sea and what fills it resound;
> let the plains be joyful and all that is in them!

Then shall all the trees of the forest exult. ℟.

They shall exult before the Lord, for he comes;
> for he comes to rule the earth.

He shall rule the world with justice
> and the peoples with his constancy. ℟.

Reading II (Titus 2:11-14)

A reading from the Letter of Saint Paul to Titus

The grace of God has appeared to all.

Beloved:
> **The grace of God has appeared, saving all**
> **and training us to reject godless ways and worldly desires**
> **and to live temperately, justly, and devoutly in this age,**
> **as we await the blessed hope,**
> **the appearance of the glory of our great God**
> **and savior Jesus Christ,**
> **who gave himself for us to deliver us from all lawlessness**
> **and to cleanse for himself a people as his own,**
> **eager to do what is good.**

The word of the Lord. All: **Thanks be to God.**

Gospel (Luke 2:1-14)
Alleluia (Luke 2:10-11)

℣. Alleluia, alleluia. ℟. **Alleluia, alleluia.**
℣. I proclaim to you good news of great joy:
> today a Savior is born for us,
> Christ the Lord. ℟.

✠ **A reading from the holy Gospel according to Luke**

All: **Glory to you, O Lord.**

Today a Savior has been born for you.

In those days a decree went out from Caesar Augustus
   that the whole world should be enrolled.
This was the first enrollment,
   when Quirinius was governor of Syria.
So all went to be enrolled, each to his own town.
And Joseph too went up from Galilee from the town of Nazareth
   to Judea, to the city of David that is called Bethlehem,
   because he was of the house and family of David,
   to be enrolled with Mary, his betrothed, who was with child.
While they were there,
   the time came for her to have her child,
   and she gave birth to her firstborn son.
She wrapped him in swaddling clothes and laid him in a manger,
   because there was no room for them in the inn.
Now there were shepherds in that region living in the fields
   and keeping the night watch over their flock.
The angel of the Lord appeared to them
   and the glory of the Lord shone around them,
   and they were struck with great fear.
The angel said to them,
   "Do not be afraid;
   for behold, I proclaim to you good news of great joy
   that will be for all the people.
For today in the city of David
   a savior has been born for you who is Christ and Lord.
And this will be a sign for you:
   you will find an infant wrapped in swaddling clothes
   and lying in a manger."
And suddenly there was a multitude of the heavenly host with the angel,
   praising God and saying:

> "Glory to God in the highest
> and on earth peace to those on whom his favor rests."

The Gospel of the Lord. **All: Praise to you, Lord Jesus Christ.**

Prayer over the Offerings
May the oblation of this day's feast
be pleasing to you, O Lord, we pray,
that through this most holy exchange
we may be found in the likeness of Christ,
in whom our nature is united to you.
Who lives and reigns for ever and ever. **All: Amen.**

Communion Antiphon (John 1:14)
The Word became flesh, and we have seen his glory.

Prayer after Communion
Grant us, we pray, O Lord our God,
that we, who are gladdened by participation
in the feast of our Redeemer's Nativity,
may through an honorable way of life become worthy of union with him.
Who lives and reigns for ever and ever. **All: Amen.**

AT THE MASS AT DAWN

Entrance Antiphon
(Cf. Isaiah 9:1, 5; Luke 1:33)
Today a light will shine upon us, for the Lord is born for us;
and he will be called Wondrous God,
Prince of peace, Father of future ages:
and his reign will be without end.

Collect
Grant, we pray, almighty God,
that, as we are bathed in the new radiance of your incarnate Word,

the light of faith, which illumines our minds,
may also shine through in our deeds.
Through our Lord Jesus Christ, your Son,
who lives and reigns with you in the unity of the Holy Spirit,
one God, for ever and ever. All: **Amen.**

READING I (L 15) (Isaiah 62:11-12)
A reading from the Book of the Prophet Isaiah

Behold, your Savior comes!

> **See, the L**ORD **proclaims
> to the ends of the earth:
> say to daughter Zion,
> your savior comes!
> Here is his reward with him,
> his recompense before him.
> They shall be called the holy people,
> the redeemed of the L**ORD**,
> and you shall be called "Frequented,"
> a city that is not forsaken.**

The word of the Lord. All: **Thanks be to God.**

RESPONSORIAL PSALM 97

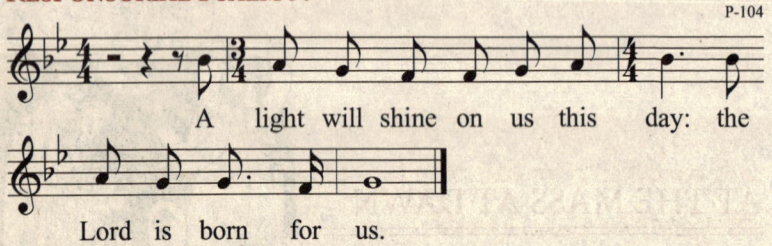

A light will shine on us this day: the Lord is born for us.

Music: Jay F. Hunstiger, © 1990, administered by Liturgical Press. All rights reserved.

Psalm 97:1, 6, 11-12

℟. **A light will shine on us this day: the Lord is born for us.**

> The LORD is king; let the earth rejoice;
>   let the many isles be glad.
> The heavens proclaim his justice,
>   and all peoples see his glory. ℟.
>
> Light dawns for the just;
>   and gladness, for the upright of heart.

> Be glad in the LORD, you just,
> and give thanks to his holy name. R̂.

READING II (Titus 3:4-7)
A reading from the Letter of Saint Paul to Titus

Because of his mercy, he saved us.

Beloved:
> **When the kindness and generous love
> of God our savior appeared,
> not because of any righteous deeds we had done
> but because of his mercy,
> he saved us through the bath of rebirth
> and renewal by the Holy Spirit,
> whom he richly poured out on us
> through Jesus Christ our savior,
> so that we might be justified by his grace
> and become heirs in hope of eternal life.**

The word of the Lord. All: **Thanks be to God.**

GOSPEL (Luke 2:15-20)
ALLELUIA (Luke 2:14)

V̂. Alleluia, alleluia. R̂. **Alleluia, alleluia.**
V̂. Glory to God in the highest,
and on earth peace to those
on whom his favor rests. R̂.

✠ **A reading from the holy Gospel according to Luke**

All: **Glory to you, O Lord.**

The shepherds found Mary and Joseph and the infant.

**When the angels went away from them to heaven,
the shepherds said to one another,
"Let us go, then, to Bethlehem
to see this thing that has taken place,
which the Lord has made known to us."
So they went in haste and found Mary and Joseph,
and the infant lying in the manger.**

When they saw this,
  they made known the message
  that had been told them about this child.
All who heard it were amazed
  by what had been told them by the shepherds.
And Mary kept all these things,
  reflecting on them in her heart.
Then the shepherds returned,
  glorifying and praising God
  for all they had heard and seen,
  just as it had been told to them.

The Gospel of the Lord. All: **Praise to you, Lord Jesus Christ.**

Prayer over the Offerings
May our offerings be worthy, we pray, O Lord,
of the mysteries of the Nativity this day,
that, just as Christ was born a man and also shone forth as God,
so these earthly gifts may confer on us what is divine.
Through Christ our Lord. All: **Amen.**

Communion Antiphon (Cf. Zechariah 9:9)
Rejoice, O Daughter Sion; lift up praise, Daughter Jerusalem:
Behold, your King will come, the Holy One and Savior of
  the world.

Prayer after Communion
Grant us, Lord, as we honor with joyful devotion
the Nativity of your Son,
that we may come to know with fullness of faith
the hidden depths of this mystery
and to love them ever more and more.
Through Christ our Lord. All: **Amen.**

AT THE MASS DURING THE DAY

Entrance Antiphon (Cf. Isaiah 9:5)
A child is born for us, and a son is given to us;
his scepter of power rests upon his shoulder,
and his name will be called Messenger of great counsel.

Collect
O God, who wonderfully created the dignity of human nature
and still more wonderfully restored it,
grant, we pray,
that we may share in the divinity of Christ,
who humbled himself to share in our humanity.
Who lives and reigns with you in the unity of the Holy Spirit,
one God, for ever and ever. All: **Amen.**

Reading I (L 16) (Isaiah 52:7-10)
A reading from the Book of the Prophet Isaiah

All the ends of the earth will behold the salvation of our God.

> **How beautiful upon the mountains
>   are the feet of him who brings glad tidings,
> announcing peace, bearing good news,
>   announcing salvation, and saying to Zion,
>   "Your God is King!"**
>
> **Hark! Your sentinels raise a cry,
>   together they shout for joy,
> for they see directly, before their eyes,
>   the Lord restoring Zion.
> Break out together in song,
>   O ruins of Jerusalem!
> For the Lord comforts his people,
>   he redeems Jerusalem.**

> The LORD has bared his holy arm
> > in the sight of all the nations;
> all the ends of the earth will behold
> > the salvation of our God.

The word of the Lord. All: Thanks be to God.

RESPONSORIAL PSALM 98

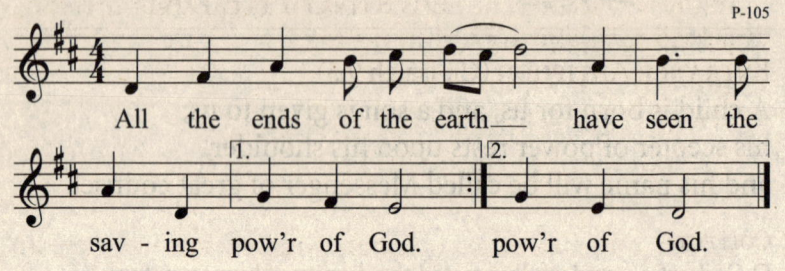

All the ends of the earth have seen the sav-ing pow'r of God. pow'r of God.

Music: Jay F. Hunstiger, © 1990, administered by Liturgical Press. All rights reserved.

Psalm 98:1, 2-3, 3-4, 5-6

℟. (3c) **All the ends of the earth have seen the saving power of God.**

Sing to the LORD a new song,
> for he has done wondrous deeds;
his right hand has won victory for him,
> his holy arm. ℟.

The LORD has made his salvation known:
> in the sight of the nations he has revealed his justice.
He has remembered his kindness and his faithfulness
> toward the house of Israel. ℟.

All the ends of the earth have seen
> the salvation by our God.
Sing joyfully to the LORD, all you lands;
> break into song; sing praise. ℟.

Sing praise to the LORD with the harp,
> with the harp and melodious song.
With trumpets and the sound of the horn
> sing joyfully before the King, the LORD. ℟.

Reading II (Hebrews 1:1-6)
A reading from the beginning of the Letter to the Hebrews

God has spoken to us through the Son.

Brothers and sisters:
In times past, God spoke in partial and various ways
    to our ancestors through the prophets;
    in these last days, he has spoken to us through the Son,
    whom he made heir of all things
    and through whom he created the universe,
        who is the refulgence of his glory,
            the very imprint of his being,
        and who sustains all things by his mighty word.
        When he had accomplished purification from sins,
        he took his seat at the right hand of the Majesty
            on high,
        as far superior to the angels
        as the name he has inherited is more excellent than
            theirs.

For to which of the angels did God ever say:
You are my son; this day I have begotten you?
Or again:
I will be a father to him, and he shall be a son to me?
And again, when he leads the firstborn into the world,
    he says:
Let all the angels of God worship him.

The word of the Lord. **All: Thanks be to God.**

Gospel (John 1:1-18) *or* Shorter Form [ ] (John 1:1-5, 9-14)
Alleluia
℣. Alleluia, alleluia. ℟. **Alleluia, alleluia.**
℣. A holy day has dawned upon us.
    Come, you nations, and adore the Lord.
    For today a great light has come upon the earth. ℟.

✢ A reading from the holy Gospel according to John
All: Glory to you, O Lord.

The Word became flesh and made his dwelling among us.

[In the beginning was the Word,
>   and the Word was with God,
>   and the Word was God.
> He was in the beginning with God.
> All things came to be through him,
>   and without him nothing came to be.
> What came to be through him was life,
>   and this life was the light of the human race;
> the light shines in the darkness,
>   and the darkness has not overcome it.]
A man named John was sent from God.
He came for testimony, to testify to the light,
>   so that all might believe through him.
He was not the light,
>   but came to testify to the light.
[The true light, which enlightens everyone,
>   was coming into the world.
> He was in the world,
>   and the world came to be through him,
>   but the world did not know him.
> He came to what was his own,
>   but his own people did not accept him.

But to those who did accept him
> he gave power to become children of God,
> to those who believe in his name,
> who were born not by natural generation
> nor by human choice nor by a man's decision
> but of God.
>   And the Word became flesh
>   and made his dwelling among us,
>   and we saw his glory,
>   the glory as of the Father's only Son,
>   full of grace and truth.]
John testified to him and cried out, saying,
>   "This was he of whom I said,

'The one who is coming after me ranks ahead of me
because he existed before me.'"
From his fullness we have all received,
grace in place of grace,
because while the law was given through Moses,
grace and truth came through Jesus Christ.
No one has ever seen God.
The only Son, God, who is at the Father's side,
has revealed him.

The Gospel of the Lord. All: **Praise to you, Lord Jesus Christ.**

Prayer over the Offerings
Make acceptable, O Lord, our oblation on this solemn day,
when you manifested the reconciliation
that makes us wholly pleasing in your sight
and inaugurated for us the fullness of divine worship.
Through Christ our Lord. All: **Amen.**

Communion Antiphon (Cf. Psalm 98[97]:3)
All the ends of the earth have seen the salvation of our God.

Prayer after Communion
Grant, O merciful God,
that, just as the Savior of the world, born this day,
is the author of divine generation for us,
so he may be the giver even of immortality.
Who lives and reigns for ever and ever. All: **Amen.**

The Holy Family of Jesus, Mary, and Joseph

SUNDAY WITHIN THE OCTAVE OF THE NATIVITY OF THE LORD (Christmas)

December 28, 2014

Reflection on the Gospel
Mary and Joseph bring Jesus to the temple "according to the law," fulfilling their obligation as new parents. Simeon is open to the Holy Spirit's Presence, guidance, and revelation to him of the "Christ of the Lord." Anna spoke prophetically to others about the redemption that was at hand. Faithfulness to the law, openness to the Holy Spirit, prophetically speaking about what has been revealed deepen our right relationship with God. Families are holy when they, too, act as did Mary and Joseph, Simeon, and Anna.

- Being open to the Holy Spirit is to . . .

—*Living Liturgy*™, *Holy Family 2014*

Entrance Antiphon (Luke 2:16)
The shepherds went in haste,
and found Mary and Joseph and the Infant lying in a manger.

Collect
O God, who were pleased to give us
the shining example of the Holy Family,
graciously grant that we may imitate them
in practicing the virtues of family life and in the bonds of charity,
and so, in the joy of your house,
delight one day in eternal rewards.
Through our Lord Jesus Christ, your Son,
who lives and reigns with you in the unity of the Holy Spirit,
one God, for ever and ever. All: **Amen.**

Reading I (L 17) (Sirach 3:2-6, 12-14) *for this year additional options can be found in the Lectionary*
A reading from the Book of Sirach
Those who fear the Lord honor their parents.

God sets a father in honor over his children;
  a mother's authority he confirms over her sons.
Whoever honors his father atones for sins,
  and preserves himself from them.
When he prays, he is heard;
  he stores up riches who reveres his mother.
Whoever honors his father is gladdened by children,
  and, when he prays, is heard.
Whoever reveres his father will live a long life;
  he who obeys his father brings comfort to his mother.

My son, take care of your father when he is old;
  grieve him not as long as he lives.
Even if his mind fail, be considerate of him;
  revile him not all the days of his life;
kindness to a father will not be forgotten,
  firmly planted against the debt of your sins
    —a house raised in justice to you.

The word of the Lord. All: **Thanks be to God.**

Responsorial Psalm 128

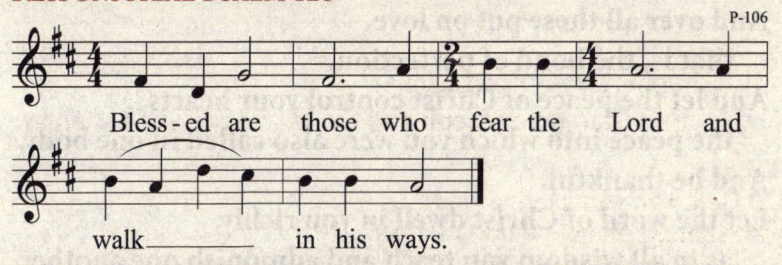

Bless-ed are those who fear the Lord and walk in his ways.

Music: Jay F. Hunstiger, © 1998, administered by Liturgical Press. All rights reserved.

Psalm 128:1-2, 3, 4-5

℟. (See 1) **Blessed are those who fear the Lord and walk in his ways.**

Blessed is everyone who fears the LORD,
  who walks in his ways!
For you shall eat the fruit of your handiwork;
  blessed shall you be, and favored. ℟.

Your wife shall be like a fruitful vine
  in the recesses of your home;

(continued)

your children like olive plants
   around your table. ℟.

Behold, thus is the man blessed
   who fears the Lord.
The Lord bless you from Zion:
   may you see the prosperity of Jerusalem
   all the days of your life. ℟.

Reading II (Colossians 3:12-21) *or* Shorter Form [ ]
(Colossians 3:12-17) *for this year additional options can be found in the Lectionary*

A reading from the Letter of Saint Paul to the Colossians

Family life in the Lord.

[Brothers and sisters:
Put on, as God's chosen ones, holy and beloved,
   heartfelt compassion, kindness, humility, gentleness,
      and patience,
   bearing with one another and forgiving one another,
   if one has a grievance against another;
   as the Lord has forgiven you, so must you also do.
And over all these put on love,
   that is, the bond of perfection.
And let the peace of Christ control your hearts,
   the peace into which you were also called in one body.
And be thankful.
Let the word of Christ dwell in you richly,
   as in all wisdom you teach and admonish one another,
   singing psalms, hymns, and spiritual songs
   with gratitude in your hearts to God.
And whatever you do, in word or in deed,
   do everything in the name of the Lord Jesus,
   giving thanks to God the Father through him.]

Wives, be subordinate to your husbands,
   as is proper in the Lord.
Husbands, love your wives,
   and avoid any bitterness toward them.

Children, obey your parents in everything,
 for this is pleasing to the Lord.
Fathers, do not provoke your children,
 so they may not become discouraged.

The word of the Lord. All: **Thanks be to God.**

GOSPEL (Luke 2:22-40) *or* Shorter Form [ ] (Luke 2:22, 39-40)
ALLELUIA (Colossians 3:15a, 16a)
℣. Alleluia, alleluia.   ℟. **Alleluia, alleluia.**
℣. Let the peace of Christ control your hearts;
 let the word of Christ dwell in you richly. ℟.

or:

ALLELUIA (Hebrews 1:1-2)
℣. Alleluia, alleluia.   ℟. **Alleluia, alleluia.**
℣. In the past God spoke to our ancestors through the prophets;
 in these last days, he has spoken to us through the Son. ℟.

✠ **A reading from the holy Gospel according to Luke**

All: **Glory to you, O Lord.**

The child grew and became strong, filled with wisdom.

[**When the days were completed for their purification**
 according to the law of Moses,
 they took him up to Jerusalem
 to present him to the Lord,]
 just as it is written in the law of the Lord,
 Every male that opens the womb shall be consecrated
   to the Lord,
 and to offer the sacrifice of
 a pair of turtledoves or two young pigeons,
 in accordance with the dictate in the law of the Lord.
Now there was a man in Jerusalem whose name was Simeon.
This man was righteous and devout,
 awaiting the consolation of Israel,
 and the Holy Spirit was upon him.

It had been revealed to him by the Holy Spirit
    that he should not see death
    before he had seen the Christ of the Lord.
He came in the Spirit into the temple;
    and when the parents brought in the child Jesus
    to perform the custom of the law in regard to him,
    he took him into his arms and blessed God, saying:
        "Now, Master, you may let your servant go
            in peace, according to your word,
        for my eyes have seen your salvation,
            which you prepared in sight of all the peoples,
        a light for revelation to the Gentiles,
            and glory for your people Israel."
The child's father and mother were amazed at what was
    said about him;
    and Simeon blessed them and said to Mary his mother,
    "Behold, this child is destined
    for the fall and rise of many in Israel,
    and to be a sign that will be contradicted
    —and you yourself a sword will pierce—
    so that the thoughts of many hearts may be revealed."
There was also a prophetess, Anna,
    the daughter of Phanuel, of the tribe of Asher.
She was advanced in years,
    having lived seven years with her husband after her
        marriage,
    and then as a widow until she was eighty-four.
She never left the temple,
    but worshiped night and day with fasting and prayer.
And coming forward at that very time,
    she gave thanks to God and spoke about the child
    to all who were awaiting the redemption of Jerusalem.

[When they had fulfilled all the prescriptions
    of the law of the Lord,
    they returned to Galilee,
    to their own town of Nazareth.

The child grew and became strong, filled with wisdom;
   and the favor of God was upon him.]

The Gospel of the Lord. All: **Praise to you, Lord Jesus Christ.**

Prayer over the Offerings
We offer you, Lord, the sacrifice of conciliation,
humbly asking that,
through the intercession of the Virgin Mother of God and Saint Joseph,
you may establish our families firmly in your grace and your peace.
Through Christ our Lord. All: **Amen.**

Communion Antiphon (Baruch 3:38)
Our God has appeared on the earth, and lived among us.

Prayer after Communion
Bring those you refresh with this heavenly Sacrament,
most merciful Father,
to imitate constantly the example of the Holy Family,
so that, after the trials of this world,
we may share their company for ever.
Through Christ our Lord. All: **Amen.**

Solemnity of Mary, the Holy Mother of God

OCTAVE DAY OF THE NATIVITY OF THE LORD (Christmas)

January 1, 2015

World Day of Peace

Reflection on the Gospel

This infant conceived by the Holy Spirit in Mary's womb is both God and man. No doubt Mary reflected "in her heart" on this great mystery throughout her life, a reflection that preserved her as the holy and faithful Mother of God. Our reflection on the mystery of the incarnation must be so deep as Mary's that it brings us to greater holiness and faithfulness. It must bring us, like the shepherds, to come in haste to encounter the One who deserves all glory and praise.

- *Theotokos, the mystery of God and man, Mary's son is . . .*

—Living Liturgy™, *Mary, Mother of God 2015*

ENTRANCE ANTIPHON

Hail, Holy Mother, who gave birth to the King
who rules heaven and earth for ever.

Or:

(Cf. Isaiah 9:1, 5; Luke 1:33)
Today a light will shine upon us, for the Lord is born for us;
and he will be called Wondrous God,
Prince of peace, Father of future ages:
and his reign will be without end.

COLLECT

O God, who through the fruitful virginity of Blessed Mary
bestowed on the human race
the grace of eternal salvation,
grant, we pray,
that we may experience the intercession of her,
through whom we were found worthy
to receive the author of life,

our Lord Jesus Christ, your Son.
Who lives and reigns with you in the unity of the Holy Spirit,
one God, for ever and ever. All: **Amen.**

READING I (L 18) (Numbers 6:22-27)
A reading from the Book of Numbers

They shall invoke my name upon the Israelites, and I will bless them.

The LORD said to Moses:
   "Speak to Aaron and his sons and tell them:
   This is how you shall bless the Israelites.
Say to them:
   The LORD bless you and keep you!
   The LORD let his face shine upon
      you, and be gracious to you!
   The LORD look upon you kindly and
      give you peace!
So shall they invoke my name upon the Israelites,
   and I will bless them."

The word of the Lord. All: **Thanks be to God.**

RESPONSORIAL PSALM 67

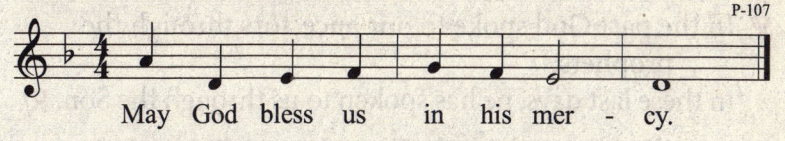

May God bless us in his mercy.

Music: Jay F. Hunstiger, © 1990, administered by Liturgical Press. All rights reserved.

Psalm 67:2-3, 5, 6, 8

℟. (2a) **May God bless us in his mercy.**

   May God have pity on us and bless us;
      may he let his face shine upon us.
   So may your way be known upon earth;
      among all nations, your salvation. ℟.

   May the nations be glad and exult
      because you rule the peoples in equity;
      the nations on the earth you guide. ℟.

   May the peoples praise you, O God;
      may all the peoples praise you!

(continued)

May God bless us,
> and may all the ends of the earth fear him! ℟.

Reading II (Galatians 4:4-7)
A reading from the Letter of Saint Paul to the Galatians

God sent his Son, born of a woman.

Brothers and sisters:
When the fullness of time had come, God sent his Son,
> **born of a woman, born under the law,**
> **to ransom those under the law,**
> **so that we might receive adoption as sons.**
As proof that you are sons,
> **God sent the Spirit of his Son into our hearts,**
> **crying out, "Abba, Father!"**
So you are no longer a slave but a son,
> **and if a son then also an heir, through God.**

The word of the Lord. All: **Thanks be to God.**

Gospel (Luke 2:16-21)
Alleluia (Hebrews 1:1-2)
℣. Alleluia, alleluia. ℟. **Alleluia, alleluia.**
℣. In the past God spoke to our ancestors through the prophets;
> in these last days, he has spoken to us through the Son. ℟.

✠ **A reading from the holy Gospel according to Luke**

All: **Glory to you, O Lord.**

They found Mary and Joseph and the infant. When the eight days were completed, he was named Jesus.

The shepherds went in haste to Bethlehem and found
> **Mary and Joseph,**
> **and the infant lying in the manger.**
When they saw this,
> **they made known the message**
> **that had been told them about this child.**
All who heard it were amazed
> **by what had been told them by the shepherds.**

**And Mary kept all these things,
  reflecting on them in her heart.
Then the shepherds returned,
  glorifying and praising God
  for all they had heard and seen,
  just as it had been told to them.**

**When eight days were completed for his circumcision,
  he was named Jesus, the name given him by the angel
  before he was conceived in the womb.**

The Gospel of the Lord. All: **Praise to you, Lord Jesus Christ.**

Prayer over the Offerings
O God, who in your kindness begin all good things
and bring them to fulfillment,
grant to us, who find joy in the Solemnity of the holy Mother of God,
that, just as we glory in the beginnings of your grace,
so one day we may rejoice in its completion.
Through Christ our Lord. All: **Amen.**

Communion Antiphon (Hebrews 13:8)
Jesus Christ is the same yesterday, today, and for ever.

Prayer after Communion
We have received this heavenly Sacrament with joy, O Lord:
grant, we pray,
that it may lead us to eternal life,
for we rejoice to proclaim the blessed ever-Virgin Mary
Mother of your Son and Mother of the Church.
Through Christ our Lord. All: **Amen.**

The Epiphany of the Lord

AT THE VIGIL MASS

January 4, 2015

This Mass is used on the evening of the day before the Solemnity, either before or after First Vespers (Evening Prayer I) of the Epiphany.

Reflection on the Gospel

This gospel uncovers a number of contrasts: the magi-Gentiles from the east vs. Herod and the Jews of all Jerusalem; the light of the star that guided the magi vs. the darkness of Herod's heart; the "newborn king of the Jews" thought to be found in Jerusalem vs. this Child being found in the small village of Bethlehem; Herod breeding evil in his heart to keep his power and status vs. the magi who paid homage and offered gifts to the Child. Searching for and finding the Christ necessitates a choice in face of contrasts.

- I am guided to Christ by . . .

—Living Liturgy™, *Epiphany 2015*

Entrance Antiphon (Cf. Baruch 5:5)
Arise, Jerusalem, and look to the East
and see your children gathered from the rising to the setting of the sun.

Collect
May the splendor of your majesty, O Lord, we pray,
shed its light upon our hearts,
that we may pass through the shadows of this world
and reach the brightness of our eternal home.
Through our Lord Jesus Christ, your Son,
who lives and reigns with you in the unity of the Holy Spirit,
one God, for ever and ever. All: **Amen.**

(Note readings are those of the day.)

Prayer over the Offerings
Accept we pray, O Lord, our offerings,
in honor of the appearing of your Only Begotten Son
and the first fruits of the nations,
that to you praise may be rendered
and eternal salvation be ours.
Through Christ our Lord. All: **Amen.**

Communion Antiphon (Cf. Revelation 21:23)
The brightness of God illumined the holy city Jerusalem,
and the nations will walk by its light.

Prayer after Communion
Renewed by sacred nourishment,
we implore your mercy, O Lord,
that the star of your justice
may shine always bright in our minds
and that our true treasure may ever consist in our confession of you.
Through Christ our Lord. All. **Amen.**

January 5

AT THE MASS DURING THE DAY

Entrance Antiphon (Cf. Malachi 3:1; 1 Chronicles 29:12)
Behold, the Lord, the Mighty One, has come;
and kingship is in his grasp, and power and dominion.

Collect
O God, who on this day
revealed your Only Begotten Son to the nations
by the guidance of a star,
grant in your mercy
that we, who know you already by faith,
may be brought to behold the beauty of your sublime glory.
Through our Lord Jesus Christ, your Son,
who lives and reigns with you in the unity of the Holy Spirit,
one God, for ever and ever. All: **Amen.**

Reading I (L 20) (Isaiah 60:1-6)
A reading from the Book of the Prophet Isaiah

The glory of the Lord shines upon you.

Rise up in splendor, Jerusalem! Your light has come,
  the glory of the Lord shines upon you.
See, darkness covers the earth,
  and thick clouds cover the peoples;
but upon you the LORD shines,
  and over you appears his glory.
Nations shall walk by your light,
  and kings by your shining radiance.
Raise your eyes and look about;
  they all gather and come to you:
your sons come from afar,
  and your daughters in the arms of their nurses.

Then you shall be radiant at what you see,
  your heart shall throb and overflow,
for the riches of the sea shall be emptied out before you,
  the wealth of nations shall be brought to you.
Caravans of camels shall fill you,
  dromedaries from Midian and Ephah;
all from Sheba shall come
  bearing gold and frankincense,
    and proclaiming the praises of the LORD.

The word of the Lord. All: Thanks be to God.

RESPONSORIAL PSALM 72

Lord, ev-'ry na-tion on earth will a-dore you.

Music: Jay F. Hunstiger, © 1990, administered by Liturgical Press. All rights reserved.

Psalm 72:1-2, 7-8, 10-11, 12-13

℟. (*See* 11) **Lord, every nation on earth will adore you.**

O God, with your judgment endow the king,
  and with your justice, the king's son;
he shall govern your people with justice
  and your afflicted ones with judgment. ℟.

Justice shall flower in his days,
  and profound peace, till the moon be no more.
May he rule from sea to sea,
  and from the River to the ends of the earth. ℟.

The kings of Tarshish and the Isles shall offer gifts;
  the kings of Arabia and Seba shall bring tribute.
All kings shall pay him homage,
  all nations shall serve him. ℟.

For he shall rescue the poor when he cries out,
  and the afflicted when he has no one to help him.
He shall have pity for the lowly and the poor;
  the lives of the poor he shall save. ℟.

READING II (Ephesians 3:2-3a, 5-6)
A reading from the Letter of Saint Paul to the Ephesians

Now it has been revealed that the Gentiles are coheirs of the promise.

Brothers and sisters:
You have heard of the stewardship of God's grace
  that was given to me for your benefit,
    namely, that the mystery was made known to me by revelation.
It was not made known to people in other generations
  as it has now been revealed
  to his holy apostles and prophets by the Spirit:
  that the Gentiles are coheirs, members of the same body,
  and copartners in the promise in Christ Jesus through the gospel.

The word of the Lord. All: **Thanks be to God.**

GOSPEL (Matthew 2:1-12)
ALLELUIA (Matthew 2:2)
℣. Alleluia, alleluia. ℟. **Alleluia, alleluia.**
℣. We saw his star at its rising
  and have come to do him homage. ℟.

✠ **A reading from the holy Gospel according to Matthew**
All: **Glory to you, O Lord.**

We saw his star at its rising and have come to do him homage.

When Jesus was born in Bethlehem of Judea,
>   in the days of King Herod,
>> behold, magi from the east arrived in Jerusalem, saying,
>> "Where is the newborn king of the Jews?
We saw his star at its rising
> and have come to do him homage."
When King Herod heard this,
> he was greatly troubled,
> and all Jerusalem with him.
Assembling all the chief priests and the scribes of the people,
> he inquired of them where the Christ was to be born.
They said to him, "In Bethlehem of Judea,
> for thus it has been written through the prophet:
>> *And you, Bethlehem, land of Judah,*
>>> *are by no means least among the rulers of Judah;*
>> *since from you shall come a ruler,*
>>> *who is to shepherd my people Israel."*
Then Herod called the magi secretly
> and ascertained from them the time of the star's appearance.
He sent them to Bethlehem and said,
> "Go and search diligently for the child.
When you have found him, bring me word,
> that I too may go and do him homage."
After their audience with the king they set out.
And behold, the star that they had seen at its rising preceded them,
> until it came and stopped over the place where the child was.
They were overjoyed at seeing the star,
> and on entering the house
> they saw the child with Mary his mother.
They prostrated themselves and did him homage.
Then they opened their treasures
> and offered him gifts of gold, frankincense, and myrrh.

**And having been warned in a dream not to return to
   Herod,
  they departed for their country by another way.**

The Gospel of the Lord. All: **Praise to you, Lord Jesus Christ.**

Prayer over the Offerings
Look with favor, Lord, we pray,
on these gifts of your Church,
in which are offered now not gold or frankincense or myrrh,
but he who by them is proclaimed,
sacrificed and received, Jesus Christ.
Who lives and reigns for ever and ever. All: **Amen.**

Communion Antiphon (Cf. Matthew 2:2)
We have seen his star in the East,
and have come with gifts to adore the Lord.

Prayer after Communion
Go before us with heavenly light, O Lord,
always and everywhere,
that we may perceive with clear sight
and revere with true affection
the mystery in which you have willed us to participate.
Through Christ our Lord. All: **Amen.**

The Baptism of the Lord

January 11, 2015

Reflection on the Gospel

Jesus' baptism did not change his identity, but revealed who he was. John prophesied that Jesus, however, would bring an entirely different baptism, for he would baptize us with the Holy Spirit. The event of our baptism with the Spirit announces to all present who we become: beloved children with whom God is also "well pleased." Our whole Christian life is a journey of taking ownership of the ownership God has already taken of us. Through baptism God claims us.

- *Jesus is revealed to me by . . . and I am claimed by God as his own child.*

—Living Liturgy™, *Baptism of the Lord, 2015*

Entrance Antiphon (Cf. Matthew 3:16-17)

After the Lord was baptized, the heavens were opened,
and the Spirit descended upon him like a dove,
and the voice of the Father thundered:
This is my beloved Son, with whom I am well pleased.

Collect

Almighty ever-living God,
who, when Christ had been baptized in the River Jordan
and as the Holy Spirit descended upon him,
solemnly declared him your beloved Son,
grant that your children by adoption,
reborn of water and the Holy Spirit,
may always be well pleasing to you.
Through our Lord Jesus Christ, your Son,
who lives and reigns with you in the unity of the Holy Spirit,
one God, for ever and ever. All: **Amen.**

Or:

O God, whose Only Begotten Son
has appeared in our very flesh,
grant, we pray, that we may be inwardly transformed
through him whom we recognize as outwardly like ourselves.
Who lives and reigns with you in the unity of the Holy Spirit,
one God, for ever and ever. All: **Amen.**

Reading I (L 21) (Isaiah 42:1-4, 6-7) *for this year additional options can be found in the Lectionary*

A reading from the Book of the Prophet Isaiah

Behold my servant with whom I am well pleased.

Thus says the Lord:
Here is my servant whom I uphold,
>my chosen one with whom I am pleased,
upon whom I have put my spirit;
>he shall bring forth justice to the nations,
not crying out, not shouting,
>not making his voice heard in the street.
A bruised reed he shall not break,
>and a smoldering wick he shall not quench,
until he establishes justice on the earth;
>the coastlands will wait for his teaching.

I, the Lord, have called you for the victory of justice,
>I have grasped you by the hand;
I formed you, and set you
>as a covenant of the people,
>a light for the nations,
to open the eyes of the blind,
>to bring out prisoners from confinement,
>and from the dungeon, those who live in darkness.

The word of the Lord. All: **Thanks be to God.**

Responsorial Psalm 29

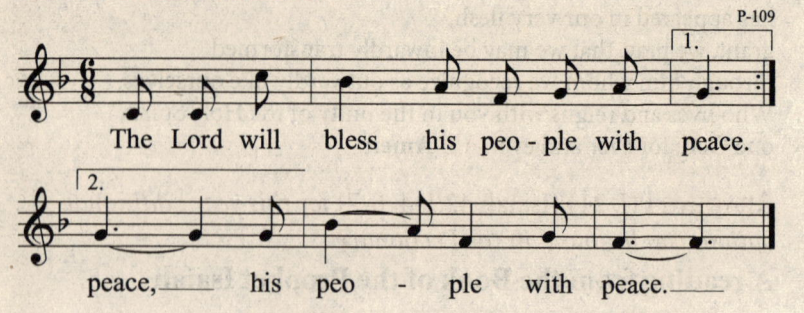

The Lord will bless his people with peace.
peace, his people with peace.

Music: Jay F. Hunstiger, © 1990, administered by Liturgical Press. All rights reserved.

Psalm 29:1-2, 3-4, 3, 9-10

℟. (11b) **The Lord will bless his people with peace.**

> Give to the LORD, you sons of God,
>   give to the LORD glory and praise,
> give to the LORD the glory due his name;
>   adore the LORD in holy attire. ℟.

> The voice of the LORD is over the waters,
>   the LORD, over vast waters.
> The voice of the LORD is mighty;
>   the voice of the LORD is majestic. ℟.

> The God of glory thunders,
>   and in his temple all say, "Glory!"
> The LORD is enthroned above the flood;
>   the LORD is enthroned as king forever. ℟.

Reading II (Acts of the Apostles 10:34-38) *for this year additional options can be found in the Lectionary*

A reading from the Acts of the Apostles

God anointed him with the Holy Spirit.

**Peter proceeded to speak to those gathered
  in the house of Cornelius, saying:
  "In truth, I see that God shows no partiality.
Rather, in every nation whoever fears him and acts
    uprightly
  is acceptable to him.**

You know the word that he sent to the Israelites
> as he proclaimed peace through Jesus Christ, who is
> > Lord of all,
> what has happened all over Judea,
> beginning in Galilee after the baptism
> that John preached,
> how God anointed Jesus of Nazareth
> with the Holy Spirit and power.

He went about doing good
> and healing all those oppressed by the devil,
> for God was with him."

The word of the Lord. All: Thanks be to God.

GOSPEL (Mark 1:7-11)
ALLELUIA (See Mark 9:7)
℣. Alleluia, alleluia. ℟. **Alleluia, alleluia.**
℣. The heavens were opened and the voice of the Father
> > thundered:
> This is my beloved Son, listen to him. ℟.

Or:

ALLELUIA (See John 1:29)
℣. Alleluia, alleluia. ℟. **Alleluia, alleluia.**
℣. John saw Jesus approaching him, and said:
> Behold the Lamb of God who takes away the sin of
> > the world. ℟.

✢ **A reading from the holy Gospel according to Mark**

All: **Glory to you, O Lord.**

You are my beloved Son; with you I am well pleased.

This is what John the Baptist proclaimed:
> "One mightier than I is coming after me.

I am not worthy to stoop and loosen the thongs of his
> sandals.

I have baptized you with water;
> he will baptize you with the Holy Spirit."

It happened in those days that Jesus came from Nazareth of Galilee
  and was baptized in the Jordan by John.
On coming up out of the water he saw the heavens being torn open
  and the Spirit, like a dove, descending upon him.
And a voice came from the heavens,
  "You are my beloved Son; with you I am well pleased."

The Gospel of the Lord. All: **Praise to you, Lord Jesus Christ.**

Prayer over the Offerings
Accept, O Lord, the offerings
we have brought to honor the revealing of your beloved Son,
so that the oblation of your faithful
may be transformed into the sacrifice of him
who willed in his compassion
to wash away the sins of the world.
Who lives and reigns for ever and ever. All: **Amen.**

Communion Antiphon (John 1:32, 34)
Behold the One of whom John said:
I have seen and testified that this is the Son of God.

Prayer after Communion
Nourished with these sacred gifts,
we humbly entreat your mercy, O Lord,
that, faithfully listening to your Only Begotten Son,
we may be your children in name and in truth.
Through Christ our Lord. All: **Amen.**

Second Sunday in Ordinary Time

January 18, 2015

Reflection on the Gospel

The two disciples in the gospel would have interpreted John the Baptist's cry, "Behold, the Lamb of God," within the Passover and temple tradition of sacrifice of lambs. What is startling about John's cry is that he uses this sacrificial reference not for a lamb, an animal, but for a human being who was walking by—Jesus. John is pointing to Jesus as the One who will be sacrificed. Little did they know at this point that the core of following Jesus is sacrifice—a total self-giving. Still, they followed him.

- *"Behold, the Lamb of God" . . .*

—Living Liturgy™, *Second Sunday in Ordinary Time 2015*

Entrance Antiphon (Psalm 66[65]:4)

**All the earth shall bow down before you, O God,
and shall sing to you,
shall sing to your name, O Most High!**

Collect

Almighty ever-living God,
who govern all things,
both in heaven and on earth,
mercifully hear the pleading of your people
and bestow your peace on our times.
Through our Lord Jesus Christ, your Son,
who lives and reigns with you in the unity of the Holy Spirit,
one God, for ever and ever. **All: Amen.**

Reading I (L 65-B) (1 Samuel 3:3b-10, 19)

A reading from the first Book of Samuel

Speak, Lord, for your servant is listening.

**Samuel was sleeping in the temple of the Lord
 where the ark of God was.
The Lord called to Samuel, who answered, "Here I am."**

Samuel ran to Eli and said, "Here I am. You called me."
"I did not call you," Eli said. "Go back to sleep."
So he went back to sleep.
Again the Lord called Samuel, who rose and went to Eli.
"Here I am," he said. "You called me."
But Eli answered, "I did not call you, my son. Go back to sleep."

At that time Samuel was not familiar with the Lord,
> because the Lord had not revealed anything to him as yet.

The Lord called Samuel again, for the third time.
Getting up and going to Eli, he said, "Here I am. You called me."
Then Eli understood that the Lord was calling the youth.
So he said to Samuel, "Go to sleep, and if you are called, reply,
> Speak, Lord, for your servant is listening."

When Samuel went to sleep in his place,
> the Lord came and revealed his presence,
> calling out as before, "Samuel, Samuel!"

Samuel answered, "Speak, for your servant is listening."

Samuel grew up, and the Lord was with him,
> not permitting any word of his to be without effect.

The word of the Lord. **All:** Thanks be to God.

Responsorial Psalm 40

Here am I, Lord;— I come to do your will. Here am I, Lord;— I come to do your will. will.

Music: Jay F. Hunstiger, © 1992, administered by Liturgical Press. All rights reserved.

Psalm 40:2, 4, 7-8, 8-9, 10

℟. (8a and 9a) **Here am I, Lord; I come to do your will.**

I have waited, waited for the LORD,
  and he stooped toward me and heard my cry.
And he put a new song into my mouth,
  a hymn to our God. ℟.

Sacrifice or offering you wished not,
  but ears open to obedience you gave me.
Holocausts or sin-offerings you sought not;
  then said I, "Behold I come." ℟.

"In the written scroll it is prescribed for me,
to do your will, O my God, is my delight,
  and your law is within my heart!" ℟.

I announced your justice in the vast assembly;
  I did not restrain my lips, as you, O LORD, know. ℟.

READING II (1 Corinthians 6:13c-15a, 17-20)

A reading from the first Letter of Saint Paul to the Corinthians

Your bodies are members of Christ.

Brothers and sisters:
The body is not for immorality, but for the Lord,
  and the Lord is for the body;
    God raised the Lord and will also raise us by his power.
Do you not know that your bodies are members of Christ?
But whoever is joined to the Lord becomes one Spirit with him.
Avoid immorality.
Every other sin a person commits is outside the body,
  but the immoral person sins against his own body.
Do you not know that your body
  is a temple of the Holy Spirit within you,
    whom you have from God, and that you are not your own?

For you have been purchased at a price.
Therefore glorify God in your body.

The word of the Lord. All: **Thanks be to God.**

GOSPEL (John 1:35-42)
ALLELUIA (John 1:41, 17b)
℣. Alleluia, alleluia. ℟. **Alleluia, alleluia.**
℣. We have found the Messiah:
Jesus Christ, who brings us truth and grace. ℟.

✠ **A reading from the holy Gospel according to John**

All: **Glory to you, O Lord.**

They saw where he was staying and they stayed with him.

**John was standing with two of his disciples,
and as he watched Jesus walk by, he said,
"Behold, the Lamb of God."
The two disciples heard what he said and followed Jesus.
Jesus turned and saw them following him and said to them,
"What are you looking for?"
They said to him, "Rabbi"—which translated means
Teacher—,
"where are you staying?"
He said to them, "Come, and you will see."
So they went and saw where Jesus was staying,
and they stayed with him that day.
It was about four in the afternoon.
Andrew, the brother of Simon Peter,
was one of the two who heard John and followed Jesus.
He first found his own brother Simon and told him,
"We have found the Messiah"—which is translated
Christ—.
Then he brought him to Jesus.
Jesus looked at him and said,
"You are Simon the son of John;
you will be called Cephas" — which is translated Peter.**

The Gospel of the Lord. All: **Praise to you, Lord Jesus Christ.**

Prayer over the Offerings
Grant us, O Lord, we pray,
that we may participate worthily in these mysteries,
for whenever the memorial of this sacrifice is celebrated
the work of our redemption is accomplished.
Through Christ our Lord. All: **Amen.**

Communion Antiphon (Cf. Psalm 23[22]:5)
You have prepared a table before me,
and how precious is the chalice that quenches my thirst.

Or:

(1 John 4:16)
We have come to know and to believe
in the love that God has for us.

Prayer after Communion
Pour on us, O Lord, the Spirit of your love,
and in your kindness
make those you have nourished
by this one heavenly Bread
one in mind and heart.
Through Christ our Lord. All: **Amen.**

Third Sunday in Ordinary Time

January 25, 2015

Reflection on the Gospel

John preached repentance, and was arrested in spite of his goodness and innocence. Jesus preached the Gospel and suffered and died in spite of his goodness and innocence. Hearing Jesus' call to discipleship and choosing to follow him faithfully literally assures us we will meet adversity and suffering, as did both John and Jesus. The surprise of the

gospel is not that we will face adversity, however. The surprise is that in preaching repentance and changing our lives, "the time of fulfillment" is upon us. To enter into this "time of fulfillment," we must leave everything behind and answer Jesus' call to follow him.

• *Choosing and following Jesus is . . .*

—*Living Liturgy*™, *Third Sunday in Ordinary Time 2015*

Entrance Antiphon (Cf. Psalm 96[95]:1, 6)

O sing a new song to the Lord;
sing to the Lord, all the earth.
In his presence are majesty and splendor,
strength and honor in his holy place.

Collect

Almighty ever-living God,
direct our actions according to your good pleasure,
that in the name of your beloved Son
we may abound in good works.
Through our Lord Jesus Christ, your Son,
who lives and reigns with you in the unity of the Holy Spirit,
one God, for ever and ever. All: **Amen.**

Reading I (L- 68-B) (Jonah 3:1-5, 10)

A reading from the Book of the Prophet Jonah

The Ninevites turned from their evil way.

The word of the Lord came to Jonah, saying:
  "Set out for the great city of Nineveh,
    and announce to it the message that I will tell you."
So Jonah made ready and went to Nineveh,
  according to the Lord's bidding.
Now Nineveh was an enormously large city;
  it took three days to go through it.
Jonah began his journey through the city,
  and had gone but a single day's walk announcing,
  "Forty days more and Nineveh shall be destroyed,"
  when the people of Nineveh believed God;
  they proclaimed a fast
  and all of them, great and small, put on sackcloth.

When God saw by their actions how they turned from their evil way,
> **he repented of the evil that he had threatened to do to them;**
> **he did not carry it out.**

The word of the Lord. All: **Thanks be to God.**

Responsorial Psalm 25

Teach me your ways, O— Lord, teach me your ways.

Music: Jay F. Hunstiger, © 1990, administered by Liturgical Press. All rights reserved.

Psalm 25:4-5, 6-7, 8-9

℟. (4a) **Teach me your ways, O Lord.**

> Your ways, O Lord, make known to me;
>> teach me your paths,
> guide me in your truth and teach me,
>> for you are God my savior. ℟.

> Remember that your compassion, O Lord,
>> and your love are from of old.
> In your kindness remember me,
>> because of your goodness, O Lord. ℟.

> Good and upright is the Lord;
>> thus he shows sinners the way.
> He guides the humble to justice
>> and teaches the humble his way. ℟.

Reading II (1 Corinthians 7:29-31)

A reading from the first Letter of Saint Paul to the Corinthians

The world in its present form is passing away.

I tell you, brothers and sisters, the time is running out. From now on, let those having wives act as not having them,
> **those weeping as not weeping,**
> **those rejoicing as not rejoicing,**

those buying as not owning,
those using the world as not using it fully.
For the world in its present form is passing away.

The word of the Lord. All: **Thanks be to God.**

GOSPEL (Mark 1:14-20)
ALLELUIA (Mark 1:15)

℣. Alleluia, alleluia. ℟. **Alleluia, alleluia.**
℣. The kingdom of God is at hand.
 Repent and believe in the Gospel. ℟.

✠ **A reading from the holy Gospel according to Mark**

All: **Glory to you, O Lord.**

Repent and believe in the Gospel.

After John had been arrested,
 Jesus came to Galilee proclaiming the gospel of God:
 "This is the time of fulfillment.
The kingdom of God is at hand.
Repent, and believe in the gospel."

As he passed by the Sea of Galilee,
 he saw Simon and his brother Andrew casting their
  nets into the sea;
 they were fishermen.
Jesus said to them,
 "Come after me, and I will make you fishers of men."
Then they abandoned their nets and followed him.
He walked along a little farther
 and saw James, the son of Zebedee, and his brother
  John.
They too were in a boat mending their nets.
Then he called them.
So they left their father Zebedee in the boat
 along with the hired men and followed him.

The Gospel of the Lord. All: **Praise to you, Lord Jesus Christ.**

Prayer over the Offerings
Accept our offerings, O Lord, we pray,
and in sanctifying them
grant that they may profit us for salvation.
Through Christ our Lord. All: **Amen.**

Communion Antiphon (Cf. Psalm 34[33]:6)
Look toward the Lord and be radiant;
let your faces not be abashed.

Or:

(John 8:12)
I am the light of the world, says the Lord;
whoever follows me will not walk in darkness,
but will have the light of life.

Prayer after Communion
Grant, we pray, almighty God,
that, receiving the grace
by which you bring us to new life,
we may always glory in your gift.
Through Christ our Lord. All: **Amen.**

Fourth Sunday in Ordinary Time

February 1, 2015

Reflection on the Gospel

All of us must confront many battles waged between good and evil throughout our lives. For us to destroy the evil that confronts us, we must be "of God," we must be holy. We have the authority to banish evil because, baptized into Christ, we are holy ones "of God." The authority of holiness is our baptismal birthright. It is God's Life given us that makes us holy; it is God's Life that makes us, too, "of God." Like Jesus, we must be the authority of holiness incarnate.

• *Baptized into Christ, we are the holy ones "of God" . . .*

—Living Liturgy™, *Fourth Sunday in Ordinary Time 2015*

Entrance Antiphon (Psalm 106[105]:47)
Save us, O Lord our God!
And gather us from the nations,
to give thanks to your holy name,
and make it our glory to praise you.

Collect
Grant us, Lord our God,
that we may honor you with all our mind,
and love everyone in truth of heart.
Through our Lord Jesus Christ, your Son,
who lives and reigns with you in the unity of the Holy Spirit,
one God, for ever and ever. All: **Amen.**

Reading I (L 71-B) (Deuteronomy 18:15-20)
A reading from the Book of Deuteronomy

I will raise up a prophet and I will put my words into his mouth.

Moses spoke to all the people, saying:
   "A prophet like me will the Lord, your God, raise up
      for you
   from among your own kin;
   to him you shall listen.
This is exactly what you requested of the Lord, your
      God, at Horeb
   on the day of the assembly, when you said,
   'Let us not again hear the voice of the Lord, our God,
   nor see this great fire any more, lest we die.'
And the Lord said to me, 'This was well said.
I will raise up for them a prophet like you from among
      their kin,
   and will put my words into his mouth;
   he shall tell them all that I command him.
Whoever will not listen to my words which he speaks in
      my name,
   I myself will make him answer for it.
But if a prophet presumes to speak in my name
   an oracle that I have not commanded him to speak,
   or speaks in the name of other gods, he shall die.'"

The word of the Lord. All: **Thanks be to God.**

Responsorial Psalm 95

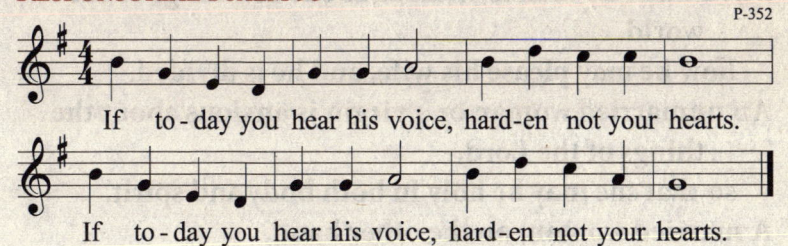

(musical notation)

If to-day you hear his voice, hard-en not your hearts.

If to-day you hear his voice, hard-en not your hearts.

Music: Jay F. Hunstiger, © 1993, administered by Liturgical Press. All rights reserved.

Psalm 95:1-2, 6-7, 7-9

℟. (8) **If today you hear his voice, harden not your hearts.**

Come, let us sing joyfully to the Lord;
  let us acclaim the rock of our salvation.
Let us come into his presence with thanksgiving;
  let us joyfully sing psalms to him. ℟.

Come, let us bow down in worship;
  let us kneel before the Lord who made us.
For he is our God,
  and we are the people he shepherds, the flock he guides. ℟.

Oh, that today you would hear his voice:
  "Harden not your hearts as at Meribah,
  as in the day of Massah in the desert,
where your fathers tempted me;
  they tested me though they had seen my works." ℟.

Reading II (1 Corinthians 7:32-35)

A reading from the first Letter of Saint Paul to the Corinthians

A virgin is anxious about the things of the Lord, that she may be holy.

Brothers and sisters:
I should like you to be free of anxieties.
An unmarried man is anxious about the things of the Lord,
  how he may please the Lord.

But a married man is anxious about the things of the world,
> how he may please his wife, and he is divided.

An unmarried woman or a virgin is anxious about the things of the Lord,
> so that she may be holy in both body and spirit.

A married woman, on the other hand,
> is anxious about the things of the world,
> how she may please her husband.

I am telling you this for your own benefit,
> not to impose a restraint upon you,
> but for the sake of propriety
> and adherence to the Lord without distraction.

The word of the Lord. All: Thanks be to God.

Gospel (Mark 1:21-28)
Alleluia (Matthew 4:16)

℣. Alleluia, alleluia. ℟. **Alleluia, alleluia.**
℣. The people who sit in darkness have seen a great light;
on those dwelling in a land overshadowed by death,
light has arisen. ℟.

✠ **A reading from the holy Gospel according to Mark**

All: **Glory to you, O Lord.**

He taught them as one having authority.

Then they came to Capernaum,
> and on the sabbath Jesus entered the synagogue and taught.

The people were astonished at his teaching,
> for he taught them as one having authority and not as the scribes.

In their synagogue was a man with an unclean spirit;
> he cried out, "What have you to do with us, Jesus of Nazareth?

Have you come to destroy us?
I know who you are—the Holy One of God!"

Jesus rebuked him and said,
  "Quiet! Come out of him!"
The unclean spirit convulsed him and with a loud cry
  came out of him.
All were amazed and asked one another,
  "What is this?
A new teaching with authority.
He commands even the unclean spirits and they obey
  him."
His fame spread everywhere throughout the whole
  region of Galilee.

The Gospel of the Lord. All: **Praise to you, Lord Jesus Christ.**

Prayer over the Offerings
O Lord, we bring to your altar
these offerings of our service:
be pleased to receive them, we pray,
and transform them
into the Sacrament of our redemption.
Through Christ our Lord. All: **Amen.**

Communion Antiphon (Cf. Psalm 31[30]:17-18)
Let your face shine on your servant.
Save me in your merciful love.
O Lord, let me never be put to shame, for I call on you.

Or:

(Matthew 5:3-4)
Blessed are the poor in spirit,
for theirs is the kingdom of heaven.
Blessed are the meek, for they shall possess the land.

Prayer after Communion
Nourished by these redeeming gifts,
we pray, O Lord,
that through this help to eternal salvation
true faith may ever increase.
Through Christ our Lord. All: **Amen.**

Fifth Sunday in Ordinary Time

February 8, 2015

Reflection on the Gospel

In the gospel Simon says to Jesus, "Everyone is looking for you." Jesus is having great success healing many people and driving out demons. All who encounter him adore him. People are paying great attention to him—"The whole town was gathered" at the door of Simon and Andrew's house. Nonetheless, Jesus moves on to other villages. His ministry is not about drawing attention to himself, but about preaching the Good News of salvation. Yet his ministry is about himself, for he is the Good News.

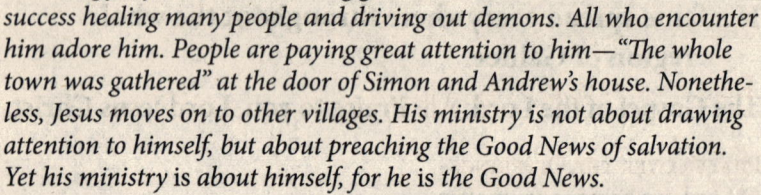

• I share the Good News by . . .

—Living Liturgy™, *Fifth Sunday in Ordinary Time 2015*

Entrance Antiphon (Psalm 95[94]:6-7)

O come, let us worship God
and bow low before the God who made us,
for he is the Lord our God.

Collect

Keep your family safe, O Lord, with unfailing care,
that, relying solely on the hope of heavenly grace,
they may be defended always by your protection.
Through our Lord Jesus Christ, your Son,
who lives and reigns with you in the unity of the Holy Spirit,
one God, for ever and ever. **All: Amen.**

Reading I (L 74-B) (Job 7:1-4, 6-7)

A reading from the Book of Job

I am filled with restlessness until the dawn.

Job spoke, saying:
 Is not man's life on earth a drudgery?
  Are not his days those of hirelings?
 He is a slave who longs for the shade,
  a hireling who waits for his wages.

So I have been assigned months of misery,
   and troubled nights have been allotted to me.
If in bed I say, "When shall I arise?"
   then the night drags on;
   I am filled with restlessness until the dawn.
My days are swifter than a weaver's shuttle;
   they come to an end without hope.
Remember that my life is like the wind;
   I shall not see happiness again.

The word of the Lord. All: **Thanks be to God.**

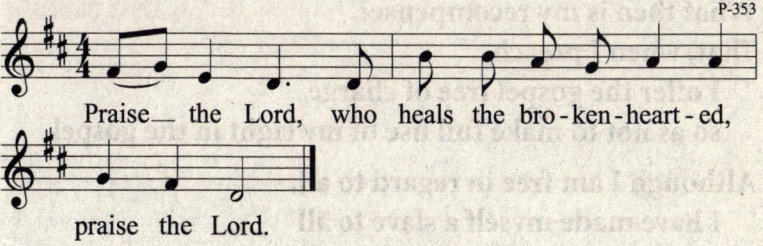

Responsorial Psalm 147

Praise the Lord, who heals the broken-hearted, praise the Lord.

Music: Jay F. Hunstiger, © 1990, administered by Liturgical Press. All rights reserved.

Psalm 147:1-2, 3-4, 5-6

℟. (See 3a) **Praise the Lord, who heals the brokenhearted.**
   or: ℟. **Alleluia.**

Praise the LORD, for he is good;
   sing praise to our God, for he is gracious;
   it is fitting to praise him.
The LORD rebuilds Jerusalem;
   the dispersed of Israel he gathers. ℟.

He heals the brokenhearted
   and binds up their wounds.
He tells the number of the stars;
   he calls each by name. ℟.

Great is our Lord and mighty in power;
   to his wisdom there is no limit.
The LORD sustains the lowly;
   the wicked he casts to the ground. ℟.

Reading II (1 Corinthians 9:16-19, 22-23)

A reading from the first Letter of Saint Paul to the Corinthians

Woe to me if I do not preach the Gospel.

Brothers and sisters:
If I preach the gospel, this is no reason for me to boast,
   for an obligation has been imposed on me,
   and woe to me if I do not preach it!
If I do so willingly, I have a recompense,
   but if unwillingly, then I have been entrusted with a stewardship.
What then is my recompense?
That, when I preach,
   I offer the gospel free of charge
   so as not to make full use of my right in the gospel.

Although I am free in regard to all,
   I have made myself a slave to all
   so as to win over as many as possible.
To the weak I became weak, to win over the weak.
I have become all things to all, to save at least some.
All this I do for the sake of the gospel,
   so that I too may have a share in it.

The word of the Lord. All: **Thanks be to God.**

Gospel (Mark 1:29-39)

Alleluia (Matthew 8:17)

℣. Alleluia, alleluia. ℟. **Alleluia, alleluia.**
℣. Christ took away our infirmities
   and bore our diseases. ℟.

✠ **A reading from the holy Gospel according to Mark**

All: **Glory to you, O Lord.**

Jesus cured many who were sick with various diseases.

On leaving the synagogue
   Jesus entered the house of Simon and Andrew with
      James and John.

Simon's mother-in-law lay sick with a fever.
They immediately told him about her.
He approached, grasped her hand, and helped her up.
Then the fever left her and she waited on them.

When it was evening, after sunset,
>they brought to him all who were ill or possessed by demons.

The whole town was gathered at the door.
He cured many who were sick with various diseases,
>and he drove out many demons,
>>not permitting them to speak because they knew him.

Rising very early before dawn, he left
>and went off to a deserted place, where he prayed.
Simon and those who were with him pursued him
>and on finding him said, "Everyone is looking for you."
He told them, "Let us go on to the nearby villages
>that I may preach there also.
For this purpose have I come."
So he went into their synagogues,
>preaching and driving out demons throughout the whole of Galilee.

The Gospel of the Lord. All: **Praise to you, Lord Jesus Christ.**

Prayer over the Offerings
O Lord, our God,
who once established these created things
to sustain us in our frailty,
grant, we pray,
that they may become for us now
the Sacrament of eternal life.
Through Christ our Lord. All: **Amen.**

Communion Antiphon (Cf. Psalm 107[106]:8-9)
Let them thank the Lord for his mercy,
his wonders for the children of men,
for he satisfies the thirsty soul,
and the hungry he fills with good things.

Or:

(Matthew 5:5-6)
Blessed are those who mourn, for they shall be consoled.
Blessed are those who hunger and thirst for righteousness,
for they shall have their fill.

PRAYER AFTER COMMUNION
O God, who have willed that we be partakers
in the one Bread and the one Chalice,
grant us, we pray, so to live
that, made one in Christ,
we may joyfully bear fruit
for the salvation of the world.
Through Christ our Lord. All: **Amen.**

Sixth Sunday in Ordinary Time

February 15, 2015

Reflection on the Gospel

This healing account between a leper and Jesus dramatically unfolds in a conversation punctuated by concrete and very personal gestures. The leper comes to Jesus, kneels, and boldly begs for cleansing, gestures expressing his sense of unworthiness. Moved with pity, Jesus stretches out his hand and touches the leper, gestures revealing the leper's inherent dignity. Freed from pain and isolation, the leper can let his inherent dignity spill over into proclaiming the Good News of a new Presence, a new Awakening, a new Life.

- I continue the work of Jesus by doing . . .

—Living Liturgy™, *Sixth Sunday in Ordinary Time 2015*

ENTRANCE ANTIPHON (Cf. Psalm 31[30]:3-4)
Be my protector, O God,
a mighty stronghold to save me.
For you are my rock, my stronghold!
Lead me, guide me, for the sake of your name.

Collect

O God, who teach us that you abide
in hearts that are just and true,
grant that we may be so fashioned by your grace
as to become a dwelling pleasing to you.
Through our Lord Jesus Christ, your Son,
who lives and reigns with you in the unity of the Holy Spirit,
one God, for ever and ever. **All: Amen.**

Reading I (L 77-B) (Leviticus 13:1-2, 44-46)

A reading from the Book of Leviticus

The leper will dwell apart, making an abode outside the camp.

**The Lord said to Moses and Aaron,
"If someone has on his skin a scab or pustule or blotch
which appears to be the sore of leprosy,
he shall be brought to Aaron, the priest,
or to one of the priests among his descendants.
If the man is leprous and unclean,
the priest shall declare him unclean
by reason of the sore on his head.**

**"The one who bears the sore of leprosy
shall keep his garments rent and his head bare,
and shall muffle his beard;
he shall cry out, 'Unclean, unclean!'
As long as the sore is on him he shall declare himself
unclean,
since he is in fact unclean.
He shall dwell apart, making his abode outside the camp."**

The word of the Lord. **All: Thanks be to God.**

Responsorial Psalm 32

*I turn to you, Lord, in time of trouble,
and you fill me with the joy of salvation.*

Music: Jay F. Hunstiger, © 1990, administered by Liturgical Press. All rights reserved.

Psalm 32:1-2, 5, 11

℟. (7) **I turn to you, Lord, in time of trouble, and you fill me with the joy of salvation.**

Blessed is he whose fault is taken away,
 whose sin is covered.
Blessed the man to whom the Lord imputes not guilt,
 in whose spirit there is no guile. ℟.

Then I acknowledged my sin to you,
 my guilt I covered not.
I said, "I confess my faults to the Lord, "
 and you took away the guilt of my sin. ℟.

Be glad in the Lord and rejoice, you just;
 exult, all you upright of heart. ℟.

READING II (1 Corinthians 10:31—11:1)

A reading from the first Letter of Saint Paul to the Corinthians

Be imitators of me, as I am of Christ.

Brothers and sisters,
Whether you eat or drink, or whatever you do,
 do everything for the glory of God.
Avoid giving offense, whether to the Jews or Greeks or the church of God,
 just as I try to please everyone in every way,
 not seeking my own benefit but that of the many,
 that they may be saved.
Be imitators of me, as I am of Christ.

The word of the Lord. All: **Thanks be to God.**

GOSPEL (Mark 1:40-45)

ALLELUIA (Luke 7:16)
℣. Alleluia, alleluia. ℟. **Alleluia, alleluia.**
℣. A great prophet has arisen in our midst,
 God has visited his people. ℟.

✠ **A reading from the holy Gospel according to Mark**
All: **Glory to you, O Lord.**

The leprosy left him, and he was made clean.

A leper came to Jesus and kneeling down begged him
    and said,
  "If you wish, you can make me clean."
Moved with pity, he stretched out his hand,
    touched him, and said to him,
  "I do will it. Be made clean."
The leprosy left him immediately, and he was made clean.
Then, warning him sternly, he dismissed him at once.

He said to him, "See that you tell no one anything,
    but go, show yourself to the priest
    and offer for your cleansing what Moses prescribed;
    that will be proof for them."

The man went away and began to publicize the whole
    matter.
He spread the report abroad
    so that it was impossible for Jesus to enter a town
    openly.
He remained outside in deserted places,
    and people kept coming to him from everywhere.

The Gospel of the Lord. All: **Praise to you, Lord Jesus Christ.**

Prayer over the Offerings
May this oblation, O Lord, we pray,
cleanse and renew us
and may it become for those who do your will
the source of eternal reward.
Through Christ our Lord. All: **Amen.**

Communion Antiphon (Cf. Psalm 78[77]:29-30)
They ate and had their fill,
and what they craved the Lord gave them;
they were not disappointed in what they craved.

Or:

(John 3:16)
God so loved the world
that he gave his Only Begotten Son,
so that all who believe in him may not perish,
but may have eternal life.

Prayer after Communion
Having fed upon these heavenly delights,
we pray, O Lord,
that we may always long
for that food by which we truly live.
Through Christ our Lord. All: **Amen.**

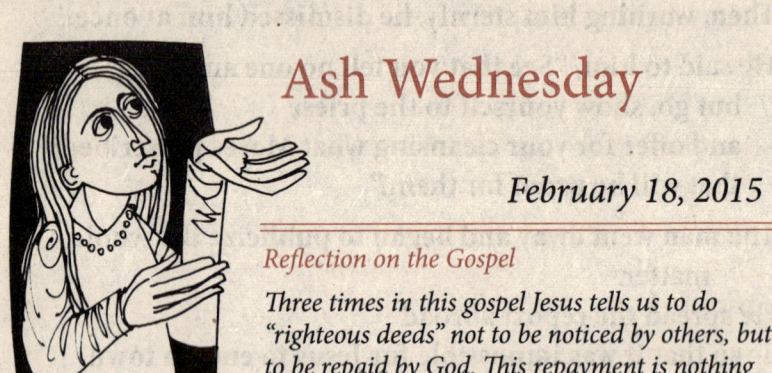

Ash Wednesday

February 18, 2015

Reflection on the Gospel

Three times in this gospel Jesus tells us to do "righteous deeds" not to be noticed by others, but to be repaid by God. This repayment is nothing less than the righteousness of a deepened relationship with God. Our "righteous deeds"—our Lenten penances—are to be directed to forming a new habit of righteous relationship. Ironically, what we have done "in secret" will be noticed by others—not for the deeds themselves, but for who, through these deeds, we become.

• I proclaim the Gospel by . . .

—*Living Liturgy*™, *Ash Wednesday 2015*

Entrance Antiphon (Wisdom 11:24, 25, 27)
You are merciful to all, O Lord,
and despise nothing that you have made.
You overlook people's sins, to bring them to repentance,
and you spare them, for you are the Lord our God.

Collect
Grant, O Lord, that we may begin with holy fasting
this campaign of Christian service,
so that, as we take up battle against spiritual evils,
we may be armed with weapons of self-restraint.
Through our Lord Jesus Christ, your Son,
who lives and reigns with you in the unity of the Holy Spirit,
one God, for ever and ever. All: **Amen.**

Reading I (L 219) (Joel 2:12-18)

A reading from the Book of the Prophet Joel

Rend your hearts, not your garments.

Even now, says the Lord,
 return to me with your whole heart,
 with fasting, and weeping, and mourning;
Rend your hearts, not your garments,
 and return to the Lord, your God.
For gracious and merciful is he,
 slow to anger, rich in kindness,
 and relenting in punishment.
Perhaps he will again relent
 and leave behind him a blessing,
Offerings and libations
 for the Lord, your God.

Blow the trumpet in Zion!
 proclaim a fast,
 call an assembly;
Gather the people,
 notify the congregation;
Assemble the elders,
 gather the children
 and the infants at the breast;
Let the bridegroom quit his room
 and the bride her chamber.
Between the porch and the altar
 let the priests, the ministers of the Lord, weep,
And say, "Spare, O Lord, your people,
 and make not your heritage a reproach,
 with the nations ruling over them!
Why should they say among the peoples,
 'Where is their God?'"

Then the Lord was stirred to concern for his land
 and took pity on his people.

The word of the Lord. All: **Thanks be to God.**

Responsorial Psalm 51

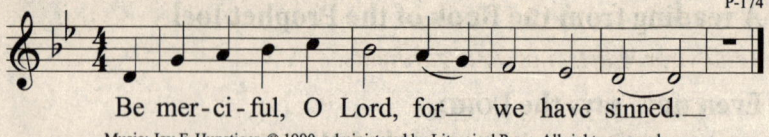

Be merciful, O Lord, for we have sinned.

Music: Jay F. Hunstiger, © 1990, administered by Liturgical Press. All rights reserved.

Psalm 51:3-4, 5-6ab, 12-13, 14 and 17

℟. (*See* 3a) **Be merciful, O Lord, for we have sinned.**

Have mercy on me, O God, in your goodness;
> in the greatness of your compassion wipe out my offense.

Thoroughly wash me from my guilt
> and of my sin cleanse me. ℟.

For I acknowledge my offense,
> and my sin is before me always:

"Against you only have I sinned,
> and done what is evil in your sight." ℟.

A clean heart create for me, O God,
> and a steadfast spirit renew within me.

Cast me not out from your presence,
> and your Holy Spirit take not from me. ℟.

Give me back the joy of your salvation,
> and a willing spirit sustain in me.

O Lord, open my lips,
> and my mouth shall proclaim your praise. ℟.

Reading II (2 Corinthians 5:20—6:2)

A reading from the second Letter of Saint Paul to the Corinthians

Be reconciled to God. Behold, now is the acceptable time.

Brothers and sisters:
We are ambassadors for Christ,
> **as if God were appealing through us.**

We implore you on behalf of Christ,
> **be reconciled to God.**

For our sake he made him to be sin who did not know sin,
   so that we might become the righteousness of God
      in him.
Working together, then,
   we appeal to you not to receive the grace of God in vain.
For he says:

   In an acceptable time I heard you,
      and on the day of salvation I helped you.

Behold, now is a very acceptable time;
   behold, now is the day of salvation.
The word of the Lord. All: **Thanks be to God.**

GOSPEL (Matthew 6:1-6, 16-18)
VERSE BEFORE THE GOSPEL (*See* Psalm 95:8)
℣. Praise to you, Lord Jesus Christ, king of endless glory!
℟. **Praise to you, Lord Jesus Christ, king of endless glory!**
℣. If today you hear his voice,
   harden not your hearts. ℟.

✠ **A reading from the holy Gospel according to Matthew**

All: **Glory to you, O Lord.**

Your Father who sees in secret will repay you.

Jesus said to his disciples:
   "Take care not to perform righteous deeds
   in order that people may see them;
      otherwise, you will have no recompense from your
         heavenly Father.
When you give alms,
   do not blow a trumpet before you,
   as the hypocrites do in the synagogues and in the streets
   to win the praise of others.
Amen, I say to you,
   they have received their reward.
But when you give alms,
   do not let your left hand know what your right is doing,
   so that your almsgiving may be secret.

And your Father who sees in secret will repay you.

"When you pray,
    do not be like the hypocrites,
    who love to stand and pray in the synagogues and on
        street corners
    so that others may see them.
Amen, I say to you,
    they have received their reward.
But when you pray, go to your inner room,
    close the door, and pray to your Father in secret.
And your Father who sees in secret will repay you.

"When you fast,
    do not look gloomy like the hypocrites.
They neglect their appearance,
    so that they may appear to others to be fasting.
Amen, I say to you, they have received their reward.
But when you fast,
    anoint your head and wash your face,
    so that you may not appear to be fasting,
    except to your Father who is hidden.
And your Father who sees what is hidden will repay you."

The Gospel of the Lord. All: Praise to you, Lord Jesus Christ.

Blessing and Distribution of Ashes

Dear brethren (brothers and sisters), let us humbly ask God our Father
that he be pleased to bless with the abundance of his grace
these ashes, which we will put on our heads in penitence.

O God, who are moved by acts of humility
and respond with forgiveness to works of penance,
lend your merciful ear to our prayers
and in your kindness pour out the grace of your ✠ blessing
on your servants who are marked with these ashes,
that, as they follow the Lenten observances,
they may be worthy to come with minds made pure
to celebrate the Paschal Mystery of your Son.
Through Christ our Lord. All: **Amen.**

Or:

O God, who desire not the death of sinners,
but their conversion,
mercifully hear our prayers
and in your kindness be pleased to bless ✢ these ashes,
which we intend to receive upon our heads,
that we, who acknowledge we are but ashes
and shall return to dust,
may, through a steadfast observance of Lent,
gain pardon for sins and newness of life
after the likeness of your Risen Son.
Who lives and reigns for ever and ever. All: **Amen.**

To each who receives the ashes:
Repent, and believe in the Gospel.

or:

Remember that you are dust, and to dust you shall return.

The rite concludes with the Prayer of the Faithful.

Prayer over the Offerings
As we solemnly offer
the annual sacrifice for the beginning of Lent,
we entreat you, O Lord,
that, through works of penance and charity,
we may turn away from harmful pleasures
and, cleansed from our sins, may become worthy
to celebrate devoutly the Passion of your Son.
Who lives and reigns for ever and ever. All: **Amen.**

Communion Antiphon (Cf. Psalm 1:2-3)
He who ponders the law of the Lord day and night
will yield fruit in due season.

Prayer after Communion
May the Sacrament we have received sustain us, O Lord,
that our Lenten fast may be pleasing to you
and be for us a healing remedy.
Through Christ our Lord. All: **Amen.**

First Sunday of Lent

February 22, 2015

Reflection on the Gospel

Mark does not relay the details of Jesus' experience of temptation, but he does show its outcome: Jesus boldly enters Galilee proclaiming, "This is the time . . . Repent, and believe." Temptations always force us to make a choice. Jesus' choice is to take up his saving mission. What is our temptation? What is our choice? These are the questions of Lent, questions we must constantly ask if we wish to participate in Jesus' saving mission, proclaiming by the choices we make that the Gospel determines who we are and how we act.

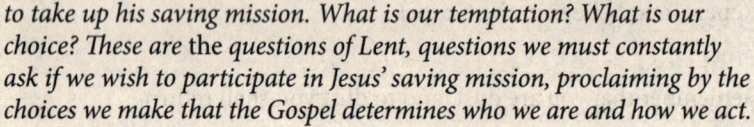

- *Remember that you are dust, and to dust you will return.*
- *Repent, and believe in the Gospel . . .*

—Living Liturgy™, *First Sunday of Lent 2015*

ENTRANCE ANTIPHON (Cf. Psalm 91[90]:15-16)
When he calls on me, I will answer him;
I will deliver him and give him glory,
I will grant him length of days.

COLLECT
Grant, almighty God,
through the yearly observances of holy Lent,
that we may grow in understanding
of the riches hidden in Christ
and by worthy conduct pursue their effects.
Through our Lord Jesus Christ, your Son,
who lives and reigns with you in the unity of the Holy Spirit,
one God, for ever and ever. All: **Amen.**

READING I (L 23-B) (Genesis 9:8-15)
A reading from the Book of Genesis

God's covenant with Noah when he was delivered from the flood.

God said to Noah and to his sons with him:
   "See, I am now establishing my covenant with you
      and your descendants after you
      and with every living creature that was with you:

all the birds, and the various tame and wild animals
that were with you and came out of the ark.
I will establish my covenant with you,
that never again shall all bodily creatures be destroyed
by the waters of a flood;
there shall not be another flood to devastate the earth."
God added:
"This is the sign that I am giving for all ages to come,
of the covenant between me and you
and every living creature with you:
I set my bow in the clouds to serve as a sign
of the covenant between me and the earth.
When I bring clouds over the earth,
and the bow appears in the clouds,
I will recall the covenant I have made
between me and you and all living beings,
so that the waters shall never again become a flood
to destroy all mortal beings."

The word of the Lord. All: Thanks be to God.

Responsorial Psalm 25

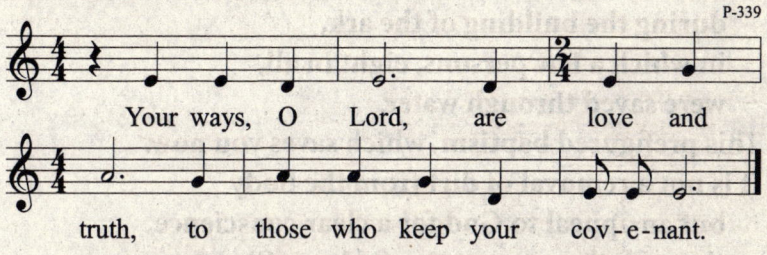

Your ways, O Lord, are love and truth, to those who keep your covenant.

Music: Jay F. Hunstiger, © 1990, administered by Liturgical Press. All rights reserved.

Psalm 25:4-5, 6-7, 8-9

℟. (See 10) **Your ways, O Lord, are love and truth to those who keep your covenant.**

Your ways, O Lord, make known to me;
  teach me your paths,
Guide me in your truth and teach me,
  for you are God my savior. ℟.

(continued)

Remember that your compassion, O Lord,
 and your love are from of old.
In your kindness remember me,
 because of your goodness, O Lord. ℟.

Good and upright is the Lord,
 thus he shows sinners the way.
He guides the humble to justice,
 and he teaches the humble his way. ℟.

Reading II (1 Peter 3:18-22)
A reading from the first Letter of Saint Peter

The water of the flood prefigured baptism, which saves you now.

**Beloved:
Christ suffered for sins once,
 the righteous for the sake of the unrighteous,
 that he might lead you to God.
Put to death in the flesh,
 he was brought to life in the Spirit.
In it he also went to preach to the spirits in prison,
 who had once been disobedient
 while God patiently waited in the days of Noah
 during the building of the ark,
 in which a few persons, eight in all,
 were saved through water.
This prefigured baptism, which saves you now.
It is not a removal of dirt from the body
 but an appeal to God for a clear conscience,
 through the resurrection of Jesus Christ,
 who has gone into heaven
 and is at the right hand of God,
 with angels, authorities, and powers subject to him.
The word of the Lord.** All: **Thanks be to God.**

Gospel (Mark 1:12-15)
Verse before the Gospel (Matthew 4:4b)
℣. Praise to you, Lord Jesus Christ, king of endless glory.
℟. **Praise to you, Lord Jesus Christ, king of endless glory.**
℣. One does not live on bread alone,
   but on every word that comes forth from the mouth of
      God. ℟.

✠ **A reading from the holy Gospel according to Mark**

All: **Glory to you, O Lord.**

Jesus was tempted by Satan, and the angels ministered to him.

**The Spirit drove Jesus out into the desert,
   and he remained in the desert for forty days,
      tempted by Satan.
He was among wild beasts,
   and the angels ministered to him.**

**After John had been arrested,
   Jesus came to Galilee proclaiming the gospel of God:
"This is the time of fulfillment.
The kingdom of God is at hand.
Repent, and believe in the gospel."**

The Gospel of the Lord. All: **Praise to you, Lord Jesus Christ.**

Prayer over the Offerings
Give us the right dispositions, O Lord, we pray,
to make these offerings,
for with them we celebrate the beginning
of this venerable and sacred time.
Through Christ our Lord. All: **Amen.**

Communion Antiphon (Matthew 4:4)
One does not live by bread alone,
but by every word that comes forth from the mouth of God.

Or:

(Cf. Psalm 91[90]:4)
The Lord will conceal you with his pinions,
and under his wings you will trust.

Prayer after Communion

Renewed now with heavenly bread,
by which faith is nourished, hope increased,
and charity strengthened,
we pray, O Lord,
that we may learn to hunger for Christ,
the true and living Bread,
and strive to live by every word
which proceeds from your mouth.
Through Christ our Lord. All: **Amen.**

Second Sunday of Lent

March 1, 2015

Reflection on the Gospel

On the mountain Peter, James, and John witness three theophanies (appearance of God): Jesus the transfigured One, Jesus the "beloved Son," Jesus the "Son of Man." Coming "down from the mountain," they would witness Jesus passing through death to the full revelation of what had been foreshadowed in his transfiguration: the theophany of his risen, glorified Body. Finally, when Peter, James, and John choose dying to self, they are transfigured by Jesus' risen Life. They too become theophanies. So can we.

- *I can become the appearance of God by . . .*

—Living Liturgy™, *Second Sunday of Lent 2015*

Entrance Antiphon (Cf. Psalm 27[26]:8-9)

Of you my heart has spoken: Seek his face.
It is your face, O Lord, that I seek;
hide not your face from me.

Or:

(Cf. Psalm 25[24]:6, 2, 22)
Remember your compassion, O Lord,
and your merciful love, for they are from of old.
Let not our enemies exult over us.
Redeem us, O God of Israel, from all our distress.

Collect
O God, who have commanded us
to listen to your beloved Son,
be pleased, we pray,
to nourish us inwardly by your word,
that, with spiritual sight made pure,
we may rejoice to behold your glory.
Through our Lord Jesus Christ, your Son,
who lives and reigns with you in the unity of the Holy Spirit,
one God, for ever and ever. **All: Amen.**

Reading I (L 26-B) (Genesis 22:1-2, 9a, 10-13, 15-18)
A reading from the Book of Genesis

The sacrifice of Abraham, our father in faith.

**God put Abraham to the test.
He called to him, "Abraham!"
"Here I am!" he replied.
Then God said:**
   **"Take your son Isaac, your only one, whom you love,
   and go to the land of Moriah.
There you shall offer him up as a holocaust
   on a height that I will point out to you."**

When they came to the place of which God had told him,
   Abraham built an altar there and arranged the wood
      on it.
Then he reached out and took the knife to slaughter his
   son.
But the Lord's messenger called to him from heaven,
   "Abraham, Abraham!"
"Here I am!" he answered.
"Do not lay your hand on the boy," said the messenger.
"Do not do the least thing to him.

I know now how devoted you are to God,
> since you did not withhold from me your own beloved son."

As Abraham looked about,
> he spied a ram caught by its horns in the thicket.

So he went and took the ram
> and offered it up as a holocaust in place of his son.

Again the Lord's messenger called to Abraham from heaven and said:
> "I swear by myself, declares the Lord,
> that because you acted as you did
> in not withholding from me your beloved son,
> I will bless you abundantly
> and make your descendants as countless
> as the stars of the sky and the sands of the seashore;
> your descendants shall take possession
> of the gates of their enemies,
> and in your descendants all the nations of the earth
> shall find blessing—
> all this because you obeyed my command."

The word of the Lord. All: Thanks be to God.

Responsorial Psalm 116

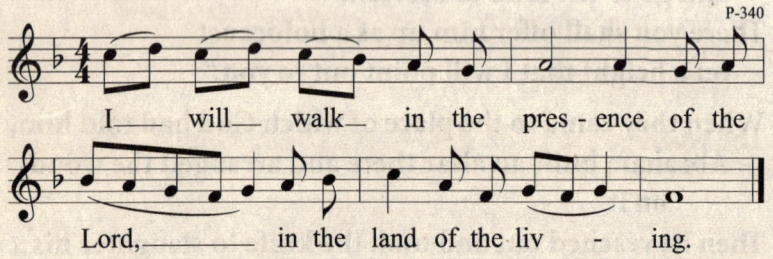

I will walk in the presence of the Lord, in the land of the living.

Music: Jay F. Hunstiger, © 1990, administered by Liturgical Press. All rights reserved.

Psalm 116:10, 15, 16-17, 18-19

R℣. (9) **I will walk before the Lord, in the land of the living.**

> I believed, even when I said,
> "I am greatly afflicted."

Precious in the eyes of the Lord
   is the death of his faithful ones. ℟.

O Lord, I am your servant;
   I am your servant, the son of your handmaid;
   you have loosed my bonds.
To you will I offer sacrifice of thanksgiving,
   and I will call upon the name of the Lord. ℟.

My vows to the Lord I will pay
   in the presence of all his people,
In the courts of the house of the Lord,
   in your midst, O Jerusalem. ℟.

Reading II (Romans 8:31b-34)

A reading from the Letter of Saint Paul to the Romans

God did not spare his own Son.

Brothers and sisters:
If God is for us, who can be against us?
He who did not spare his own Son
   but handed him over for us all,
   how will he not also give us everything else along with him?
Who will bring a charge against God's chosen ones?
   It is God who acquits us, who will condemn?
Christ Jesus it is who died—or, rather, was raised—
   who also is at the right hand of God,
   who indeed intercedes for us.

The word of the Lord. All: **Thanks be to God.**

Gospel (Mark 9:2-10)

Verse before the Gospel (See Matthew 17:5)

℣. Praise and honor to you, Lord Jesus Christ!
℟. **Praise and honor to you, Lord Jesus Christ!**
℣. From the shining cloud the Father's voice is heard:
   This is my beloved Son, listen to him. ℟.

✠ **A reading from the holy Gospel according to Mark**

All: **Glory to you, O Lord.**

This is my beloved Son.

Jesus took Peter, James, and John
    and led them up a high mountain apart by themselves.
And he was transfigured before them,
    and his clothes became dazzling white,
    such as no fuller on earth could bleach them.
Then Elijah appeared to them along with Moses,
    and they were conversing with Jesus.
Then Peter said to Jesus in reply,
    "Rabbi, it is good that we are here!
Let us make three tents:
    one for you, one for Moses, and one for Elijah."
He hardly knew what to say, they were so terrified.
Then a cloud came, casting a shadow over them;
    from the cloud came a voice,
    "This is my beloved Son. Listen to him."
Suddenly, looking around, they no longer saw anyone
    but Jesus alone with them.

As they were coming down from the mountain,
    he charged them not to relate what they had seen to anyone,
    except when the Son of Man had risen from the dead.
So they kept the matter to themselves,
    questioning what rising from the dead meant.

The Gospel of the Lord. All: **Praise to you, Lord Jesus Christ.**

Prayer over the Offerings
May this sacrifice, O Lord, we pray,
cleanse us of our faults
and sanctify your faithful in body and mind
for the celebration of the paschal festivities.
Through Christ our Lord. All: **Amen.**

Communion Antiphon (Matthew 17:5)
This is my beloved Son, with whom I am well pleased;
listen to him.

Prayer after Communion
As we receive these glorious mysteries,
we make thanksgiving to you, O Lord,

for allowing us while still on earth
to be partakers even now of the things of heaven.
Through Christ our Lord. **All: Amen.**

Third Sunday of Lent

March 8, 2015

Reflection on the Gospel

The temple in Jerusalem was a sign to the Jews of God's Presence and saving works. This sign could be corrupted, however, by human beings who turn away from the temple's true purpose. Enraged, Jesus takes "a whip" and drives out of the temple area those who corrupt the sign. Then Jesus announces both a new temple (his own body) that could not be corrupted and a new sign ("raised from the dead"). Now we are the new temple: the living sign of the new things God is doing for us.

- *The Body of Christ is . . .*

—Living Liturgy™, *Third Sunday of Lent 2015*

ENTRANCE ANTIPHON (Cf. Psalm 25[24]:15-16)
My eyes are always on the Lord,
for he rescues my feet from the snare.
Turn to me and have mercy on me,
for I am alone and poor.

Or:

(Cf. Ezekiel 36:23-26)
When I prove my holiness among you,
I will gather you from all the foreign lands;
and I will pour clean water upon you
and cleanse you from all your impurities,
and I will give you a new spirit, says the Lord.

Collect

O God, author of every mercy and of all goodness,
who in fasting, prayer and almsgiving
have shown us a remedy for sin,
look graciously on this confession of our lowliness,
that we, who are bowed down by our conscience,
may always be lifted up by your mercy.
Through our Lord Jesus Christ, your Son,
who lives and reigns with you in the unity of the Holy Spirit,
one God, for ever and ever. All: **Amen.**

The readings given for Year A, n. 28, may be used in place of these.

Reading I (L 29-B) (Exodus 20:1-17) *or* Shorter Form [ ] (Exodus 20:1-3, 7-8, 12-17)

A reading from the Book of Exodus

The law was given through Moses.

[In those days, God delivered all these commandments:
"I, the Lord, am your God,
who brought you out of the land of Egypt, that place of slavery.
You shall not have other gods besides me.]
You shall not carve idols for yourselves
in the shape of anything in the sky above
or on the earth below or in the waters beneath the earth;
you shall not bow down before them or worship them.
For I, the Lord, your God, am a jealous God,
inflicting punishment for their fathers' wickedness
on the children of those who hate me,
down to the third and fourth generation;
but bestowing mercy down to the thousandth generation
on the children of those who love me and keep my commandments.

["You shall not take the name of the Lord, your God, in vain.
For the Lord will not leave unpunished
the one who takes his name in vain.

"Remember to keep holy the sabbath day.]
Six days you may labor and do all your work,
> but the seventh day is the sabbath of the Lord,
> > your God.

No work may be done then either by you, or your son or daughter,
> or your male or female slave, or your beast,
> or by the alien who lives with you.

In six days the Lord made the heavens and the earth,
> the sea and all that is in them;
> but on the seventh day he rested.

That is why the Lord has blessed the sabbath day and made it holy.

["Honor your father and your mother,
> that you may have a long life in the land
> which the Lord, your God, is giving you.

You shall not kill.
You shall not commit adultery.
You shall not steal.
You shall not bear false witness against your neighbor.
You shall not covet your neighbor's house.
You shall not covet your neighbor's wife,
> nor his male or female slave, nor his ox or ass,
> nor anything else that belongs to him."]

The word of the Lord. **All: Thanks be to God.**

Responsorial Psalm 19

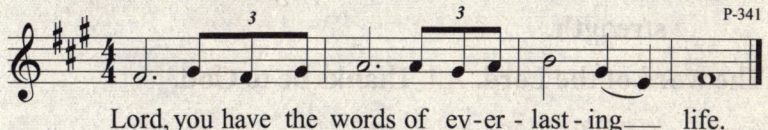

Lord, you have the words of ev-er-last-ing life.

Music: Jay F. Hunstiger, © 1990, administered by Liturgical Press. All rights reserved.

Psalm 19:8, 9, 10, 11

℟. (John 6:68c) **Lord, you have the words of everlasting life.**

> The law of the Lord is perfect,
> refreshing the soul;

(continued)

The decree of the L{ORD} is trustworthy,
> giving wisdom to the simple. ℟.

The precepts of the L{ORD} are right,
> rejoicing the heart;
the command of the L{ORD} is clear,
> enlightening the eye. ℟.

The fear of the L{ORD} is pure,
> enduring forever;
the ordinances of the L{ORD} are true,
> all of them just. ℟.

They are more precious than gold,
> than a heap of purest gold;
sweeter also than syrup
> or honey from the comb. ℟.

R{EADING} II (1 Corinthians 1:22-25)

A reading from the first Letter of Saint Paul to the Corinthians

We proclaim Christ crucified, a stumbling block to many, but to those who are called, the wisdom of God.

Brothers and sisters:
Jews demand signs and Greeks look for wisdom,
> **but we proclaim Christ crucified,**
> **a stumbling block to Jews and foolishness to Gentiles,**
> **but to those who are called, Jews and Greeks alike,**
> **Christ the power of God and the wisdom of God.**
For the foolishness of God is wiser than human wisdom,
> **and the weakness of God is stronger than human strength.**

The word of the Lord. All: **Thanks be to God.**

G{OSPEL} (John 2:13-25)
V{ERSE} {BEFORE THE} G{OSPEL} (John 3:16)

℣. Praise to you, Lord Jesus Christ, king of endless glory!
℟. **Praise to you, Lord Jesus Christ, king of endless glory!**
℣. God so loved the world that he gave his only Son,
> so that everyone who believes in him might have
> > eternal life. ℟.

✣ **A reading from the holy Gospel according to John**

All: Glory to you, O Lord.

Destroy this temple, and in three days I will raise it up.

Since the Passover of the Jews was near,
> Jesus went up to Jerusalem.

He found in the temple area those who sold oxen, sheep, and doves,
> as well as the money changers seated there.

He made a whip out of cords
> and drove them all out of the temple area, with the sheep and oxen,
> and spilled the coins of the money changers
> and overturned their tables,
> and to those who sold doves he said,
> "Take these out of here,
>> and stop making my Father's house a marketplace."

His disciples recalled the words of Scripture,
> ***Zeal for your house will consume me.***

At this the Jews answered and said to him,
> "What sign can you show us for doing this?"

Jesus answered and said to them,
> "Destroy this temple and in three days I will raise it up."

The Jews said,
> "This temple has been under construction for forty-six years,
> and you will raise it up in three days?"

But he was speaking about the temple of his body.

Therefore, when he was raised from the dead,
> his disciples remembered that he had said this,
> and they came to believe the Scripture
> and the word Jesus had spoken.

While he was in Jerusalem for the feast of Passover,
> many began to believe in his name
> when they saw the signs he was doing.

**But Jesus would not trust himself to them because he
   knew them all,
 and did not need anyone to testify about human nature.
He himself understood it well.**

The Gospel of the Lord. All: **Praise to you, Lord Jesus Christ.**

Prayer over the Offerings
Be pleased, O Lord, with these sacrificial offerings,
and grant that we who beseech pardon for our own sins,
may take care to forgive our neighbor.
Through Christ our Lord. All: **Amen.**

Communion Antiphon (Cf. Psalm 84[83]:4-5)
The sparrow finds a home,
and the swallow a nest for her young:
by your altars, O Lord of hosts, my King and my God.
Blessed are they who dwell in your house,
for ever singing your praise.

Prayer after Communion
As we receive the pledge
of things yet hidden in heaven
and are nourished while still on earth
with the Bread that comes from on high,
we humbly entreat you, O Lord,
that what is being brought about in us in mystery
may come to true completion.
Through Christ our Lord. All: **Amen.**

Fourth Sunday of Lent

March 15, 2015

Reflection on the Gospel

There are two parts to this gospel, separated by the line "And this is the verdict." The first part concerns the evidence: God "gave his only Son" in whom we choose to believe or not. The second part gives the judgment: those are saved who believe in Jesus, live the truth, and come to the light. Those are condemned who do not believe in Jesus, prefer darkness, and do "wicked things." Our whole life is working out our own verdict. Thank God we are at the mercy of a gracious and forgiving God!

- *I live the truth and come to the light when I . . .*

—*Living Liturgy*™, *Fourth Sunday of Lent 2015*

ENTRANCE ANTIPHON (Cf. Isaiah 66:10-11)

Rejoice, Jerusalem, and all who love her.
Be joyful, all who were in mourning;
exult and be satisfied at her consoling breast.

COLLECT

O God, who through your Word
reconcile the human race to yourself in a wonderful way,
grant, we pray,
that with prompt devotion and eager faith
the Christian people may hasten
toward the solemn celebrations to come.
Through our Lord Jesus Christ, your Son,
who lives and reigns with you in the unity of the Holy Spirit,
one God, for ever and ever. All: **Amen.**

The readings given for Year A, n. 31, may be used in place of these.

READING I (L 32-B) (2 Chronicles 36:14-16, 19-23)

A reading from the second Book of Chronicles

The wrath and the mercy of the Lord are revealed in the exile and liberation of his people.

In those days, all the princes of Judah, the priests, and the people
   added infidelity to infidelity,
   practicing all the abominations of the nations
   and polluting the Lord's temple
   which he had consecrated in Jerusalem.

Early and often did the Lord, the God of their fathers,
   send his messengers to them,
      for he had compassion on his people and his dwelling place.
But they mocked the messengers of God,
   despised his warnings, and scoffed at his prophets,
      until the anger of the Lord against his people was so inflamed
   that there was no remedy.
Their enemies burnt the house of God,
   tore down the walls of Jerusalem,
   set all its palaces afire,
   and destroyed all its precious objects.
Those who escaped the sword were carried captive to Babylon,
   where they became servants of the king of the Chaldeans and his sons
   until the kingdom of the Persians came to power.
All this was to fulfill the word of the Lord spoken by Jeremiah:
   "Until the land has retrieved its lost sabbaths,
   during all the time it lies waste it shall have rest
   while seventy years are fulfilled."

In the first year of Cyrus, king of Persia,
   in order to fulfill the word of the Lord spoken by Jeremiah,
   the Lord inspired King Cyrus of Persia
   to issue this proclamation throughout his kingdom,
   both by word of mouth and in writing:

"Thus says Cyrus, king of Persia:
All the kingdoms of the earth
the LORD, the God of heaven, has given to me,
and he has also charged me to build him a house
in Jerusalem, which is in Judah.
Whoever, therefore, among you belongs to any part of his people,
let him go up, and may his God be with him!"

The word of the Lord. All: Thanks be to God.

RESPONSORIAL PSALM 137

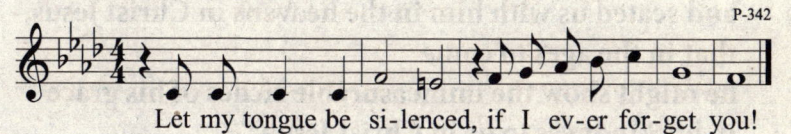

Let my tongue be silenced, if I ever forget you!

Music: Jay F. Hunstiger, © 1990, administered by Liturgical Press. All rights reserved.

Psalm 137:1-2, 3, 4-5, 6

℟. (6ab) **Let my tongue be silenced, if I ever forget you!**

By the streams of Babylon
  we sat and wept
  when we remembered Zion.
On the aspens of that land
  we hung up our harps. ℟.

For there our captors asked of us
  the lyrics of our songs,
And our despoilers urged us to be joyous:
  "Sing for us the songs of Zion!" ℟.

How could we sing a song of the LORD
  in a foreign land?
If I forget you, Jerusalem,
  may my right hand be forgotten! ℟.

May my tongue cleave to my palate
  if I remember you not,
If I place not Jerusalem
  ahead of my joy. ℟.

Reading II (Ephesians 2:4-10)
A reading from the Letter of Saint Paul to the Ephesians

Though dead in your transgressions, by grace you have been saved.

Brothers and sisters:
God, who is rich in mercy,
   because of the great love he had for us,
   even when we were dead in our transgressions,
   brought us to life with Christ—by grace you have been saved—,
   raised us up with him,
   and seated us with him in the heavens in Christ Jesus,
   that in the ages to come
   he might show the immeasurable riches of his grace
   in his kindness to us in Christ Jesus.
For by grace you have been saved through faith,
   and this is not from you; it is the gift of God;
   it is not from works, so no one may boast.
For we are his handiwork, created in Christ Jesus for the good works
   that God has prepared in advance,
   that we should live in them.

The word of the Lord. All: **Thanks be to God.**

Gospel (John 3:14-21)
Verse before the Gospel (John 3:16)

℣. Praise to you, Lord Jesus Christ, king of endless glory!
℟. **Praise to you, Lord Jesus Christ, king of endless glory!**
℣. God so loved the world that he gave his only Son,
so everyone who believes in him might have eternal life. ℟.

✠ **A reading from the holy Gospel according to John**

All: **Glory to you, O Lord.**

God sent his Son so that the world might be saved through him.

Jesus said to Nicodemus:
   "Just as Moses lifted up the serpent in the desert,

> so must the Son of Man be lifted up,
> so that everyone who believes in him may have eternal life."

For God so loved the world that he gave his only Son,
> so that everyone who believes in him might not perish but might have eternal life.

For God did not send his Son into the world to condemn the world,
> but that the world might be saved through him.

Whoever believes in him will not be condemned,
> but whoever does not believe has already been condemned,
> because he has not believed in the name of the only Son of God.

And this is the verdict,
> that the light came into the world,
> but people preferred darkness to light,
> because their works were evil.

For everyone who does wicked things hates the light
> and does not come toward the light,
> so that his works might not be exposed.

But whoever lives the truth comes to the light,
> so that his works may be clearly seen as done in God.

The Gospel of the Lord. All: **Praise to you, Lord Jesus Christ.**

Prayer over the Offerings

We place before you with joy these offerings,
which bring eternal remedy, O Lord,
praying that we may both faithfully revere them
and present them to you, as is fitting,
for the salvation of all the world.
Through Christ our Lord. All: **Amen.**

Communion Antiphon (Cf. Psalm 122[121]:3-4)

Jerusalem is built as a city bonded as one together.
It is there that the tribes go up, the tribes of the Lord,
to praise the name of the Lord.

Prayer after Communion

O God, who enlighten everyone who comes into this world,
illuminate our hearts, we pray,
with the splendor of your grace,
that we may always ponder
what is worthy and pleasing to your majesty
and love you in all sincerity.
Through Christ our Lord. All: **Amen.**

Fifth Sunday of Lent

March 22, 2015

Reflection on the Gospel

Jesus reveals his "hour . . . to be glorified" in surprisingly inglorious ways: dying grain, losing life, serving others. Jesus himself struggled with this: "I am troubled now." When we focus only on the giving up and the giving over of our lives, we fail to take into account the glorification. The Father is glorified in the very giving over of the Son. The Son is glorified in giving himself over to the cross. We are glorified in giving ourselves over to following Jesus to the cross. And this glorification is fullness of Life.

- *In reality the fullness of life comes through . . .*

—Living Liturgy™, *Fifth Sunday of Lent 2015*

Entrance Antiphon (Cf. Psalm 43[42]:1-2)

Give me justice, O God,
and plead my cause against a nation that is faithless.
From the deceitful and cunning rescue me,
for you, O God, are my strength.

Collect

By your help, we beseech you, Lord our God,
may we walk eagerly in that same charity
with which, out of love for the world,
your Son handed himself over to death.
Through our Lord Jesus Christ, your Son,
who lives and reigns with you in the unity of the Holy Spirit,
one God, for ever and ever. All: **Amen.**

The readings given for Year A, n. 34, may be used in place of these.

Reading I (L 35-B) (Jeremiah 31:31-34)

A reading from the Book of the Prophet Jeremiah

I will make a new covenant and remember their sin no more.

The days are coming, says the Lord,
  when I will make a new covenant with the house of Israel
  and the house of Judah.
It will not be like the covenant I made with their fathers
  the day I took them by the hand
  to lead them forth from the land of Egypt;
  for they broke my covenant,
  and I had to show myself their master, says the Lord.
But this is the covenant that I will make
  with the house of Israel after those days, says the Lord.
I will place my law within them and write it upon their hearts;
  I will be their God, and they shall be my people.
No longer will they have need to teach their friends and relatives
  how to know the Lord.
All, from least to greatest, shall know me, says the Lord,
  for I will forgive their evildoing and remember their sin no more.

The word of the Lord. All: **Thanks be to God.**

Responsorial Psalm 51

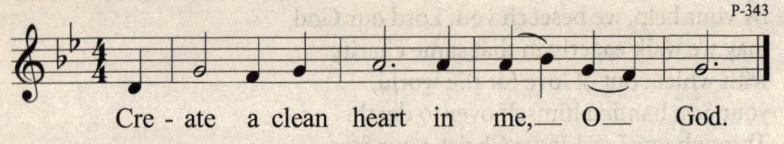

Create a clean heart in me, O God.

Music: Jay F. Hunstiger, © 1990, administered by Liturgical Press. All rights reserved.

Psalm 51:3-4, 12-13, 14-15

℟. (12a) **Create a clean heart in me, O God.**

Have mercy on me, O God, in your goodness;
 in the greatness of your compassion wipe out my
  offense.
Thoroughly wash me from my guilt
 and of my sin cleanse me. ℟.

A clean heart create for me, O God,
 and a steadfast spirit renew within me.
Cast me not out from your presence,
 and your Holy Spirit take not from me. ℟.

Give me back the joy of your salvation,
 and a willing spirit sustain in me.
I will teach transgressors your ways,
 and sinners shall return to you. ℟.

Reading II (Hebrews 5:7-9)

A reading from the Letter to the Hebrews

Christ learned obedience and became the source of eternal salvation.

**In the days when Christ Jesus was in the flesh,
 he offered prayers and supplications with loud cries
  and tears
 to the one who was able to save him from death,
 and he was heard because of his reverence.
Son though he was, he learned obedience from what he
  suffered;
 and when he was made perfect,
 he became the source of eternal salvation for all who
  obey him.**

The word of the Lord. All: **Thanks be to God.**

Gospel (John 12:20-33)
Verse before the gospel (John 12:26)
℣. Glory to you, Word of God, Lord Jesus Christ!
℟. **Glory to you, Word of God, Lord Jesus Christ!**
℣. Whoever serves me must follow me, says the Lord; and where I am, there also will my servant be. ℟.

✠ **A reading from the holy Gospel according to John**

All: **Glory to you, O Lord.**

If a grain of wheat falls to the ground and dies, it produces much fruit.

Some Greeks who had come to worship at the Passover Feast
came to Philip, who was from Bethsaida in Galilee,
and asked him, "Sir, we would like to see Jesus."
Philip went and told Andrew;
then Andrew and Philip went and told Jesus.
Jesus answered them,
"The hour has come for the Son of Man to be glorified.
Amen, amen, I say to you,
unless a grain of wheat falls to the ground and dies,
it remains just a grain of wheat;
but if it dies, it produces much fruit.
Whoever loves his life loses it,
and whoever hates his life in this world
will preserve it for eternal life.
Whoever serves me must follow me,
and where I am, there also will my servant be.
The Father will honor whoever serves me.

"I am troubled now. Yet what should I say?
'Father, save me from this hour'?
But it was for this purpose that I came to this hour.
Father, glorify your name."
Then a voice came from heaven,
"I have glorified it and will glorify it again."

The crowd there heard it and said it was thunder;
    but others said, "An angel has spoken to him."
Jesus answered and said,
    "This voice did not come for my sake but for yours.
Now is the time of judgment on this world;
    now the ruler of this world will be driven out.
And when I am lifted up from the earth,
    I will draw everyone to myself."
He said this indicating the kind of death he would die.

The Gospel of the Lord. All: **Praise to you, Lord Jesus Christ.**

Prayer over the Offerings
Hear us, almighty God,
and, having instilled in your servants
the teachings of the Christian faith,
graciously purify them
by the working of this sacrifice.
Through Christ our Lord. All: **Amen.**

Communion Antiphon (John 12:24)
Amen, Amen I say to you: Unless a grain of wheat
falls to the ground and dies, it remains a single grain.
But if it dies, it bears much fruit.

Prayer after Communion
We pray, almighty God,
that we may always be counted among the members of Christ,
in whose Body and Blood we have communion.
Who lives and reigns for ever and ever. All: **Amen.**

Palm Sunday of the Lord's Passion

March 29, 2015

Reflection on the Gospel

In Mark's account of Jesus' passion, many persons respond to Jesus in many different ways. At the Last Supper, Peter and the rest of the Twelve swear they will never deny him. Judas betrays Jesus with a kiss. Peter denies Jesus three times. Soldiers mock him. Soldiers crucify him. The centurion proclaims Jesus to be the "Son of God." During Jesus' last hours, only a few faithful people stand by Jesus. Most do not. As we hear this passion proclaimed, where do we stand?

- *I stand by Jesus when . . .*

—Living Liturgy™, *Palm Sunday 2015*

THE COMMEMORATION OF THE LORD'S ENTRANCE INTO JERUSALEM

FIRST FORM: THE PROCESSION

The congregation assembles in a secondary church or chapel or in some other suitable place distinct from the church to which the procession will move. The faithful carry palm branches.

ANTIPHON

Hosanna to the Son of David;
blessed is he who comes in the name of the Lord, the King of Israel.
Hosanna in the highest.

Priest: In the name of the Father, and of the Son, and of the Holy Spirit.
  All: Amen.

Then he greets the people in the usual way. A brief address is given, in which the faithful are invited to participate actively and consciously in the celebration of this day, in these or similar words:

Dear brethren (brothers and sisters),
since the beginning of Lent until now
we have prepared our hearts by penance and charitable works.
Today we gather together to herald with the whole Church
the beginning of the celebration
of our Lord's Paschal Mystery,
that is to say, of his Passion and Resurrection.
For it was to accomplish this mystery
that he entered his own city of Jerusalem.
Therefore, with all faith and devotion,
let us commemorate
the Lord's entry into the city for our salvation,
following in his footsteps,
so that, being made by his grace partakers of the Cross,
we may have a share also in his Resurrection and in his life.

Let us pray.

A Almighty ever-living God,
sanctify ✛ these branches with your blessing,
that we, who follow Christ the King in exultation,
may reach the eternal Jerusalem through him.
Who lives and reigns for ever and ever. All: **Amen.**

B Increase the faith of those who place their hope in you, O God,
and graciously hear the prayers of those who call on you,
that we, who today hold high these branches
to hail Christ in his triumph,
may bear fruit for you by good works accomplished in him.
Who lives and reigns for ever and ever. All: **Amen.**

THE READING OF THE GOSPEL

GOSPEL (L 37-B) (*A*: Mark 11:1-10)

✛ **A reading from the holy Gospel according to Mark**

All: **Glory to you, O Lord.**

Blessed is he who comes in the name of the Lord.

**When Jesus and his disciples drew near to Jerusalem,
to Bethphage and Bethany at the Mount of Olives,
he sent two of his disciples and said to them,
"Go into the village opposite you,
and immediately on entering it,
you will find a colt tethered on which no one has ever sat.**

Untie it and bring it here.
If anyone should say to you,
>'Why are you doing this?' reply,
>'The Master has need of it
>and will send it back here at once.'"

So they went off
>and found a colt tethered at a gate outside on the street,
>and they untied it.

Some of the bystanders said to them,
>"What are you doing, untying the colt?"

They answered them just as Jesus had told them to,
>and they permitted them to do it.

So they brought the colt to Jesus
>and put their cloaks over it.

And he sat on it.
Many people spread their cloaks on the road,
>and others spread leafy branches
>that they had cut from the fields.

Those preceding him as well as those following kept
>crying out:
>"Hosanna!
>>Blessed is he who comes in the name of the Lord!
>>Blessed is the kingdom of our father David that
>>>is to come!
>>Hosanna in the highest!"

The Gospel of the Lord. All: **Praise to you, Lord Jesus Christ.**

Or:

(B: John 12:12-16)

✢ **A reading from the holy Gospel according to John**

All: **Glory to you, O Lord.**

Blessed is he who comes in the name of the Lord.

When the great crowd that had come to the feast heard
>that Jesus was coming to Jerusalem,

> they took palm branches and went out to meet him,
> and cried out:
> "Hosanna!
> Blessed is he who comes in the name of the Lord,
> the king of Israel."

Jesus found an ass and sat upon it, as is written:
> *Fear no more, O daughter Zion;*
> *see, your king comes, seated upon an ass's colt.*

His disciples did not understand this at first,
> but when Jesus had been glorified
> they remembered that these things were written about him
> and that they had done this for him.

The Gospel of the Lord. All: **Praise to you, Lord Jesus Christ.**

PROCESSION WITH THE BLESSED BRANCHES

SECOND FORM: THE SOLEMN ENTRANCE
The commemoration of the Lord's entrance may be celebrated before the principal Mass with the solemn entrance, which takes place within the church.

THIRD FORM: THE SIMPLE ENTRANCE
The Lord's entrance is commemorated with the following simple entrance.

ENTRANCE ANTIPHON (Cf. John 12:1, 12-13; Psalm 24[23]:9-10)
Six days before the Passover,
when the Lord came into the city of Jerusalem,
the children ran to meet him;
in their hands they carried palm branches
and with a loud voice cried out:
*Hosanna in the highest!
Blessed are you, who have come in your abundant mercy!

O gates, lift high your heads;
grow higher, ancient doors.
Let him enter, the king of glory!
Who is this king of glory?
He, the Lord of hosts, he is the king of glory.
*Hosanna in the highest!
Blessed are you, who have come in your abundant mercy!

Collect

Almighty ever-living God,
who as an example of humility for the human race to follow
caused our Savior to take flesh and submit to the Cross,
graciously grant that we may heed his lesson of patient suffering
and so merit a share in his Resurrection.
Who lives and reigns with you in the unity of the Holy Spirit,
one God, for ever and ever. All: **Amen.**

Reading I (L 38-ABC) (Isaiah 50:4-7)

A reading from the Book of the Prophet Isaiah

My face I did not shield from buffets and spitting, knowing that I shall not be put to shame.

> **The Lord God has given me**
>   **a well-trained tongue,**
> **that I might know how to speak to the weary**
>   **a word that will rouse them.**
> **Morning after morning**
>   **he opens my ear that I may hear;**
> **and I have not rebelled,**
>   **have not turned back.**
> **I gave my back to those who beat me,**
>   **my cheeks to those who plucked my beard;**
> **my face I did not shield**
>   **from buffets and spitting.**
> **The Lord God is my help,**
>   **therefore I am not disgraced;**
> **I have set my face like flint,**
>   **knowing that I shall not be put to shame.**

The word of the Lord. All: **Thanks be to God.**

Responsorial Psalm 22

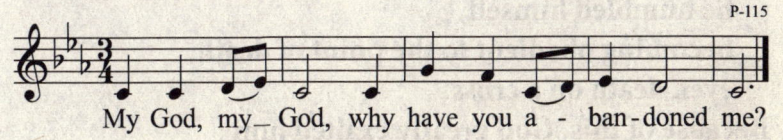

P-115

My God, my God, why have you a-ban-doned me?

Music: Jay F. Hunstiger, © 1990, administered by Liturgical Press. All rights reserved.

Psalm 22:8-9, 17-18, 19-20, 23-24

℟. (2a) **My God, my God, why have you abandoned me?**

> All who see me scoff at me;
> > they mock me with parted lips, they wag their heads:
> "He relied on the Lord; let him deliver him,
> > let him rescue him, if he loves him." ℟.
>
> Indeed, many dogs surround me,
> > a pack of evildoers closes in upon me;
> they have pierced my hands and my feet;
> > I can count all my bones. ℟.
>
> They divide my garments among them,
> > and for my vesture they cast lots.
> But you, O Lord, be not far from me;
> > O my help, hasten to aid me. ℟.
>
> I will proclaim your name to my brethren;
> > in the midst of the assembly I will praise you:
> "You who fear the Lord, praise him;
> > all you descendants of Jacob, give glory to him;
> > revere him, all you descendants of Israel!" ℟.

Reading II (Philippians 2:6-11)

A reading from the Letter of Saint Paul to the Philippians

Christ humbled himself. Because of this God greatly exalted him.

**Christ Jesus, though he was in the form of God,
did not regard equality with God
something to be grasped.
Rather, he emptied himself,
taking the form of a slave,
coming in human likeness;
and found human in appearance,
he humbled himself,
becoming obedient to the point of death,
even death on a cross.
Because of this, God greatly exalted him
and bestowed on him the name
which is above every name,**

> that at the name of Jesus
> every knee should bend,
> of those in heaven and on earth and under the earth,
> and every tongue confess that
> Jesus Christ is Lord,
> to the glory of God the Father.

The word of the Lord. All: **Thanks be to God.**

* The message of the liturgy in proclaiming the passion narratives in full is to enable the assembly to see vividly the love of Christ for each person, despite their sins, a love that even death could not vanquish. The crimes during the Passion of Christ cannot be attributed indiscriminately to all Jews of that time, nor to Jews today. The Jewish people should not be referred to as though rejected or cursed, as if this view followed from Scripture. The Church ever keeps in mind that Jesus, his mother Mary, and the Apostles all were Jewish. As the Church has always held, Christ freely suffered his passion and death because of the sins of all, that all might be saved.

GOSPEL (Mark 14:1—15:47) *or* Shorter Form [ ] (Mark 15:1-39)
VERSE BEFORE THE GOSPEL (Philippians 2:8-9)

℣. Praise to you, Lord Jesus Christ, king of endless glory!
℟. **Praise to you, Lord Jesus Christ, king of endless glory!**
℣. Christ became obedient to the point of death,
even death on a cross.
Because of this, God greatly exalted him
and bestowed on him the name which is above every
    name. ℟.

The symbols in the following passion narrative represent:

    C.   Narrator;
    ✛   Christ;
    S.   speakers other than Christ;
    SS.   groups of speakers.

The Passion of our Lord Jesus Christ according to Mark

The Passion of our Lord Jesus Christ.

C. **The Passover and the Feast of Unleavened Bread
        were to take place in two days' time.
    So the chief priests and the scribes were seeking a way
        to arrest him by treachery and put him to death.
    They said,**

SS. "Not during the festival,
   for fear that there may be a riot among the people."

C. When he was in Bethany reclining at table
   in the house of Simon the leper,
      a woman came with an alabaster jar of perfumed oil,
      costly genuine spikenard.
   She broke the alabaster jar and poured it on his head.
   There were some who were indignant.

SS. "Why has there been this waste of perfumed oil?
   It could have been sold for more than three hundred
         days' wages
      and the money given to the poor."

C. They were infuriated with her.
   Jesus said,

✞ "Let her alone.
   Why do you make trouble for her?
   She has done a good thing for me.
   The poor you will always have with you,
      and whenever you wish you can do good to them,
      but you will not always have me.
   She has done what she could.
   She has anticipated anointing my body for burial.
   Amen, I say to you,
      wherever the gospel is proclaimed to the whole
            world,
      what she has done will be told in memory of her."

C. Then Judas Iscariot, one of the Twelve,
   went off to the chief priests to hand him over to them.
   When they heard him they were pleased and promised
         to pay him money.
   Then he looked for an opportunity to hand him over.

   On the first day of the Feast of Unleavened Bread,
      when they sacrificed the Passover lamb,
      his disciples said to him,

SS.	"Where do you want us to go and prepare for you to eat the Passover?"
C.	He sent two of his disciples and said to them,

✠	"Go into the city and a man will meet you,
	    carrying a jar of water.
	Follow him.
	Wherever he enters, say to the master of the house,
	    'The Teacher says, "Where is my guest room
	        where I may eat the Passover with my disciples?"'
	Then he will show you a large upper room furnished
	        and ready.
	Make the preparations for us there."

C.	The disciples then went off, entered the city,
	    and found it just as he had told them;
	    and they prepared the Passover.
	When it was evening, he came with the Twelve.
	And as they reclined at table and were eating,
	    Jesus said,

✠	"Amen, I say to you, one of you will betray me, one who is eating with me."
C.	They began to be distressed and to say to him, one by one,
S.	"Surely it is not I?"
C.	He said to them,

✠	"One of the Twelve, the one who dips with me into
	        the dish.
	For the Son of Man indeed goes, as it is written of him,
	    but woe to that man by whom the Son of Man is
	        betrayed.
	It would be better for that man if he had never been
	        born."

C.	While they were eating,
	    he took bread, said the blessing,
	    broke it, and gave it to them, and said,

✠	"Take it; this is my body."

C. Then he took a cup, gave thanks, and gave it to them,
   and they all drank from it.
   He said to them,
✠   "This is my blood of the covenant,
   which will be shed for many.
   Amen, I say to you,
      I shall not drink again the fruit of the vine
      until the day when I drink it new in the kingdom
         of God."
C. Then, after singing a hymn,
   they went out to the Mount of Olives.

   Then Jesus said to them,
✠   "All of you will have your faith shaken, for it is
      written:
   I will strike the shepherd,
      and the sheep will be dispersed.
   But after I have been raised up,
      I shall go before you to Galilee."
C. Peter said to him,
S.   "Even though all should have their faith shaken,
      mine will not be."
C. Then Jesus said to him,
✠   "Amen, I say to you,
   this very night before the cock crows twice
   you will deny me three times."
C. But he vehemently replied,
S.   "Even though I should have to die with you,
      I will not deny you."
C. And they all spoke similarly.

   Then they came to a place named Gethsemane,
      and he said to his disciples,
✠   "Sit here while I pray."
C. He took with him Peter, James, and John,
   and began to be troubled and distressed.
   Then he said to them,

✢   "My soul is sorrowful even to death.
Remain here and keep watch."
C. He advanced a little and fell to the ground and prayed
that if it were possible the hour might pass by him;
he said,
✢ "Abba, Father, all things are possible to you.
Take this cup away from me,
but not what I will but what you will."
C. When he returned he found them asleep.
He said to Peter,
✢   "Simon, are you asleep?
Could you not keep watch for one hour?
Watch and pray that you may not undergo the test.
The spirit is willing but the flesh is weak."
C. Withdrawing again, he prayed, saying the same thing.
Then he returned once more and found them asleep,
for they could not keep their eyes open
and did not know what to answer him.
He returned a third time and said to them,
✢   "Are you still sleeping and taking your rest?
It is enough. The hour has come.
Behold, the Son of Man is to be handed over to sinners.
Get up, let us go.
See, my betrayer is at hand."
C. Then, while he was still speaking,
Judas, one of the Twelve, arrived,
accompanied by a crowd with swords and clubs
who had come from the chief priests,
the scribes, and the elders.
His betrayer had arranged a signal with them, saying,
S. "The man I shall kiss is the one;
arrest him and lead him away securely."
C. He came and immediately went over to him and said,
S. "Rabbi."

C.   And he kissed him.
At this they laid hands on him and arrested him.
One of the bystanders drew his sword,
   struck the high priest's servant, and cut off his ear.
Jesus said to them in reply,
✠   "Have you come out as against a robber,
with swords and clubs, to seize me?
Day after day I was with you teaching in the temple area,
   yet you did not arrest me;
but that the Scriptures may be fulfilled."
C.   And they all left him and fled.
Now a young man followed him
   wearing nothing but a linen cloth about his body.
They seized him,
   but he left the cloth behind and ran off naked.

They led Jesus away to the high priest,
   and all the chief priests and the elders and the scribes came together.
Peter followed him at a distance into the high priest's courtyard
   and was seated with the guards, warming himself at the fire.
The chief priests and the entire Sanhedrin
   kept trying to obtain testimony against Jesus
   in order to put him to death, but they found none.
Many gave false witness against him,
   but their testimony did not agree.
Some took the stand and testified falsely against him, alleging,
SS.   "We heard him say,
   'I will destroy this temple made with hands
   and within three days I will build another
   not made with hands.'"

C.	Even so their testimony did not agree.
	The high priest rose before the assembly and questioned Jesus, saying,
S.	"Have you no answer?
	What are these men testifying against you?"
C.	But he was silent and answered nothing.
	Again the high priest asked him and said to him,
S.	"Are you the Christ, the son of the Blessed One?"
C.	Then Jesus answered,
✠	"I am;
	and 'you will see the Son of Man
	seated at the right hand of the Power
	and coming with the clouds of heaven.'"
C.	At that the high priest tore his garments and said,
S.	"What further need have we of witnesses?
	You have heard the blasphemy.
	What do you think?"
C.	They all condemned him as deserving to die.
	Some began to spit on him.
	They blindfolded him and struck him and said to him,
SS.	"Prophesy!"
C.	And the guards greeted him with blows.
	While Peter was below in the courtyard, one of the high priest's maids came along.
	Seeing Peter warming himself, she looked intently at him and said,
S.	"You too were with the Nazarene, Jesus."
C.	But he denied it saying,
S.	"I neither know nor understand what you are talking about."
C.	So he went out into the outer court.
	Then the cock crowed.
	The maid saw him and began again to say to the bystanders,
S.	"This man is one of them."

C.	Once again he denied it.
	A little later the bystanders said to Peter once more,
SS.	"Surely you are one of them; for you too are a Galilean."
C.	He began to curse and to swear,
S.	"I do not know this man about whom you are talking."
C.	And immediately a cock crowed a second time.
	Then Peter remembered the word that Jesus had said to him,
✝	"Before the cock crows twice you will deny me three times."
C.	He broke down and wept.

[As soon as morning came,
 the chief priests with the elders and the scribes,
 that is, the whole Sanhedrin, held a council.
They bound Jesus, led him away, and handed him
  over to Pilate.
Pilate questioned him,

S.	"Are you the king of the Jews?"
C.	He said to him in reply,
✝	"You say so."
C.	The chief priests accused him of many things.
	Again Pilate questioned him,
S.	"Have you no answer?
	See how many things they accuse you of."
C.	Jesus gave him no further answer, so that Pilate was amazed.

Now on the occasion of the feast he used to release to them
   one prisoner whom they requested.
A man called Barabbas was then in prison
   along with the rebels who had committed murder
     in a rebellion.

The crowd came forward and began to ask him
  to do for them as he was accustomed.
Pilate answered,
S.   "Do you want me to release to you the king of
  the Jews?"
C. For he knew that it was out of envy
  that the chief priests had handed him over.
But the chief priests stirred up the crowd
  to have him release Barabbas for them instead.
Pilate again said to them in reply,
S.   "Then what do you want me to do
  with the man you call the king of the Jews?"
C. They shouted again,
SS. "Crucify him."
C. Pilate said to them,
S. "Why? What evil has he done?"
C. They only shouted the louder,
SS. "Crucify him."
C. So Pilate, wishing to satisfy the crowd,
  released Barabbas to them and, after he had Jesus
    scourged,
  handed him over to be crucified.

The soldiers led him away inside the palace,
  that is, the praetorium, and assembled the whole
    cohort.
They clothed him in purple and,
  weaving a crown of thorns, placed it on him.
They began to salute him with,
SS. "Hail, King of the Jews!"
C.   and kept striking his head with a reed and
    spitting upon him.
They knelt before him in homage.
And when they had mocked him,
  they stripped him of the purple cloak,
  dressed him in his own clothes,
  and led him out to crucify him.

They pressed into service a passer-by, Simon,
  a Cyrenian, who was coming in from the country,
  the father of Alexander and Rufus,
  to carry his cross.

They brought him to the place of Golgotha
—which is translated Place of the Skull—.
They gave him wine drugged with myrrh,
  but he did not take it.
Then they crucified him and divided his garments
  by casting lots for them to see what each should take.
It was nine o'clock in the morning when they
    crucified him.
The inscription of the charge against him read,
"The King of the Jews."
With him they crucified two revolutionaries,
  one on his right and one on his left.
Those passing by reviled him,
  shaking their heads and saying,

SS. "Aha! You who would destroy the temple
  and rebuild it in three days,
    save yourself by coming down from the cross."

C. Likewise the chief priests, with the scribes,
  mocked him among themselves and said,

SS. "He saved others; he cannot save himself.
Let the Christ, the King of Israel,
  come down now from the cross
  that we may see and believe."

C. Those who were crucified with him also kept
    abusing him.

At noon darkness came over the whole land
  until three in the afternoon.
And at three o'clock Jesus cried out in a loud voice,

✟ *"Eloi, Eloi, lema sabachthani?"*

C. which is translated,

☩ "My God, my God, why have you forsaken me?"
C. Some of the bystanders who heard it said,
SS. "Look, he is calling Elijah."
C. One of them ran, soaked a sponge with wine, put it
   on a reed
   and gave it to him to drink saying,
S. "Wait, let us see if Elijah comes to take him down."
C. Jesus gave a loud cry and breathed his last.

Here all kneel and pause for a short time.

The veil of the sanctuary was torn in two from top
   to bottom.
When the centurion who stood facing him
   saw how he breathed his last he said,
S.   "Truly this man was the Son of God!"]
C. There were also women looking on from a distance.
Among them were Mary Magdalene,
   Mary the mother of the younger James and of Joses,
   and Salome.
These women had followed him when he was in Galilee
   and ministered to him.
There were also many other women
   who had come up with him to Jerusalem.

When it was already evening,
   since it was the day of preparation,
   the day before the sabbath, Joseph of Arimathea,
   a distinguished member of the council,
   who was himself awaiting the kingdom of God,
   came and courageously went to Pilate
   and asked for the body of Jesus.
Pilate was amazed that he was already dead.
He summoned the centurion
   and asked him if Jesus had already died.
And when he learned of it from the centurion,
   he gave the body to Joseph.

**Having bought a linen cloth, he took him down,
wrapped him in the linen cloth,
and laid him in a tomb that had been hewn out of
the rock.
Then he rolled a stone against the entrance to the tomb.
Mary Magdalene and Mary the mother of Joses
watched where he was laid.**

The Gospel of the Lord. All: **Praise to you, Lord Jesus Christ.**

Prayer over the Offerings
Through the Passion of your Only Begotten Son, O Lord,
may our reconciliation with you be near at hand,
so that, though we do not merit it by our own deeds,
yet by this sacrifice made once for all,
we may feel already the effects of your mercy.
Through Christ our Lord. All: **Amen.**

Communion Antiphon (Matthew 26:42)
Father, if this chalice cannot pass without my drinking it,
your will be done.

Prayer after Communion
Nourished with these sacred gifts,
we humbly beseech you, O Lord,
that, just as through the death of your Son
you have brought us to hope for what we believe,
so by his Resurrection
you may lead us to where you call.
Through Christ our Lord. All: **Amen.**

The Sacred Paschal Triduum

Reflection on the Gospel

Suffering in itself is not the focus of these three days. Jesus suffered because he was faithful to his Father's will, because he called people back to faithfulness to their covenant with God, because he never swerved from his message of salvation for all people. Jesus suffered because he did not put human laws above divine Law, angering some religious leaders. Jesus suffered because he loved. His suffering manifested his utter self-giving, his care and compassion, his righteousness and goodness. His suffering can teach us much.

• I hear Jesus' message of faithfulness when I . . .

—*Living Liturgy*™, *Easter Triduum 2015*

Holy Thursday solemnly inaugurates "the triduum during which the Lord died, was buried and rose again" (St. Augustine). To these days Jesus referred when he prophesied: "Destroy this temple and in three days I will raise it up again" (John 2:14).

Thursday of the Lord's Supper

AT THE EVENING MASS

April 2, 2015

Reflection on the Gospel

Jesus gave us a profound witness to what self-giving love looks like: he washed his disciples' feet. This act of humble service is our "model to follow." We wash the feet of others when we love with the same kind of unreserved love as Jesus showed us. This footwashing is more than a ritual act. It is a way of living and loving. This sums up all Jesus taught. This sums up the meaning of the Supper. This sums up this night. This sums up Jesus' whole life. So must it sum up ours.

• I truly wash the feet of others by . . .

—*Living Liturgy*™, *Holy Thursday 2015*

Entrance Antiphon (Cf. Galatians 6:14)
We should glory in the Cross of our Lord Jesus Christ,
in whom is our salvation, life and resurrection,
through whom we are saved and delivered.

Collect
O God, who have called us to participate
in this most sacred Supper,
in which your Only Begotten Son,
when about to hand himself over to death,
entrusted to the Church a sacrifice new for all eternity,
the banquet of his love,
grant, we pray,
that we may draw from so great a mystery,
the fullness of charity and of life.
Through our Lord Jesus Christ, your Son,
who lives and reigns with you in the unity of the Holy Spirit,
one God, for ever and ever. All: **Amen.**

Reading I (L 39-ABC) (Exodus 12:1-8, 11-14)
A reading from the Book of Exodus

The law regarding the Passover meal.

**The Lord said to Moses and Aaron in the land of Egypt,
"This month shall stand at the head of your calendar;
you shall reckon it the first month of the year.
Tell the whole community of Israel:
On the tenth of this month every one of your families
must procure for itself a lamb, one apiece for each
household.
If a family is too small for a whole lamb,
it shall join the nearest household in procuring one
and shall share in the lamb
in proportion to the number of persons who partake
of it.
The lamb must be a year-old male and without blemish.
You may take it from either the sheep or the goats.
You shall keep it until the fourteenth day of this month,
and then, with the whole assembly of Israel present,
it shall be slaughtered during the evening twilight.**

They shall take some of its blood
   and apply it to the two doorposts and the lintel
   of every house in which they partake of the lamb.
That same night they shall eat its roasted flesh
   with unleavened bread and bitter herbs.

"This is how you are to eat it:
   with your loins girt, sandals on your feet and your
      staff in hand,
   you shall eat like those who are in flight.
It is the Passover of the Lord.
For on this same night I will go through Egypt,
   striking down every firstborn of the land, both man
      and beast,
   and executing judgment on all the gods of Egypt—
      I, the Lord!
But the blood will mark the houses where you are.
Seeing the blood, I will pass over you;
   thus, when I strike the land of Egypt,
   no destructive blow will come upon you.

"This day shall be a memorial feast for you,
   which all your generations shall celebrate
   with pilgrimage to the Lord, as a perpetual institution."

The word of the Lord. All: Thanks be to God.

Responsorial Psalm 116

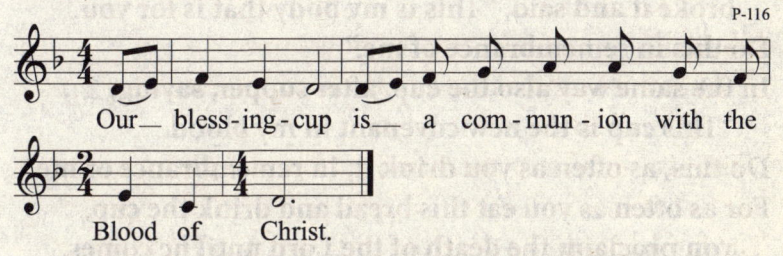

Our blessing-cup is a communion with the Blood of Christ.

Music: Jay F. Hunstiger, © 1990, administered by Liturgical Press. All rights reserved.

Psalm 116:12-13, 15-16bc, 17-18

℟. (*See* 1 Corinthians 10:16) **Our blessing-cup is a communion with the Blood of Christ.**

How shall I make a return to the Lord
    for all the good he has done for me?
The cup of salvation I will take up,
    and I will call upon the name of the Lord. ℟.

Precious in the eyes of the Lord
    is the death of his faithful ones.
I am your servant, the son of your handmaid;
    you have loosed my bonds. ℟.

To you will I offer sacrifice of thanksgiving,
    and I will call upon the name of the Lord.
My vows to the Lord I will pay
    in the presence of all his people. ℟.

Reading II (1 Corinthians 11:23-26)

A reading from the first Letter of Saint Paul to the Corinthians

For as often as you eat this bread and drink the cup, you proclaim the death of the Lord.

**Brothers and sisters:
I received from the Lord what I also handed on to you,
    that the Lord Jesus, on the night he was handed over,
    took bread, and, after he had given thanks,
    broke it and said, "This is my body that is for you.
Do this in remembrance of me."
In the same way also the cup, after supper, saying,
    "This cup is the new covenant in my blood.
Do this, as often as you drink it, in remembrance of me."
For as often as you eat this bread and drink the cup,
    you proclaim the death of the Lord until he comes.**

The word of the Lord. All: **Thanks be to God.**

Gospel (John 13:1-15)
Verse before the Gospel (John 13:34)

℣. Praise to you, Lord Jesus Christ, king of endless glory!
℟. **Praise to you, Lord Jesus Christ, king of endless glory!**
℣. I give you a new commandment, says the Lord:
love one another as I have loved you. ℟.

✣ A reading from the holy Gospel according to John

All: **Glory to you, O Lord.**

Jesus loved them to the end.

**Before the feast of Passover, Jesus knew that his hour had come
   to pass from this world to the Father.
He loved his own in the world and he loved them to the end.
The devil had already induced Judas, son of Simon the Iscariot, to hand him over.
So, during supper,
   fully aware that the Father had put everything into his power
   and that he had come from God and was returning to God,
   he rose from supper and took off his outer garments.
He took a towel and tied it around his waist.
Then he poured water into a basin
   and began to wash the disciples' feet
   and dry them with the towel around his waist.
He came to Simon Peter, who said to him,
   "Master, are you going to wash my feet?"
Jesus answered and said to him,
   "What I am doing, you do not understand now,
   but you will understand later."
Peter said to him, "You will never wash my feet."
Jesus answered him,
   "Unless I wash you, you will have no inheritance with me."**

Simon Peter said to him,
> "Master, then not only my feet, but my hands and head as well."

Jesus said to him,
> "Whoever has bathed has no need except to have his feet washed,
> for he is clean all over;
> so you are clean, but not all."

For he knew who would betray him;
> for this reason, he said, "Not all of you are clean."

So when he had washed their feet
> and put his garments back on and reclined at table again,
> he said to them, "Do you realize what I have done for you?

You call me 'teacher' and 'master,' and rightly so,
> for indeed I am.

If I, therefore, the master and teacher, have washed your feet,
> you ought to wash one another's feet.

I have given you a model to follow,
> so that as I have done for you, you should also do."

The Gospel of the Lord. All: **Praise to you, Lord Jesus Christ.**

WASHING OF FEET
Antiphons or other appropriate songs are sung.

Prayer over the Offerings
Grant us, O Lord, we pray,
that we may participate worthily in these mysteries,
for whenever the memorial of this sacrifice is celebrated
the work of our redemption is accomplished.
Through Christ our Lord. All: **Amen.**

Communion Antiphon (1 Corinthians 11:24-25)
This is the Body that will be given up for you;
this is the Chalice of the new covenant in my Blood,
    says the Lord;
do this, whenever you receive it, in memory of me.

Prayer after Communion
Grant, almighty God,
that, just as we are renewed
by the Supper of your Son in this present age,
so we may enjoy his banquet for all eternity.
Who lives and reigns for ever and ever. All: **Amen.**

TRANSFER OF THE HOLY EUCHARIST

Friday of the Passion of the Lord (Good Friday)

April 3, 2015 (First Friday)

Reflection on the Gospel

Jesus accepted mockery and rejection rather than compromise the goodness he was. He accepted suffering and death as a climactic act of fidelity and love. He "handed over the spirit" in an awe-inspiring act of self-giving. Even after death, he poured forth "blood and water" from his side, foreshadowing our own baptismal entry into his mystery and our participation in his perpetual self-giving in the eucharistic sacrifice. On this "Good" Friday we are invited to choose good. We are invited to embrace Jesus' self-giving love.

- *Choose good, hand over your spirit, by . . .*

—*Living Liturgy*™, *Good Friday 2015*

Celebration of the Lord's Passion

Prayer (Let us pray is not said)
Remember your mercies, O Lord,
and with your eternal protection sanctify your servants,
for whom Christ your Son,
by the shedding of his Blood,
established the Paschal Mystery.
Who lives and reigns for ever and ever. All: **Amen.**

Or:

O God, who by the Passion of Christ your Son, our Lord,
abolished the death inherited from ancient sin
by every succeeding generation,
grant that just as, being conformed to him,
we have borne by the law of nature
the image of the man of earth,
so by the sanctification of grace
we may bear the image of the Man of heaven.
Through Christ our Lord. All: **Amen.**

FIRST PART: LITURGY OF THE WORD

READING I (L 40-ABC) (Isaiah 52:13—53:12)
A reading from the Book of the Prophet Isaiah

He himself was wounded for our sins.
(Fourth oracle of the Servant of the Lord.)

See, my servant shall prosper,
  he shall be raised high and greatly exalted.
Even as many were amazed at him—
  so marred was his look beyond human semblance
  and his appearance beyond that of the sons of man—
so shall he startle many nations,
  because of him kings shall stand speechless;
for those who have not been told shall see,
  those who have not heard shall ponder it.

Who would believe what we have heard?
  To whom has the arm of the LORD been revealed?
He grew up like a sapling before him,
  like a shoot from the parched earth;
there was in him no stately bearing to make us look
    at him,
  nor appearance that would attract us to him.
He was spurned and avoided by people,
  a man of suffering, accustomed to infirmity,
one of those from whom people hide their faces,
  spurned, and we held him in no esteem.

Yet it was our infirmities that he bore,
    our sufferings that he endured,
while we thought of him as stricken,
    as one smitten by God and afflicted.
But he was pierced for our offenses,
    crushed for our sins;
upon him was the chastisement that makes us whole,
    by his stripes we were healed.
We had all gone astray like sheep,
    each following his own way;
but the LORD laid upon him
    the guilt of us all.

Though he was harshly treated, he submitted
    and opened not his mouth;
like a lamb led to the slaughter
    or a sheep before the shearers,
    he was silent and opened not his mouth.
Oppressed and condemned, he was taken away,
    and who would have thought any more of his destiny?
When he was cut off from the land of the living,
    and smitten for the sin of his people,
a grave was assigned him among the wicked
    and a burial place with evildoers,
though he had done no wrong
    nor spoken any falsehood.
But the LORD was pleased
    to crush him in infirmity.

If he gives his life as an offering for sin,
    he shall see his descendants in a long life,
    and the will of the LORD shall be accomplished
        through him.
Because of his affliction
    he shall see the light in fullness of days;
through his suffering, my servant shall justify many,
    and their guilt he shall bear.

> Therefore I will give him his portion among the great,
> and he shall divide the spoils with the mighty,
> because he surrendered himself to death
> and was counted among the wicked;
> and he shall take away the sins of many,
> and win pardon for their offenses.

The word of the Lord. All: **Thanks be to God.**

Responsorial Psalm 31

Father, into your hands I commend my spirit.

Music: Bartholomew Sayles, O.S.B., and Cecile Gertken, O.S.B., adapt., © 1977, 1989, Order of Saint Benedict.

Psalm 31:2, 6, 12-13, 15-16, 17, 25

℟. (Luke 23:46) **Father, into your hands I commend my spirit.**

In you, O Lord, I take refuge;
 let me never be put to shame.
In your justice rescue me.
Into your hands I commend my spirit;
 you will redeem me, O Lord, O faithful God. ℟.

For all my foes I am an object of reproach,
 a laughingstock to my neighbors, and a dread to my friends;
 they who see me abroad flee from me.
I am forgotten like the unremembered dead;
 I am like a dish that is broken. ℟.

But my trust is in you, O Lord;
 I say, "You are my God.
In your hands is my destiny; rescue me
 from the clutches of my enemies and my persecutors." ℟.

Let your face shine upon your servant;
 save me in your kindness.
Take courage and be stouthearted,
 all you who hope in the Lord. ℟.

Reading II (Hebrews 4:14-16; 5:7-9)
A reading from the Letter to the Hebrews

Jesus learned obedience and became the source of salvation for all who obey him.

Brothers and sisters:
Since we have a great high priest who has passed through the heavens,
> **Jesus, the Son of God,**
> **let us hold fast to our confession.**

For we do not have a high priest
> **who is unable to sympathize with our weaknesses,**
> **but one who has similarly been tested in every way,**
> **yet without sin.**

So let us confidently approach the throne of grace
> **to receive mercy and to find grace for timely help.**

In the days when Christ was in the flesh,
> **he offered prayers and supplications with loud cries and tears**
> **to the one who was able to save him from death,**
> **and he was heard because of his reverence.**

Son though he was, he learned obedience from what he suffered;
> **and when he was made perfect,**
> **he became the source of eternal salvation for all who obey him.**

The word of the Lord. All: **Thanks be to God.**

* See **statement on page 153.**

Gospel (John 18:1—19:42)
Verse before the Gospel (Philippians 2:8-9)

℣. Praise to you, Lord Jesus Christ, king of endless glory!
℟. **Praise to you, Lord Jesus Christ, king of endless glory!**
℣. Christ became obedient to the point of death,
> even death on a cross.
> Because of this, God greatly exalted him
> and bestowed on him the name which is above every other name. ℟.

The symbols in the following passion narrative represent:

- C.   Narrator;
- ✠   Christ;
- S.   speakers other than Christ;
- SS. groups of speakers.

The Passion of our Lord Jesus Christ according to John

The Passion of our Lord Jesus Christ.

C. Jesus went out with his disciples across the Kidron valley
   to where there was a garden,
   into which he and his disciples entered.
Judas his betrayer also knew the place,
   because Jesus had often met there with his disciples.
So Judas got a band of soldiers and guards
   from the chief priests and the Pharisees
   and went there with lanterns, torches, and weapons.
Jesus, knowing everything that was going to happen to him,
   went out and said to them,

✠ "Whom are you looking for?"

C. They answered him,

SS. "Jesus the Nazorean."

C. He said to them,

✠ "I AM."

C. Judas his betrayer was also with them.
When he said to them, "I AM,"
   they turned away and fell to the ground.
So he again asked them,

✠ "Whom are you looking for?"

C. They said,

SS. "Jesus the Nazorean."

C. Jesus answered,

✠ "I told you that I AM.
So if you are looking for me, let these men go."

C. This was to fulfill what he had said,
   "I have not lost any of those you gave me."

Then Simon Peter, who had a sword, drew it,
> struck the high priest's slave, and cut off his right ear.
The slave's name was Malchus.
Jesus said to Peter,

☩   "Put your sword into its scabbard.
Shall I not drink the cup that the Father gave me?"

C. So the band of soldiers, the tribune, and the Jewish guards seized Jesus,
> bound him, and brought him to Annas first.
He was the father-in-law of Caiaphas,
> who was high priest that year.
It was Caiaphas who had counseled the Jews
> that it was better that one man should die rather than the people.

Simon Peter and another disciple followed Jesus.
Now the other disciple was known to the high priest,
> and he entered the courtyard of the high priest with Jesus.
But Peter stood at the gate outside.
So the other disciple, the acquaintance of the high priest,
> went out and spoke to the gatekeeper and brought Peter in.
Then the maid who was the gatekeeper said to Peter,

S.   "You are not one of this man's disciples, are you?"
C. He said,
S.   "I am not."
C. Now the slaves and the guards were standing around a charcoal fire
> that they had made, because it was cold,
> and were warming themselves.
Peter was also standing there keeping warm.

The high priest questioned Jesus
> about his disciples and about his doctrine.
Jesus answered him,

✝ "I have spoken publicly to the world.
I have always taught in a synagogue
or in the temple area where all the Jews gather,
and in secret I have said nothing. Why ask me?
Ask those who heard me what I said to them.
They know what I said."
C. When he had said this,
one of the temple guards standing there struck Jesus and said,
S. "Is this the way you answer the high priest?"
C. Jesus answered him,
✝ "If I have spoken wrongly, testify to the wrong;
but if I have spoken rightly, why do you strike me?"
C. Then Annas sent him bound to Caiaphas the high priest.

Now Simon Peter was standing there keeping warm.
And they said to him,
S. "You are not one of his disciples, are you?"
C. He denied it and said,
S. "I am not."
C. One of the slaves of the high priest,
a relative of the one whose ear Peter had cut off, said,
S. "Didn't I see you in the garden with him?"
C. Again Peter denied it.
And immediately the cock crowed.

Then they brought Jesus from Caiaphas to the praetorium.
It was morning.
And they themselves did not enter the praetorium,
in order not to be defiled so that they could eat the Passover.
So Pilate came out to them and said,
S. "What charge do you bring against this man?"
C. They answered and said to him,

SS.	"If he were not a criminal, we would not have handed him over to you."
C.	At this, Pilate said to them,
S.	"Take him yourselves, and judge him according to your law."
C.	The Jews answered him,
SS.	"We do not have the right to execute anyone,"
C.	in order that the word of Jesus might be fulfilled that he said indicating the kind of death he would die. So Pilate went back into the praetorium and summoned Jesus and said to him,
S.	"Are you the King of the Jews?"
C.	Jesus answered,
✝	"Do you say this on your own or have others told you about me?"
C.	Pilate answered,
S.	"I am not a Jew, am I? Your own nation and the chief priests handed you over to me. What have you done?"
C.	Jesus answered,
✝	"My kingdom does not belong to this world. If my kingdom did belong to this world, my attendants would be fighting to keep me from being handed over to the Jews. But as it is, my kingdom is not here."
C.	So Pilate said to him,
S.	"Then you are a king?"
C.	Jesus answered,
✝	"You say I am a king. For this I was born and for this I came into the world, to testify to the truth. Everyone who belongs to the truth listens to my voice."
C.	Pilate said to him,
S.	"What is truth?"

C.	When he had said this,
	he again went out to the Jews and said to them,
S.	"I find no guilt in him.
	But you have a custom that I release one prisoner to
	you at Passover.
	Do you want me to release to you the King of the Jews?"
C.	They cried out again,
SS.	"Not this one but Barabbas!"
C.	Now Barabbas was a revolutionary.

Then Pilate took Jesus and had him scourged.
And the soldiers wove a crown out of thorns and
     placed it on his head,
   and clothed him in a purple cloak,
   and they came to him and said,

SS.	"Hail, King of the Jews!"
C.	And they struck him repeatedly.
	Once more Pilate went out and said to them,
S.	"Look, I am bringing him out to you,
	so that you may know that I find no guilt in him."
C.	So Jesus came out,
	wearing the crown of thorns and the purple cloak.
	And Pilate said to them,
S.	"Behold, the man!"
C.	When the chief priests and the guards saw him they
	cried out,
SS.	"Crucify him, crucify him!"
C.	Pilate said to them,
S.	"Take him yourselves and crucify him.
	I find no guilt in him."
C.	The Jews answered,
SS.	"We have a law, and according to that law he ought
	to die,
	because he made himself the Son of God."
C.	Now when Pilate heard this statement,
	he became even more afraid,
	and went back into the praetorium and said to Jesus,

S.   "Where are you from?"
C.   Jesus did not answer him.
So Pilate said to him,
S.   "Do you not speak to me?
Do you not know that I have power to release you
and I have power to crucify you?"
C.   Jesus answered him,
✠   "You would have no power over me
if it had not been given to you from above.
For this reason the one who handed me over to you
has the greater sin."
C.   Consequently, Pilate tried to release him; but the Jews cried out,
SS.   "If you release him, you are not a Friend of Caesar.
Everyone who makes himself a king opposes Caesar."
C.   When Pilate heard these words he brought Jesus out
and seated him on the judge's bench
in the place called Stone Pavement, in Hebrew, Gabbatha.
It was preparation day for Passover, and it was about noon.
And he said to the Jews,
S.   "Behold, your king!"
C.   They cried out,
SS.   "Take him away, take him away! Crucify him!"
C.   Pilate said to them,
S.   "Shall I crucify your king?"
C.   The chief priests answered,
SS.   "We have no king but Caesar."
C.   Then he handed him over to them to be crucified.

So they took Jesus, and, carrying the cross himself,
he went out to what is called the Place of the Skull,
in Hebrew, Golgotha.
There they crucified him, and with him two others,
one on either side, with Jesus in the middle.

      Pilate also had an inscription written and put on the cross.
      It read,
         "Jesus the Nazorean, the King of the Jews."
      Now many of the Jews read this inscription,
         because the place where Jesus was crucified was near the city;
         and it was written in Hebrew, Latin, and Greek.
      So the chief priests of the Jews said to Pilate,

SS.   "Do not write 'The King of the Jews,'
      but that he said, 'I am the King of the Jews.'"

C.   Pilate answered,

S.   "What I have written, I have written."

C.   When the soldiers had crucified Jesus,
      they took his clothes and divided them into four shares,
      a share for each soldier.
    They also took his tunic, but the tunic was seamless,
      woven in one piece from the top down.
    So they said to one another,

SS.   "Let's not tear it, but cast lots for it to see whose it will be,"

C.   in order that the passage of Scripture might be fulfilled that says:
      They divided my garments among them,
      and for my vesture they cast lots.
    This is what the soldiers did.
    Standing by the cross of Jesus were his mother
      and his mother's sister, Mary the wife of Clopas, and Mary of Magdala.
    When Jesus saw his mother and the disciple there
      whom he loved he said to his mother,

✠   "Woman, behold, your son."

C.   Then he said to the disciple,

✠   "Behold, your mother."

C.   And from that hour the disciple took her into his home.

After this, aware that everything was now finished,
   in order that the Scripture might be fulfilled,
   Jesus said,
✠ "I thirst."
C. There was a vessel filled with common wine.
   So they put a sponge soaked in wine on a sprig of
      hyssop
      and put it up to his mouth.
   When Jesus had taken the wine, he said,
✠ "It is finished."
C. And bowing his head, he handed over the spirit.

Here all kneel and pause for a short time.

Now since it was preparation day,
   in order that the bodies might not remain
      on the cross on the sabbath,
      for the sabbath day of that week was a solemn one,
   the Jews asked Pilate that their legs be broken
   and that they be taken down.
So the soldiers came and broke the legs of the first
   and then of the other one who was crucified with
      Jesus.
But when they came to Jesus and saw that he was
   already dead,
   they did not break his legs,
   but one soldier thrust his lance into his side,
   and immediately blood and water flowed out.
An eyewitness has testified, and his testimony is true;
   he knows that he is speaking the truth,
   so that you also may come to believe.
For this happened so that the Scripture passage
   might be fulfilled:
Not a bone of it will be broken.
And again another passage says:
They will look upon him whom they have pierced.

After this, Joseph of Arimathea,
    secretly a disciple of Jesus for fear of the Jews,
    asked Pilate if he could remove the body of Jesus.
And Pilate permitted it.
So he came and took his body.
Nicodemus, the one who had first come to him at night,
    also came bringing a mixture of myrrh and aloes
    weighing about one hundred pounds.
They took the body of Jesus
    and bound it with burial cloths along with the spices,
    according to the Jewish burial custom.
Now in the place where he had been crucified there
    was a garden,
    and in the garden a new tomb, in which no one
        had yet been buried.
So they laid Jesus there because of the Jewish
    preparation day;
    for the tomb was close by.

The Gospel of the Lord. All: **Praise to you, Lord Jesus Christ.**

The Solemn Intercessions

I. For Holy Church

Let us pray, dearly beloved, for the holy Church of God,
that our God and Lord be pleased to give her peace,
to guard her and to unite her throughout the whole world
and grant that, leading our life in tranquility and quiet,
we may glorify God the Father almighty.

Prayer in silence. Then the Priest sings or says:

Almighty ever-living God,
who in Christ revealed your glory to all the nations,
watch over the works of your mercy,
that your Church, spread throughout all the world,
may persevere with steadfast faith in confessing your name.
Through Christ our Lord. All: **Amen.**

II. For the Pope

Let us pray also for our most Holy Father Pope N.,
that our God and Lord,
who chose him for the Order of Bishops,

may keep him safe and unharmed for the Lord's holy Church,
to govern the holy People of God.

Prayer in silence. Then the Priest sings or says:

Almighty ever-living God,
by whose decree all things are founded,
look with favor on our prayers
and in your kindness protect the Pope chosen for us,
that, under him, the Christian people,
governed by you their maker,
may grow in merit by reason of their faith.
Through Christ our Lord. All: **Amen.**

III. FOR ALL ORDERS AND DEGREES OF THE FAITHFUL

Let us pray also for our Bishop N.,*
for all Bishops, Priests, and Deacons of the Church
and for the whole of the faithful people.

Prayer in silence. Then the Priest sings or says:

Almighty ever-living God,
by whose Spirit the whole body of the Church
is sanctified and governed,
hear our humble prayer for your ministers,
that, by the gift of your grace,
all may serve you faithfully.
Through Christ our Lord. All: **Amen.**

IV. FOR CATECHUMENS

Let us pray also for (our) catechumens,
that our God and Lord
may open wide the ears of their inmost hearts
and unlock the gates of his mercy,
that, having received forgiveness of all their sins
through the waters of rebirth,
they, too, may be one with Christ Jesus our Lord.

Prayer in silence. Then the Priest sings or says:

Almighty ever-living God,
who make your Church ever fruitful with new offspring,
increase the faith and understanding of (our) catechumens,
that, reborn in the font of Baptism,
they may be added to the number of your adopted children.
Through Christ our Lord. All: **Amen.**

---

* Mention may be made here of the Coadjutor Bishop, or Auxiliary Bishops, as noted in the *General Instruction of the Roman Missal*, no. 149.

V. For the Unity of Christians

Let us pray also for all our brothers and sisters who believe in Christ,
that our God and Lord may be pleased,
as they live the truth,
to gather them together and keep them in his one Church.

Prayer in silence. Then the Priest sings or says:

Almighty ever-living God,
who gather what is scattered
and keep together what you have gathered,
look kindly on the flock of your Son,
that those whom one Baptism has consecrated
may be joined together by integrity of faith
and united in the bond of charity.
Through Christ our Lord. All: **Amen.**

VI. For the Jewish People

Let us pray also for the Jewish people,
to whom the Lord our God spoke first,
that he may grant them to advance in love of his name
and in faithfulness to his covenant.

Prayer in silence. Then the Priest sings or says:

Almighty ever-living God,
who bestowed your promises on Abraham and his descendants,
graciously hear the prayers of your Church,
that the people you first made your own
may attain the fullness of redemption.
Through Christ our Lord. All: **Amen.**

VII. For Those Who Do Not Believe in Christ

Let us pray also for those who do not believe in Christ,
that, enlightened by the Holy Spirit,
they, too, may enter on the way of salvation.

Prayer in silence. Then the Priest sings or says:

Almighty ever-living God,
grant to those who do not confess Christ
that, by walking before you with a sincere heart,
they may find the truth
and that we ourselves, being constant in mutual love
and striving to understand more fully the mystery of your life,
may be made more perfect witnesses to your love in the world.
Through Christ our Lord. All: **Amen.**

VIII. For Those Who Do Not Believe in God

Let us pray also for those who do not acknowledge God,
that, following what is right in sincerity of heart,
they may find the way to God himself.

Prayer in silence. Then the Priest sings or says:

Almighty ever-living God,
who created all people
to seek you always by desiring you
and, by finding you, come to rest,
grant, we pray,
that, despite every harmful obstacle,
all may recognize the signs of your fatherly love
and the witness of the good works
done by those who believe in you,
and so in gladness confess you,
the one true God and Father of our human race.
Through Christ our Lord. All: **Amen.**

IX. For Those in Public Office

Let us pray also for those in public office,
that our God and Lord
may direct their minds and hearts according to his will
for the true peace and freedom of all.

Prayer in silence. Then the Priest sings or says:

Almighty ever-living God,
in whose hand lies every human heart
and the rights of peoples,
look with favor, we pray,
on those who govern with authority over us,
that throughout the whole world,
the prosperity of peoples,
the assurance of peace,
and freedom of religion
may through your gift be made secure.
Through Christ our Lord. All: **Amen.**

X. For Those in Tribulation

Let us pray, dearly beloved,
to God the Father almighty,
that he may cleanse the world of all errors,
banish disease, drive out hunger,
unlock prisons, loosen fetters,
granting to travelers safety, to pilgrims return,
health to the sick, and salvation to the dying.

Prayer in silence. Then the Priest sings or says:

Almighty ever-living God,
comfort of mourners, strength of all who toil,
may the prayers of those who cry out in any tribulation
come before you,
that all may rejoice,
because in their hour of need
your mercy was at hand.
Through Christ our Lord. **All: Amen.**

SECOND PART: THE ADORATION OF THE HOLY CROSS

The Showing of the Holy Cross

First Form
℣. Ecce lignum Crucis (Behold the wood of the Cross).
All respond: **Venite adoremus (Come, let us adore).**

Second Form
℣. Behold the wood of the Cross,
on which hung the salvation of the world.
All respond: **Come, let us adore.**

The Adoration of the Holy Cross
The Priest, clergy, and faithful approach to venerate the cross in a kind of procession.

THIRD PART: HOLY COMMUNION

At the Savior's command
and formed by divine teaching,
we dare to say:

The Priest, with hands extended says, and all present continue:
**Our Father, who art in heaven,
hallowed be thy name;
thy kingdom come,
thy will be done
on earth as it is in heaven.
Give us this day our daily bread,
and forgive us our trespasses,
as we forgive those who trespass against us;
and lead us not into temptation,
but deliver us from evil.**

April 3 . 189

With hands extended, the Priest continues alone:
Deliver us, Lord, we pray, from every evil,
graciously grant peace in our days,
that, by the help of your mercy,
we may be always free from sin
and safe from all distress,
as we await the blessed hope
and the coming of our Savior, Jesus Christ.

He joins his hands. The people conclude the prayer, acclaiming:
**For the kingdom, the power and the glory are yours
   now and for ever.**

Then the Priest, with hands joined, says quietly:
May the receiving of your Body and Blood,
Lord Jesus Christ,
not bring me to judgment and condemnation,
but through your loving mercy
be for me protection in mind and body
and a healing remedy.

The Priest then genuflects, takes a particle, and, holding it slightly raised over the ciborium, while facing the people, says aloud:
Behold the Lamb of God,
behold him who takes away the sins of the world.
Blessed are those called to the supper of the Lamb.

And together with the people he adds once:
**Lord, I am not worthy
that you should enter under my roof,
but only say the word
and my soul shall be healed.**

Prayer after Communion
Almighty ever-living God,
who have restored us to life
by the blessed Death and Resurrection of your Christ,
preserve in us the work of your mercy,
that, by partaking of this mystery,
we may have a life unceasingly devoted to you.
Through Christ our Lord. All: **Amen.**

Prayer over the People
May abundant blessing, O Lord, we pray,
descend upon your people,
who have honored the Death of your Son
in the hope of their resurrection:
may pardon come,

April 3

comfort be given,
holy faith increase,
and everlasting redemption be made secure.
Through Christ our Lord. All: **Amen.**

After genuflecting to the Cross, all depart in silence. The altar is stripped;
the cross remains, however, with four candles.

HOLY SATURDAY

The Easter Vigil in the Holy Night

April 4, 2015 (First Saturday)

Reflection on the Gospel

*This night invites us to be at home. Be comfortable.
Open ourselves to an encounter like no other we have ever had. We know
what we also find in our midst: Jesus the risen One. Not in Galilee, but
right here among us. This Jesus cannot be contained in a tomb. We do
not visit a cemetery to encounter him. This Jesus has been raised from
the dead and seeks us out, offers us new Life, prepares us to open ourselves to beauty, peace, and quiet like we have never before experienced.*

- *Jesus, raised from the dead, is here in this place, in these believers,
  here among us . . .*

—Living Liturgy™, *Easter Vigil 2015*

FIRST PART: THE SOLEMN BEGINNING OF THE VIGIL
OR LUCERNARIUM

THE BLESSING OF THE FIRE AND PREPARATION OF THE CANDLE

Priest: In the name of the Father, and of the Son, and of the Holy Spirit.
   All: **Amen.**

Then he greets the assembled people in the usual way and briefly instructs
them about the night vigil in these or similar words:

Dear brethren (brothers and sisters),
on this most sacred night,

in which our Lord Jesus Christ
passed over from death to life,
the Church calls upon her sons and daughters,
scattered throughout the world,
to come together to watch and pray.
If we keep the memorial
of the Lord's paschal solemnity in this way,
listening to his word and celebrating his mysteries,
then we shall have the sure hope
of sharing his triumph over death
and living with him in God.

Let us pray.
O God, who through your Son
bestowed upon the faithful the fire of your glory,
sanctify ✠ this new fire, we pray,
and grant that,
by these paschal celebrations,
we may be so inflamed with heavenly desires,
that with minds made pure
we may attain festivities of unending splendor.
Through Christ our Lord. All: **Amen.**

Preparation of the Candle

(1) **Christ yesterday and today** (he cuts a vertical line);
(2) **the Beginning and the End** (he cuts a horizontal line);
(3) **the Alpha** (he cuts the letter Alpha above the vertical line);
(4) **and the Omega** (he cuts the letter Omega below the vertical line).
(5) **All time belongs to him** (he cuts the first numeral of the current year in the upper left corner of the cross);
(6) **and all the ages** (he cuts the second numeral of the current year in the upper right corner of the cross).
(7) **To him be glory and power** (he cuts the third numeral of the current year in the lower left corner of the cross);
(8) **through every age and for ever. Amen.** (he cuts the fourth numeral of the current year in the lower right corner of the cross).

```
      A
    2 | 0
    1 | N
      Ω
```

(1) **By his holy**   1
(2) **and glorious wounds,**
(3) **may Christ the Lord**   4 2 5
(4) **guard us**
(5) **and protect us. Amen.**   3

May the light of Christ rising in glory
dispel the darkness of our hearts and minds.

Procession

℣. The Light of Christ.   *or*   ℣. Lumen Christi.
℟. **Thanks be to God.**   ℟. **Deo Gratias.**

℣. The Light of Christ.   *or*   ℣. Lumen Christi.
℟. **Thanks be to God.**   ℟. **Deo Gratias.**

℣. The Light of Christ.   *or*   ℣. Lumen Christi.
℟. **Thanks be to God.**   ℟. **Deo Gratias.**

The Easter Proclamation (Exsultet)
Longer Form of the Easter Proclamation
[Shorter Form]

[Exult, let them exult, the hosts of heaven,
exult, let Angel ministers of God exult,
let the trumpet of salvation
sound aloud our mighty King's triumph!
Be glad, let earth be glad, as glory floods her,
ablaze with light from her eternal King,
let all corners of the earth be glad,
knowing an end to gloom and darkness.
Rejoice, let Mother Church also rejoice,
arrayed with the lightning of his glory,
let this holy building shake with joy,
filled with the mighty voices of the peoples.]

(Therefore, dearest friends,
standing in the awesome glory of this holy light,
invoke with me, I ask you,
the mercy of God almighty,
that he, who has been pleased to number me,
though unworthy, among the Levites,
may pour into me his light unshadowed,
that I may sing this candle's perfect praises).

[(℣. The Lord be with you.   *Sung only by an ordained minister.
℟. **And with your spirit.**)

℣. Lift up your hearts.   *Sung only by an ordained minister.
℟. **We lift them up to the Lord.**

℣. Let us give thanks to the Lord our God.
℟. **It is right and just.**   *Sung only by an ordained minister.

April 4

It is truly right and just,
with ardent love of mind and heart
and with devoted service of our voice,
to acclaim our God invisible, the almighty Father,
and Jesus Christ, our Lord, his Son, his Only Begotten.

Who for our sake paid Adam's debt to the eternal Father,
and, pouring out his own dear Blood,
wiped clean the record of our ancient sinfulness.

These then are the feasts of Passover,
in which is slain the Lamb, the one true Lamb,
whose Blood anoints the doorposts of believers.

This is the night,
when once you led our forebears, Israel's children,
from slavery in Egypt
and made them pass dry-shod through the Red Sea.

This is the night
that with a pillar of fire
banished the darkness of sin.

This is the night
that even now, throughout the world,
sets Christian believers apart from worldly vices
and from the gloom of sin,
leading them to grace
and joining them to his holy ones.

This is the night,
when Christ broke the prison-bars of death
and rose victorious from the underworld.]

Our birth would have been no gain,
had we not been redeemed.
[O wonder of your humble care for us!
O love, O charity beyond all telling,
to ransom a slave you gave away your Son!

O truly necessary sin of Adam,
destroyed completely by the Death of Christ!

O happy fault
that earned so great, so glorious a Redeemer!]

O truly blessed night,
worthy alone to know the time and hour
when Christ rose from the underworld!

This is the night
of which it is written:
The night shall be as bright as day,
dazzling is the night for me,
and full of gladness.

[The sanctifying power of this night
dispels wickedness, washes faults away,
restores innocence to the fallen, and joy to mourners,]
drives out hatred, fosters concord, and brings down the
    mighty.

[**On this, your night of grace, O holy Father,
accept this candle, a solemn offering,
the work of bees and of your servants' hands,
an evening sacrifice of praise,
this gift from your most holy Church.]

But now we know the praises of this pillar,
which glowing fire ignites for God's honor,
a fire into many flames divided,
yet never dimmed by sharing of its light,
for it is fed by melting wax,
drawn out by mother bees
to build a torch so precious.

[O truly blessed night,
when things of heaven are wed to those of earth,
and divine to the human.] [**]

[Therefore, O Lord,
we pray you that this candle,
hallowed to the honor of your name,
may persevere undimmed,
to overcome the darkness of this night.
Receive it as a pleasing fragrance,
and let it mingle with the lights of heaven.
May this flame be found still burning

by the Morning Star:
the one Morning Star who never sets,
Christ your Son,
who, coming back from death's domain,
has shed his peaceful light on humanity,
and lives and reigns for ever and ever. All: **Amen.**]

SECOND PART: THE LITURGY OF THE WORD

Dear brethren (brothers and sisters),
now that we have begun our solemn Vigil,
let us listen with quiet hearts to the Word of God.
Let us meditate on how God in times past saved his people
and in these, the last days, has sent us his Son as our Redeemer.
Let us pray that our God may complete this paschal work of salvation
by the fullness of redemption.

READING I (L 41-ABC) (Genesis 1:1—2:2) or Shorter Form [ ] (Genesis 1:1, 26-31a)

A reading from the Book of Genesis

God looked at everything he had made, and he found it very good.

[In the beginning, when God created the heavens and the earth,]
  the earth was a formless wasteland, and darkness covered the abyss,
  while a mighty wind swept over the waters.
Then God said,
  "Let there be light," and there was light.
God saw how good the light was.
God then separated the light from the darkness.
God called the light "day," and the darkness he called "night."
Thus evening came, and morning followed—the first day.
Then God said,
  "Let there be a dome in the middle of the waters,
  to separate one body of water from the other."

And so it happened:
> God made the dome,
> and it separated the water above the dome from the water below it.

God called the dome "the sky."
Evening came, and morning followed—the second day.

Then God said,
> "Let the water under the sky be gathered into a single basin,
> so that the dry land may appear."

And so it happened:
> the water under the sky was gathered into its basin,
> and the dry land appeared.

God called the dry land "the earth,"
> and the basin of the water he called "the sea."

God saw how good it was.

Then God said,
> "Let the earth bring forth vegetation:
> every kind of plant that bears seed
> and every kind of fruit tree on earth
> that bears fruit with its seed in it."

And so it happened:
> the earth brought forth every kind of plant that bears seed
> and every kind of fruit tree on earth
> that bears fruit with its seed in it.

God saw how good it was.
Evening came, and morning followed—the third day.

Then God said:
> "Let there be lights in the dome of the sky,
> to separate day from night.

Let them mark the fixed times, the days and the years,
> and serve as luminaries in the dome of the sky,
> to shed light upon the earth."

And so it happened:
>God made the two great lights,
>the greater one to govern the day,
>and the lesser one to govern the night;
>and he made the stars.

God set them in the dome of the sky,
>to shed light upon the earth,
>to govern the day and the night,
>and to separate the light from the darkness.

God saw how good it was.

Evening came, and morning followed—the fourth day.

Then God said,
>"Let the water teem with an abundance of living creatures,
>and on the earth let birds fly beneath the dome of the sky."

And so it happened:
>God created the great sea monsters
>and all kinds of swimming creatures with which the water teems,
>and all kinds of winged birds.

God saw how good it was, and God blessed them, saying,
>"Be fertile, multiply, and fill the water of the seas;
>and let the birds multiply on the earth."

Evening came, and morning followed—the fifth day.

Then God said,
>"Let the earth bring forth all kinds of living creatures:
>cattle, creeping things, and wild animals of all kinds."

And so it happened:
>God made all kinds of wild animals, all kinds of cattle,
>and all kinds of creeping things of the earth.

God saw how good it was.

Then [God said:
>"Let us make man in our image, after our likeness.

Let them have dominion over the fish of the sea,
> the birds of the air, and the cattle,
> and over all the wild animals
> and all the creatures that crawl on the ground."

God created man in his image;
> in the image of God he created him;
> male and female he created them.

God blessed them, saying:
> "Be fertile and multiply;
> fill the earth and subdue it.

Have dominion over the fish of the sea, the birds of the air,
> and all the living things that move on the earth."

God also said:
> "See, I give you every seed-bearing plant all over the earth
> and every tree that has seed-bearing fruit on it to be your food;
> and to all the animals of the land, all the birds of the air,
> and all the living creatures that crawl on the ground,
> I give all the green plants for food."

And so it happened.

God looked at everything he had made, and he found it very good.]

Evening came, and morning followed—the sixth day.

Thus the heavens and the earth and all their array were completed.

Since on the seventh day God was finished
> with the work he had been doing,
> > he rested on the seventh day from all the work he had undertaken.

The word of the Lord.

The response Thanks be to God is not said after the readings.

Responsorial Psalm 104 or 33

Lord, send out your Spirit, and renew the face of the earth, and renew the face of the earth.

Music: Jay F. Hunstiger, © 1990, administered by Liturgical Press. All rights reserved.

A Psalm 104:1-2, 5-6, 10, 12, 13-14, 24, 35

℟. (30) **Lord, send out your Spirit, and renew the face of the earth.**

Bless the L ORD, O my soul!
 O L ORD, my God, you are great indeed!
You are clothed with majesty and glory,
 robed in light as with a cloak. ℟.

You fixed the earth upon its foundation,
 not to be moved forever;
with the ocean, as with a garment, you covered it;
 above the mountains the waters stood. ℟.

You send forth springs into the watercourses
 that wind among the mountains.
Beside them the birds of heaven dwell;
 from among the branches they send forth their song. ℟.

You water the mountains from your palace;
 the earth is replete with the fruit of your works.
You raise grass for the cattle,
 and vegetation for man's use,
producing bread from the earth. ℟.

How manifold are your works, O L ORD!
 In wisdom you have wrought them all—
the earth is full of your creatures.
 Bless the L ORD, O my soul! ℟.

Or:

The earth is full of the goodness of the Lord.

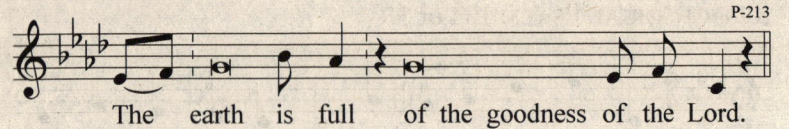

Music: Bartholomew Sayles, O.S.B., and Cecile Gertken, O.S.B., adapt., © 1977, 1989, Order of Saint Benedict.

B   Psalm 33:4-5, 6-7, 12-13, 20 and 22

℞. (5b) **The earth is full of the goodness of the Lord.**

Upright is the word of the Lord,
   and all his works are trustworthy.
He loves justice and right;
   of the kindness of the Lord the earth is full. ℞.

By the word of the Lord the heavens were made;
   by the breath of his mouth all their host.
He gathers the waters of the sea as in a flask;
   in cellars he confines the deep. ℞.

Blessed the nation whose God is the Lord,
   the people he has chosen for his own inheritance.
From heaven the Lord looks down;
   he sees all mankind. ℞.

Our soul waits for the Lord,
   who is our help and our shield.
May your kindness, O Lord, be upon us
   who have put our hope in you. ℞.

Prayer

Let us pray.

Almighty ever-living God,
who are wonderful in the ordering of all your works,
may those you have redeemed understand
that there exists nothing more marvelous
than the world's creation in the beginning
except that, at the end of the ages,
Christ our Passover has been sacrificed.
Who lives and reigns for ever and ever. All: **Amen.**

Or:

On the creation of man:
O God, who wonderfully created human nature
and still more wonderfully redeemed it,

grant us, we pray,
to set our minds against the enticements of sin,
that we may merit to attain eternal joys.
Through Christ our Lord. All: **Amen.**

Reading II (Genesis 22:1-18) *or* Shorter Form [ ]
(Genesis 22:1-2, 9a, 10-13, 15-18)

A reading from the Book of Genesis

The sacrifice of Abraham, our father in faith.

[God put Abraham to the test.
He called to him, "Abraham!"
"Here I am," he replied.
Then God said:
    "Take your son Isaac, your only one, whom you love,
        and go to the land of Moriah.
    There you shall offer him up as a holocaust
        on a height that I will point out to you."]
Early the next morning Abraham saddled his donkey,
    took with him his son Isaac and two of his servants
        as well,
    and with the wood that he had cut for the holocaust,
    set out for the place of which God had told him.

On the third day Abraham got sight of the place from afar.
Then he said to his servants:
    "Both of you stay here with the donkey,
    while the boy and I go on over yonder.
We will worship and then come back to you."
Thereupon Abraham took the wood for the holocaust
    and laid it on his son Isaac's shoulders,
    while he himself carried the fire and the knife.
As the two walked on together, Isaac spoke to his father
        Abraham:
    "Father!" Isaac said.
"Yes, son," he replied.
Isaac continued, "Here are the fire and the wood,
    but where is the sheep for the holocaust?"

"Son," Abraham answered,
  "God himself will provide the sheep for the holocaust."
Then the two continued going forward.
[When they came to the place of which God had told him,
  Abraham built an altar there and arranged the wood
    on it.]
Next he tied up his son Isaac,
  and put him on top of the wood on the altar.
[Then he reached out and took the knife to slaughter
    his son.
But the LORD's messenger called to him from heaven,
  "Abraham, Abraham!"
"Here I am!" he answered.
"Do not lay your hand on the boy," said the messenger.
"Do not do the least thing to him.
I know now how devoted you are to God,
  since you did not withhold from me your own
    beloved son."
As Abraham looked about,
  he spied a ram caught by its horns in the thicket.
So he went and took the ram
  and offered it up as a holocaust in place of his son.]
Abraham named the site Yahweh-yireh;
  hence people now say, "On the mountain the LORD
    will see."
[Again the LORD's messenger called to Abraham from
    heaven and said:
"I swear by myself, declares the LORD,
that because you acted as you did
in not withholding from me your beloved son,
I will bless you abundantly
and make your descendants as countless
as the stars of the sky and the sands of the seashore;
your descendants shall take possession
of the gates of their enemies,

and in your descendants all the nations of the earth
    shall find blessing—
all this because you obeyed my command."]

The word of the Lord.

RESPONSORIAL PSALM 16

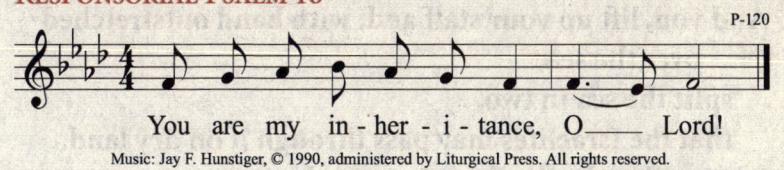

You are my in-her-i-tance, O ___ Lord!

Music: Jay F. Hunstiger, © 1990, administered by Liturgical Press. All rights reserved.

Psalm 16:5, 8, 9-10, 11

℞. (1) **You are my inheritance, O Lord.**

O LORD, my allotted portion and my cup,
    you it is who hold fast my lot.
I set the LORD ever before me;
    with him at my right hand I shall not be disturbed. ℞.

Therefore my heart is glad and my soul rejoices,
    my body, too, abides in confidence;
because you will not abandon my soul to the netherworld,
    nor will you suffer your faithful one to undergo
        corruption. ℞.

You will show me the path to life,
    fullness of joys in your presence,
    the delights at your right hand forever. ℞.

PRAYER
Let us pray.

O God, supreme Father of the faithful,
who increase the children of your promise
by pouring out the grace of adoption
throughout the whole world
and who through the Paschal Mystery
make your servant Abraham father of nations,
as once you swore,
grant, we pray,
that your peoples may enter worthily
into the grace to which you call them.
Through Christ our Lord. All: **Amen.**

READING III (Exodus 14:15—15:1)
A reading from the Book of Exodus
The Israelites marched on dry land through the midst of the sea.

The LORD said to Moses, "Why are you crying out to me?
Tell the Israelites to go forward.
And you, lift up your staff and, with hand outstretched
    over the sea,
  split the sea in two,
  that the Israelites may pass through it on dry land.
But I will make the Egyptians so obstinate
  that they will go in after them.
Then I will receive glory through Pharaoh and all his army,
  his chariots and charioteers.
The Egyptians shall know that I am the LORD,
  when I receive glory through Pharaoh
  and his chariots and charioteers."

The angel of God, who had been leading Israel's camp,
  now moved and went around behind them.
The column of cloud also, leaving the front,
  took up its place behind them,
  so that it came between the camp of the Egyptians
  and that of Israel.
But the cloud now became dark, and thus the night passed
  without the rival camps coming any closer together
    all night long.
Then Moses stretched out his hand over the sea,
  and the LORD swept the sea
  with a strong east wind throughout the night
  and so turned it into dry land.
When the water was thus divided,
  the Israelites marched into the midst of the sea on
    dry land,
  with the water like a wall to their right and to their left.

The Egyptians followed in pursuit;
> all Pharaoh's horses and chariots and charioteers went
>> after them
> right into the midst of the sea.

In the night watch just before dawn
> the LORD cast through the column of the fiery cloud
> upon the Egyptian force a glance that threw it into a
>> panic;
> and he so clogged their chariot wheels
> that they could hardly drive.

With that the Egyptians sounded the retreat before Israel,
> because the LORD was fighting for them against the
>> Egyptians.

Then the LORD told Moses, "Stretch out your hand over
> the sea,
> that the water may flow back upon the Egyptians,
> upon their chariots and their charioteers."

So Moses stretched out his hand over the sea,
> and at dawn the sea flowed back to its normal depth.

The Egyptians were fleeing head on toward the sea,
> when the LORD hurled them into its midst.

As the water flowed back,
> it covered the chariots and the charioteers of Pharaoh's
>> whole army
> which had followed the Israelites into the sea.

Not a single one of them escaped.

But the Israelites had marched on dry land
> through the midst of the sea,
> with the water like a wall to their right and to their left.

Thus the LORD saved Israel on that day
> from the power of the Egyptians.

When Israel saw the Egyptians lying dead on the seashore
> and beheld the great power that the LORD
> had shown against the Egyptians,
> they feared the LORD and believed in him and in his
>> servant Moses.

Then Moses and the Israelites sang this song to the LORD:
I will sing to the LORD, for he is gloriously triumphant;
horse and chariot he has cast into the sea.

The word of the Lord.

RESPONSORIAL PSALM (Exodus 15)

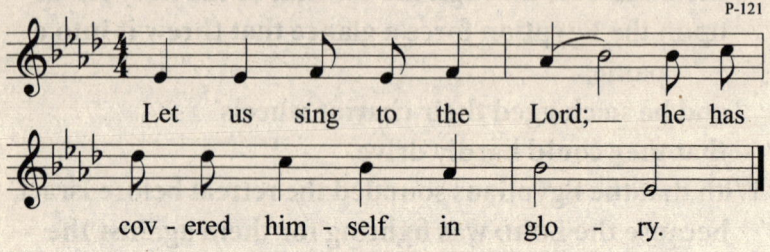

Let us sing to the Lord; he has covered himself in glory.

Music: Jay F. Hunstiger, © 1990, administered by Liturgical Press. All rights reserved.

Exodus 15:1-2, 3-4, 5-6, 17-18

℟. (1b) **Let us sing to the Lord; he has covered himself in glory.**

I will sing to the LORD, for he is gloriously triumphant;
   horse and chariot he has cast into the sea.
My strength and my courage is the LORD,
   and he has been my savior.
He is my God, I praise him;
   the God of my father, I extol him. ℟.

The LORD is a warrior,
   LORD is his name!
Pharaoh's chariots and army he hurled into the sea;
   the elite of his officers were submerged in the
      Red Sea. ℟.

The flood waters covered them,
   they sank into the depths like a stone.
Your right hand, O LORD, magnificent in power,
   your right hand, O LORD, has shattered the enemy. ℟.

You brought in the people you redeemed
   and planted them on the mountain of your inheritance—
the place where you made your seat, O LORD,
   the sanctuary, LORD, which your hands established.
The LORD shall reign forever and ever. ℟.

Prayer

Let us pray.

O God, whose ancient wonders
remain undimmed in splendor even in our day,
for what you once bestowed on a single people,
freeing them from Pharaoh's persecution
by the power of your right hand,
now you bring about as the salvation of the nations
through the waters of rebirth,
grant, we pray, that the whole world
may become children of Abraham
and inherit the dignity of Israel's birthright.
Through Christ our Lord. All: **Amen.**

Or:

O God, who by the light of the New Testament
have unlocked the meaning
of wonders worked in former times,
so that the Red Sea prefigures the sacred font
and the nation delivered from slavery
foreshadows the Christian people,
grant, we pray, that all nations,
obtaining the privilege of Israel by merit of faith,
may be reborn by partaking of your Spirit.
Through Christ our Lord. All: **Amen.**

Reading IV (Isaiah 54:5-14)

A reading from the Book of the Prophet Isaiah

With enduring love, the Lord your redeemer takes pity on you.

**The One who has become your husband is your Maker;
   his name is the Lord of hosts;
your redeemer is the Holy One of Israel,
   called God of all the earth.
The Lord calls you back,
   like a wife forsaken and grieved in spirit,
   a wife married in youth and then cast off,
   says your God.
For a brief moment I abandoned you,
   but with great tenderness I will take you back.
In an outburst of wrath, for a moment
   I hid my face from you;**

but with enduring love I take pity on you,
> says the LORD, your redeemer.
This is for me like the days of Noah,
> when I swore that the waters of Noah
> should never again deluge the earth;
so I have sworn not to be angry with you,
> or to rebuke you.
Though the mountains leave their place
> and the hills be shaken,
my love shall never leave you
> nor my covenant of peace be shaken,
> says the LORD, who has mercy on you.
O afflicted one, storm-battered and unconsoled,
> I lay your pavements in carnelians,
> and your foundations in sapphires;
I will make your battlements of rubies,
> your gates of carbuncles,
> and all your walls of precious stones.
All your children shall be taught by the LORD,
> and great shall be the peace of your children.
In justice shall you be established,
> far from the fear of oppression,
> where destruction cannot come near you.

The word of the Lord.

RESPONSISORIAL PSALM 30

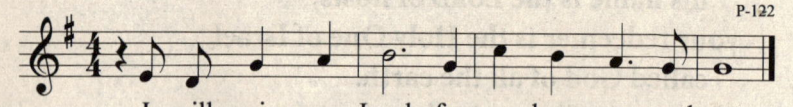

I will praise you, Lord, for you have rescued me.

Music: Jay F. Hunstiger, © 1990, administered by Liturgical Press. All rights reserved.

Psalm 30:2, 4, 5-6, 11-12, 13

℟. (2a) **I will praise you, Lord, for you have rescued me.**

I will extol you, O LORD, for you drew me clear
> and did not let my enemies rejoice over me.
O LORD, you brought me up from the netherworld;

> you preserved me from among those going down into
>   the pit. ℟.

Sing praise to the Lord, you his faithful ones,
  and give thanks to his holy name.
For his anger lasts but a moment;
  a lifetime, his good will.
At nightfall, weeping enters in,
  but with the dawn, rejoicing. ℟.

Hear, O Lord, and have pity on me;
  O Lord, be my helper.
You changed my mourning into dancing;
  O Lord, my God, forever will I give you thanks. ℟.

Prayer
Let us pray.

Almighty ever-living God,
surpass, for the honor of your name,
what you pledged to the Patriarchs by reason of their faith,
and through sacred adoption increase the children of your promise,
so that what the Saints of old never doubted would come to pass
your Church may now see in great part fulfilled.
Through Christ our Lord. All: **Amen.**

Reading V (Isaiah 55:1-11)
A reading from the Book of the Prophet Isaiah

Come to me that you may have life. I will renew with you an everlasting covenant.

Thus says the Lord:
All you who are thirsty,
  come to the water!
You who have no money,
  come, receive grain and eat;
come, without paying and without cost,
  drink wine and milk!
Why spend your money for what is not bread,
  your wages for what fails to satisfy?
Heed me, and you shall eat well,
  you shall delight in rich fare.

Come to me heedfully,
   listen, that you may have life.
I will renew with you the everlasting covenant,
   the benefits assured to David.
As I made him a witness to the peoples,
   a leader and commander of nations,
so shall you summon a nation you knew not,
   and nations that knew you not shall run to you,
because of the Lord, your God,
   the Holy One of Israel, who has glorified you.

Seek the Lord while he may be found,
   call him while he is near.
Let the scoundrel forsake his way,
   and the wicked man his thoughts;
let him turn to the Lord for mercy;
   to our God, who is generous in forgiving.
For my thoughts are not your thoughts,
   nor are your ways my ways, says the Lord.
As high as the heavens are above the earth,
   so high are my ways above your ways
   and my thoughts above your thoughts.

For just as from the heavens
   the rain and snow come down
and do not return there
   till they have watered the earth,
   making it fertile and fruitful,
giving seed to the one who sows
   and bread to the one who eats,
so shall my word be
   that goes forth from my mouth;
my word shall not return to me void,
   but shall do my will,
   achieving the end for which I sent it.

The word of the Lord.

April 4 211

Responsorial Psalm (Isaiah 12)

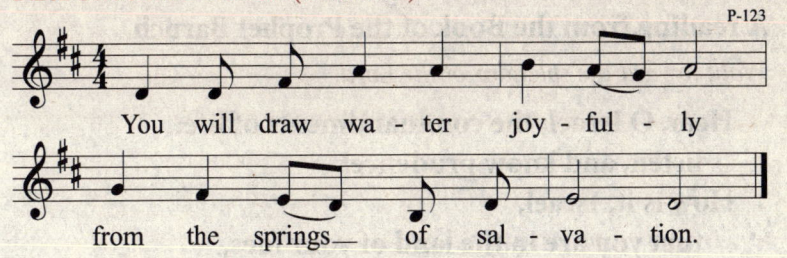

You will draw water joyfully from the springs of salvation.

Music: Jay F. Hunstiger, © 1990, administered by Liturgical Press. All rights reserved.

Isaiah 12:2-3, 4, 5-6

℟. (3) **You will draw water joyfully from the springs of salvation.**

God indeed is my savior;
 I am confident and unafraid.
My strength and my courage is the LORD,
 and he has been my savior.
With joy you will draw water
 at the fountain of salvation. ℟.

Give thanks to the LORD, acclaim his name;
 among the nations make known his deeds,
 proclaim how exalted is his name. ℟.

Sing praise to the LORD for his glorious achievement;
 let this be known throughout all the earth.
Shout with exultation, O city of Zion,
 for great in your midst
 is the Holy One of Israel! ℟.

Prayer
Let us pray.

Almighty ever-living God,
sole hope of the world,
who by the preaching of your Prophets
unveiled the mysteries of this present age,
graciously increase the longing of your people,
for only at the prompting of your grace
do the faithful progress in any kind of virtue.
Through Christ our Lord. All: **Amen.**

Reading VI (Baruch 3:9-15, 32—4:4)
A reading from the Book of the Prophet Baruch
Walk toward the splendor of the Lord.

> Hear, O Israel, the commandments of life:
>> listen, and know prudence!
>
> How is it, Israel,
>> that you are in the land of your foes,
>> grown old in a foreign land,
>
> defiled with the dead,
>> accounted with those destined for the netherworld?
>
> You have forsaken the fountain of wisdom!
>> Had you walked in the way of God,
>> you would have dwelt in enduring peace.
>
> Learn where prudence is,
>> where strength, where understanding;
>
> that you may know also
>> where are length of days, and life,
>> where light of the eyes, and peace.
>
> Who has found the place of wisdom,
>> who has entered into her treasuries?
>
> The One who knows all things knows her;
>> he has probed her by his knowledge—
>
> the One who established the earth for all time,
>> and filled it with four-footed beasts;
>
> he who dismisses the light, and it departs,
>> calls it, and it obeys him trembling;
>
> before whom the stars at their posts
>> shine and rejoice;
>
> when he calls them, they answer, "Here we are!"
>> shining with joy for their Maker.
>
> Such is our God;
>> no other is to be compared to him:
>
> he has traced out the whole way of understanding,
>> and has given her to Jacob, his servant,
>> to Israel, his beloved son.

Since then she has appeared on earth,
  and moved among people.
She is the book of the precepts of God,
  the law that endures forever;
all who cling to her will live,
  but those will die who forsake her.
Turn, O Jacob, and receive her:
  walk by her light toward splendor.
Give not your glory to another,
  your privileges to an alien race.
Blessed are we, O Israel;
  for what pleases God is known to us!

The word of the Lord.

Responsorial Psalm 19

Lord, you have the words of ev-er-last-ing life.

Music: Jay F. Hunstiger, © 1990, administered by Liturgical Press. All rights reserved.

Psalm 19:8, 9, 10, 11

℟. (John 6:68c) **Lord, you have the words of everlasting life.**

The law of the Lord is perfect,
  refreshing the soul;
the decree of the Lord is trustworthy,
  giving wisdom to the simple. ℟.

The precepts of the Lord are right,
  rejoicing the heart;
the command of the Lord is clear,
  enlightening the eye. ℟.

The fear of the Lord is pure,
  enduring forever;
the ordinances of the Lord are true,
  all of them just. ℟.

They are more precious than gold,
  than a heap of purest gold;

(continued)

sweeter also than syrup
>	or honey from the comb. ℟.

PRAYER
Let us pray.

O God, who constantly increase your Church
by your call to the nations,
graciously grant
to those you wash clean in the waters of Baptism
the assurance of your unfailing protection.
Through Christ our Lord. All: **Amen.**

READING VII (Ezekiel 36:16-17a, 18-28)

A reading from the Book of the Prophet Ezekiel

I shall sprinkle clean water upon you and I shall give you a new heart.

The word of the LORD came to me, saying:
>	Son of man, when the house of Israel lived in their land,
>	they defiled it by their conduct and deeds.
Therefore I poured out my fury upon them
>	because of the blood that they poured out on the
>		ground,
>	and because they defiled it with idols.
I scattered them among the nations,
>	dispersing them over foreign lands;
>	according to their conduct and deeds I judged them.
But when they came among the nations wherever
>		they came,
>	they served to profane my holy name,
>	because it was said of them: "These are the people of
>		the LORD,
>	yet they had to leave their land."
So I have relented because of my holy name
>	which the house of Israel profaned
>	among the nations where they came.
Therefore say to the house of Israel: Thus says the
>		Lord GOD:
>	Not for your sakes do I act, house of Israel,

but for the sake of my holy name,
  which you profaned among the nations to which
      you came.
I will prove the holiness of my great name, profaned
    among the nations,
  in whose midst you have profaned it.
Thus the nations shall know that I am the Lord, says the
    Lord God,
  when in their sight I prove my holiness through you.
For I will take you away from among the nations,
  gather you from all the foreign lands,
  and bring you back to your own land.
I will sprinkle clean water upon you
  to cleanse you from all your impurities,
  and from all your idols I will cleanse you.
I will give you a new heart and place a new spirit within
    you,
  taking from your bodies your stony hearts
  and giving you natural hearts.
I will put my spirit within you and make you live by my
    statutes,
  careful to observe my decrees.
You shall live in the land I gave your fathers;
  you shall be my people, and I will be your God.

The word of the Lord.

Responsorial Psalm

A *When baptism is celebrated*

Like the deer that longs for running streams, my soul longs for you, my God.

Music: Jay F. Hunstiger, © 1984, administered by Liturgical Press. All rights reserved.

April 4

Psalms 42:3, 5; 43:3, 4

℟. (42:2) **Like a deer that longs for running streams, my soul longs for you, my God.**

Athirst is my soul for God, the living God.
  When shall I go and behold the face of God? ℟.

I went with the throng
  and led them in procession to the house of God,
amid loud cries of joy and thanksgiving,
  with the multitude keeping festival. ℟.

Send forth your light and your fidelity;
  they shall lead me on
and bring me to your holy mountain,
  to your dwelling-place. ℟.

Then will I go in to the altar of God,
  the God of my gladness and joy;
then will I give you thanks upon the harp,
  O God, my God! ℟.

B *When baptism is not celebrated*

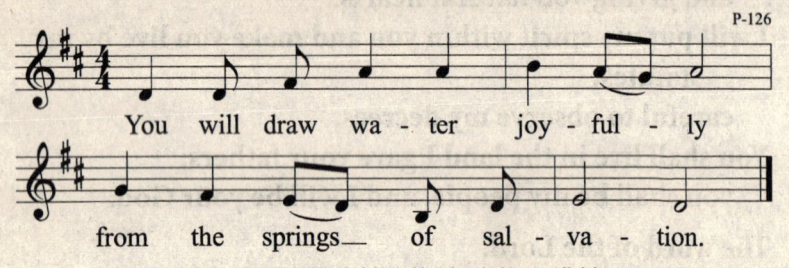

You will draw water joyfully from the springs of salvation.

Music: Jay F. Hunstiger, © 1990, administered by Liturgical Press. All rights reserved.

Isaiah 12:2-3, 4bcd, 5-6

℟. (3) **You will draw water joyfully from the springs of salvation.**

God indeed is my savior;
  I am confident and unafraid.
My strength and my courage is the LORD,
  and he has been my savior.
With joy you will draw water
  at the fountain of salvation. ℟.

Give thanks to the Lord, acclaim his name;
> among the nations make known his deeds,
> proclaim how exalted is his name. ℟.

Sing praise to the Lord for his glorious achievement;
> let this be known throughout all the earth.
Shout with exultation, O city of Zion,
> for great in your midst
> is the Holy One of Israel! ℟.

C *When baptism is not celebrated*

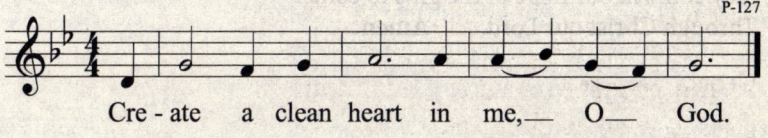

Cre - ate a clean heart in me, O God.

Music: Jay F. Hunstiger, © 1990, administered by Liturgical Press. All rights reserved.

Psalm 51:12-13, 14-15, 18-19

℟. (12a) **Create a clean heart in me, O God.**

A clean heart create for me, O God,
> and a steadfast spirit renew within me.
Cast me not out from your presence,
> and your Holy Spirit take not from me. ℟.

Give me back the joy of your salvation,
> and a willing spirit sustain in me.
I will teach transgressors your ways,
> and sinners shall return to you. ℟.

For you are not pleased with sacrifices;
> should I offer a holocaust, you would not accept it.
My sacrifice, O God, is a contrite spirit;
> a heart contrite and humbled, O God, you will not
>> spurn. ℟.

PRAYER
Let us pray.

O God of unchanging power and eternal light,
look with favor on the wondrous mystery of the whole Church
and serenely accomplish the work of human salvation,
which you planned from all eternity;
may the whole world know and see

that what was cast down is raised up,
what had become old is made new,
and all things are restored to integrity through Christ,
just as by him they came into being.
Who lives and reigns for ever and ever. All: **Amen.**

Or:

O God, who by the pages of both Testaments
instruct and prepare us to celebrate the Paschal Mystery,
grant that we may comprehend your mercy,
so that the gifts we receive from you this night
may confirm our hope of the gifts to come.
Through Christ our Lord. All: **Amen.**

GLORIA (*See* page 3).

COLLECT

O God, who make this most sacred night radiant
with the glory of the Lord's Resurrection,
stir up in your Church a spirit of adoption,
so that, renewed in body and mind,
we may render you undivided service.
Through our Lord Jesus Christ, your Son,
who lives and reigns with you in the unity of the Holy Spirit,
one God, for ever and ever. All: **Amen.**

EPISTLE (Romans 6:3-11)

A reading from the Letter of Saint Paul to the Romans

Christ, raised from the dead, dies no more.

Brothers and sisters:
Are you unaware that we who were baptized into
    Christ Jesus
    were baptized into his death?
We were indeed buried with him through baptism into
    death,
    so that, just as Christ was raised from the dead
    by the glory of the Father,
    we too might live in newness of life.

For if we have grown into union with him through a
    death like his,
    we shall also be united with him in the resurrection.

We know that our old self was crucified with him,
  so that our sinful body might be done away with,
  that we might no longer be in slavery to sin.
For a dead person has been absolved from sin.
If, then, we have died with Christ,
  we believe that we shall also live with him.
We know that Christ, raised from the dead, dies no more;
  death no longer has power over him.
As to his death, he died to sin once and for all;
  as to his life, he lives for God.
Consequently, you too must think of yourselves as being dead to sin
  and living for God in Christ Jesus.

The word of the Lord.

The Priest solemnly intones the Alleluia three times, raising his voice by a step each time, with all repeating it.

Responsorial Psalm 118

Al-le-lu-ia, al-le-lu-ia, al-le-lu-ia, al-le-lu-ia. Al-le-lu-ia, al-le-lu-ia, al-le-lu-ia, al-le-lu-ia.

Music: Jay F. Hunstiger, © 1990, administered by Liturgical Press. All rights reserved.

Psalm 118:1-2, 16-17, 22-23

℟. **Alleluia, alleluia, alleluia.**

Give thanks to the LORD, for he is good,
  for his mercy endures forever.
Let the house of Israel say,
  "His mercy endures forever." ℟.

(continued)

"The right hand of the Lord has struck with power;
　the right hand of the Lord is exalted.
I shall not die, but live,
　and declare the works of the Lord." ℟.

The stone which the builders rejected
　has become the cornerstone.
By the Lord has this been done;
　it is wonderful in our eyes. ℟.

Gospel B (Mark 16:1-7)

☩ **A reading from the holy Gospel according to Mark**

All: **Glory to you, O Lord.**

Jesus of Nazareth, the crucified, has been raised.

**When the sabbath was over,
　Mary Magdalene, Mary, the mother of James, and
　　Salome
　bought spices so that they might go and anoint him.
Very early when the sun had risen,
　on the first day of the week, they came to the tomb.
They were saying to one another,
　"Who will roll back the stone for us
　from the entrance to the tomb?"
When they looked up,
　they saw that the stone had been rolled back;
　it was very large.
On entering the tomb they saw a young man
　sitting on the right side, clothed in a white robe,
　and they were utterly amazed.
He said to them, "Do not be amazed!
You seek Jesus of Nazareth, the crucified.
He has been raised; he is not here.
Behold the place where they laid him.
But go and tell his disciples and Peter,
　'He is going before you to Galilee;
　there you will see him, as he told you.'"**

The Gospel of the Lord. All: **Praise to you, Lord Jesus Christ.**

THIRD PART: LITURGY OF BAPTISM
If there are candidates to be baptized:

Dearly beloved,
with one heart and one soul, let us by our prayers
come to the aid of these our brothers and sisters in their blessed hope,
so that, as they approach the font of rebirth,
the almighty Father may bestow on them
all his merciful help.

If the font is to be blessed, but there is no one to be baptized:

Dearly beloved,
let us humbly invoke upon this font
the grace of God the almighty Father,
that those who from it are born anew
may be numbered among the children of adoption in Christ.

The Litany is sung by two cantors, with all standing (because it is Easter Time) and responding.

THE LITANY OF THE SAINTS
If there are candidates to be baptized, the Priest says the following prayer:

Almighty ever-living God,
be present by the mysteries of your great love
and send forth the spirit of adoption
to create the new peoples
brought to birth for you in the font of Baptism,
so that what is to be carried out by our humble service
may be brought to fulfillment by your mighty power.
Through Christ our Lord. **All: Amen.**

BLESSING OF BAPTISMAL WATER

O God, who by invisible power
accomplish a wondrous effect
through sacramental signs
and who in many ways have prepared water, your creation,
to show forth the grace of Baptism;

O God, whose Spirit
in the first moments of the world's creation
hovered over the waters,
so that the very substance of water
would even then take to itself the power to sanctify;

O God, who by the outpouring of the flood
foreshadowed regeneration,
so that from the mystery of one and the same element of water
would come an end to vice and a beginning of virtue;

O God, who caused the children of Abraham
to pass dry-shod through the Red Sea,
so that the chosen people,
set free from slavery to Pharaoh,
would prefigure the people of the baptized;

O God, whose Son,
baptized by John in the waters of the Jordan,
was anointed with the Holy Spirit,
and, as he hung upon the Cross,
gave forth water from his side along with blood,
and after his Resurrection, commanded his disciples:
"Go forth, teach all nations, baptizing them
in the name of the Father and of the Son and of the Holy Spirit,"
look now, we pray, upon the face of your Church
and graciously unseal for her the fountain of Baptism.

May this water receive by the Holy Spirit
the grace of your Only Begotten Son,
so that human nature, created in your image
and washed clean through the Sacrament of Baptism
from all the squalor of the life of old,
may be found worthy to rise to the life of newborn children
through water and the Holy Spirit.

May the power of the Holy Spirit,
O Lord, we pray,
come down through your Son
into the fullness of this font,
so that all who have been buried with Christ
by Baptism into death
may rise again to life with him.
Who lives and reigns with you in the unity of the Holy Spirit,
one God, for ever and ever. **All: Amen.**

Celebration of Baptism

Renunciation of Sin and Profession of Faith

The celebrant in a series of questions to which the candidates and the parents and godparents reply **I DO**, asks the candidates and parents and godparents to renounce sin and profess their faith.

Baptism of Adults
Celebrant: Is it your will to be baptized in the faith of the Church, which we have all professed with you?
Candidate: It is.

He baptizes the candidate, saying:

N., I baptize you in the name of the Father,

He immerses the candidate or pours water upon him.

and of the Son,

He immerses the candidate or pours water upon him a second time.

and of the Holy Spirit.

He immerses the candidate or pours water upon him a third time. He asks the same question and performs the same action for each candidate.

After each baptism it is appropriate for the people to sing a short acclamation:

This is the fountain of life,
water made holy by the suffering of Christ, washing all the world.
You who are washed in this water have hope of heaven's kingdom.

Baptism of Children

Celebrant: Is it your will that N. should be baptized in the faith of the Church, which we have all professed with you?
Parents and godparents: **It is.**

He baptizes the child, saying:

N., I baptize you in the name of the Father,

He immerses the child or pours water upon it.

and of the Son,

He immerses the child or pours water upon it a second time.

and of the Holy Spirit.

He immerses the child or pours water upon it a third time. He asks the same question and performs the same action for each child.

After each baptism it is appropriate for the people to sing a short acclamation:

This is the fountain of life,
water made holy by the suffering of Christ, washing all the world.
You who are washed in this water have hope of heaven's kingdom.

Anointing with Chrism

God the Father of our Lord Jesus Christ has freed you from sin, given you a new birth by water and the Holy Spirit, and welcomed you into his holy people. He now anoints you with the chrism of salvation. As Christ was anointed Priest, Prophet, and King, so may you live always as members of his body, sharing everlasting life. All: **Amen.**

Clothing with the White Garment

(N., N.,) you have become a new creation, and have clothed yourselves in Christ. See in this white garment the outward sign of your Christian

dignity. With your family and friends to help you by word and example, bring that dignity unstained into the everlasting life of heaven.
All: **Amen.**

Celebration of Confirmation*

If the bishop has conferred baptism, he should now also confer confirmation. If the bishop is not present, the priest who conferred baptism and received the candidates into full communion is authorized to confirm. The infants who were baptized during this celebration are not confirmed. However, the newly baptized children who have gone through the RCIA process are confirmed.

Invitation
My dear friends, let us pray to God our Father, that he will pour out the Holy Spirit on these candidates for confirmation to strengthen them with his gifts and anoint them to be more like Christ, the Son of God.

Laying on of Hands
All-powerful God, Father of our Lord Jesus Christ,
by water and the Holy Spirit
you freed your sons
and daughters from sin and gave them new life.
Send your Holy Spirit upon them to be their helper and guide.
Give them the spirit of wisdom and understanding,
the spirit of right judgment and courage,
the spirit of knowledge and reverence.
Fill them with the spirit of wonder and awe in your presence.
We ask this through Christ our Lord. All: **Amen.**

Anointing with Chrism
N., be sealed with the Gift of the Holy Spirit.
Newly confirmed: **Amen.**

The minister of the sacrament adds: **Peace be with you.**
Newly confirmed: **And with your Spirit.**

The Blessing of Water
If no one is to be baptized and the font is not to be blessed, the priest blesses the water with the following prayer:

Dear brothers and sisters,
let us humbly beseech the Lord our God
to bless this water he has created,
which will be sprinkled upon us
as a memorial of our Baptism.
May he graciously renew us,

*From the RCIA, nos. 232–235.

that we may remain faithful to the Spirit
whom we have received.

And after a brief pause in silence, he proclaims the following prayer, with hands extended:

Lord our God,
in your mercy be present to your people
who keep vigil on this most sacred night,
and, for us who recall the wondrous work of our creation
and the still greater work of our redemption,
graciously bless this water.
For you created water to make the fields fruitful
and to refresh and cleanse our bodies.
You also made water the instrument of your mercy:
for through water you freed your people from slavery
and quenched their thirst in the desert;
through water the Prophets proclaimed the new covenant
you were to enter upon with the human race;
and last of all,
through water, which Christ made holy in the Jordan,
you have renewed our corrupted nature
in the bath of regeneration.
Therefore, may this water be for us
a memorial of the Baptism we have received,
and grant that we may share
in the gladness of our brothers and sisters,
who at Easter have received their Baptism.
Through Christ our Lord. All: **Amen.**

THE RENEWAL OF BAPTISMAL PROMISES
Dear brethren (brothers and sisters), through the Paschal Mystery
we have been buried with Christ in Baptism,
so that we may walk with him in newness of life.
And so, now that our Lenten observance is concluded,
let us renew the promises of Holy Baptism,
by which we once renounced Satan and his works
and promised to serve God in the holy Catholic Church.

And so I ask you:

A Priest: Do you renounce Satan? All: **I do.**
Priest: And all his works? All: **I do.**
Priest: And all his empty show? All: **I do.**

Or:

B Priest: Do you renounce sin,
so as to live in the freedom of the children of God?
All: **I do.**

Priest: Do you renounce the lure of evil,
so that sin may have no mastery over you?
All: **I do.**

Priest: Do you renounce Satan,
the author and prince of sin?
All: **I do.**

Then the priest continues:
Priest: Do you believe in God,
the Father almighty,
Creator of heaven and earth?
All: **I do.**

Priest: Do you believe in Jesus Christ, his only Son, our Lord,
who was born of the Virgin Mary,
suffered death and was buried,
rose again from the dead,
and is seated at the right hand of the Father?
All: **I do.**

Priest: Do you believe in the Holy Spirit,
the holy Catholic Church,
the communion of saints,
the forgiveness of sins,
the resurrection of the body,
and life everlasting?
All: **I do.**

And may almighty God, the Father of our Lord Jesus Christ,
who has given us new birth by water and the Holy Spirit
and bestowed on us forgiveness of our sins,
keep us by his grace,
in Christ Jesus our Lord,
for eternal life. All: **Amen.**

The Priest sprinkles the people with the blessed water, while all sing:
Ant. I saw water flowing from the Temple,
from its right-hand side, alleluia;
and all to whom this water came were saved
and shall say: Alleluia, alleluia.

PRAYER OF THE FAITHFUL

FOURTH PART: THE LITURGY OF THE EUCHARIST

PRAYER OVER THE OFFERINGS
Accept, we ask, O Lord,
the prayers of your people
with the sacrificial offerings,
that what has begun in the paschal mysteries
may, by the working of your power,
bring us to the healing of eternity.
Through Christ our Lord. **All: Amen.**

COMMUNION ANTIPHON (1 Corinthians 5:7-8)
Christ our Passover has been sacrificed;
therefore let us keep the feast
with the unleavened bread of purity and truth, alleluia.

PRAYER AFTER COMMUNION
Pour out on us, O Lord, the Spirit of your love,
and in your kindness make those you have nourished
by this paschal Sacrament
one in mind and heart.
Through Christ our Lord. **All: Amen.**

DISMISSAL
To dismiss the people the Deacon or, if there is no Deacon, the Priest himself sings or says:

Go forth, the Mass is ended, alleluia, alleluia.
Or:

Go in peace, alleluia, alleluia.
All reply: Thanks be to God, alleluia, alleluia.

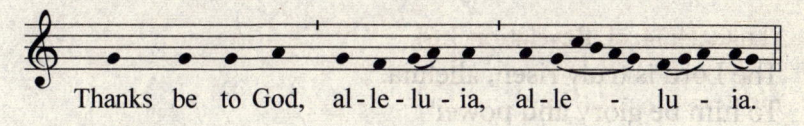

Thanks be to God, al - le - lu - ia, al - le - lu - ia.

This practice is observed throughout the Octave of Easter.

Easter Sunday

THE RESURRECTION OF THE LORD

MASS DURING THE DAY

April 5, 2015

Reflection on the Gospel

The news of an empty tomb spread from Mary to Peter and the disciple. They ran—hope quickens us. They believed—faith urges us. They witnessed to the good news—good news cannot be contained. Good news is infectious. Good news brings radiance to tired, suffering, worn faces. Good news such as an empty tomb and soon an encounter with the risen One not only cannot be contained, it changes us. Our own encounters with the risen One compel us to be witnesses, to spread Easter joy.

- *Good news, Jesus has been raised as he said and I am changed . . .*

—Living Liturgy™, *Easter Sunday 2015*

ENTRANCE ANTIPHON (Cf. Psalm 139[138]:18, 5-6)
I have risen, and I am with you still, alleluia.
You have laid your hand upon me, alleluia.
Too wonderful for me, this knowledge, alleluia, alleluia.

Or:

(Luke 24:34; cf. Revelation 1:6)
The Lord is truly risen, alleluia.
To him be glory and power
for all the ages of eternity, alleluia, alleluia.

COLLECT
O God, who on this day,
through your Only Begotten Son,
have conquered death
and unlocked for us the path to eternity,
grant, we pray, that we who keep
the solemnity of the Lord's Resurrection

may, through the renewal brought by your Spirit,
rise up in the light of life.
Through our Lord Jesus Christ, your Son,
who lives and reigns with you in the unity of the Holy Spirit,
one God, for ever and ever. All: **Amen.**

Reading I (L 42) (Acts of the Apostles 10:34a, 37-43)
A reading from the Acts of the Apostles

We ate and drank with him after he rose from the dead.

**Peter proceeded to speak and said:
   "You know what has happened all over Judea,
   beginning in Galilee after the baptism
   that John preached,
   how God anointed Jesus of Nazareth
   with the Holy Spirit and power.
He went about doing good
   and healing all those oppressed by the devil,
   for God was with him.
We are witnesses of all that he did
   both in the country of the Jews and in Jerusalem.
They put him to death by hanging him on a tree.
This man God raised on the third day and granted that
      he be visible,
   not to all the people, but to us,
   the witnesses chosen by God in advance,
   who ate and drank with him after he rose from the dead.
He commissioned us to preach to the people
   and testify that he is the one appointed by God
   as judge of the living and the dead.
To him all the prophets bear witness,
   that everyone who believes in him
   will receive forgiveness of sins through his name."

The word of the Lord.** All: **Thanks be to God.**

Responsorial Psalm 118

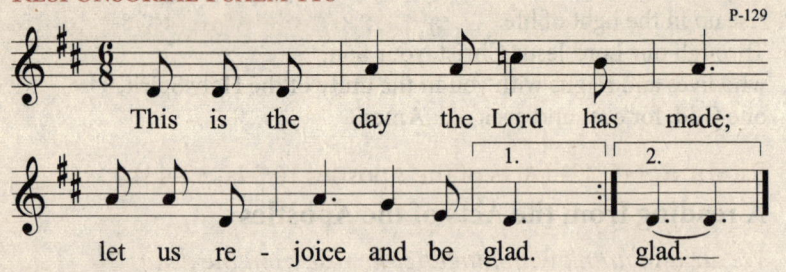

This is the day the Lord has made; let us rejoice and be glad.

Psalm 118:1-2, 16-17, 22-23

℟. (24) **This is the day the Lord has made; let us rejoice and be glad.** *or:* ℟. **Alleluia.**

Give thanks to the Lord, for he is good,
  for his mercy endures forever.
Let the house of Israel say,
  "His mercy endures forever." ℟.

"The right hand of the Lord has struck with power;
  the right hand of the Lord is exalted.
I shall not die, but live,
  and declare the works of the Lord." ℟.

The stone which the builders rejected
  has become the cornerstone.
By the Lord has this been done;
  it is wonderful in our eyes. ℟.

Reading II

A (Colossians 3:1-4)

A reading from the Letter of Saint Paul to the Colossians

Seek what is above, where Christ is.

Brothers and sisters:
If then you were raised with Christ, seek what is above,
  where Christ is seated at the right hand of God.
Think of what is above, not of what is on earth.
For you have died, and your life is hidden with Christ
  in God.

When Christ your life appears,
>   then you too will appear with him in glory.

The word of the Lord. All: **Thanks be to God.**

Or:

B (1 Corinthians 5:6b-8)

A reading from the first Letter of Saint Paul to the Corinthians

Clear out the old yeast, so that you may become a fresh batch of dough.

Brothers and sisters:
Do you not know that a little yeast leavens all the dough?
Clear out the old yeast,
>   **so that you may become a fresh batch of dough,**
>   **inasmuch as you are unleavened.**
For our paschal lamb, Christ, has been sacrificed.
Therefore, let us celebrate the feast,
>   **not with the old yeast, the yeast of malice and wickedness,**
>   **but with the unleavened bread of sincerity and truth.**

The word of the Lord. All: **Thanks be to God.**

SEQUENCE
Victimae paschali laudes

Christians, to the Paschal Victim
>   **Offer your thankful praises!**
A Lamb the sheep redeems;
>   **Christ, who only is sinless,**
>   **Reconciles sinners to the Father.**
Death and life have contended in that combat stupendous:
>   **The Prince of life, who died, reigns immortal.**
Speak, Mary, declaring
>   **What you saw, wayfaring.**
"The tomb of Christ, who is living,
>   **The glory of Jesus' resurrection;**

Bright angels attesting,
   The shroud and napkin resting.
Yes, Christ my hope is arisen;
   To Galilee he goes before you."
Christ indeed from death is risen, our new life obtaining.
   Have mercy, victor King, ever reigning!
   Amen. Alleluia.

Gospel
(John 20:1-9) *or* (Mark 16:1-7) *or* afternoon (Luke 24:13-35)
Alleluia (*See* 1 Corinthians 5:7b-8a)
℣. Alleluia, alleluia. ℟. **Alleluia, alleluia.**
℣. Christ, our paschal lamb, has been sacrificed;
   let us then feast with joy in the Lord. ℟.

✠ **A reading from the holy Gospel according to John**

All: **Glory to you, O Lord.**

He had to rise from the dead.

On the first day of the week,
   Mary of Magdala came to the tomb early in the morning,
   while it was still dark,
   and saw the stone removed from the tomb.
So she ran and went to Simon Peter
   and to the other disciple whom Jesus loved, and told them,
   "They have taken the Lord from the tomb,
   and we don't know where they put him."
So Peter and the other disciple went out and came to the tomb.
They both ran, but the other disciple ran faster than Peter and arrived at the tomb first;
   he bent down and saw the burial cloths there, but did not go in.
When Simon Peter arrived after him,
   he went into the tomb and saw the burial cloths there,
   and the cloth that had covered his head,

not with the burial cloths but rolled up in a separate
    place.
Then the other disciple also went in,
    the one who had arrived at the tomb first,
    and he saw and believed.
For they did not yet understand the Scripture
    that he had to rise from the dead.

The Gospel of the Lord. All: **Praise to you, Lord Jesus Christ.**

Renewal of Baptismal Promises
The renewal of baptismal promises may take place at all Masses today. The form followed is the same as at the Easter Vigil, page 225.

Prayer over the Offerings
Exultant with paschal gladness, O Lord,
we offer the sacrifice
by which your Church
is wondrously reborn and nourished.
Through Christ our Lord. All: **Amen.**

Communion Antiphon (1 Corinthians 5:7-8)
Christ our Passover has been sacrificed, alleluia;
therefore let us keep the feast with the unleavened bread
of purity and truth, alleluia, alleluia.

Prayer after Communion
Look upon your Church, O God,
with unfailing love and favor,
so that, renewed by the paschal mysteries,
she may come to the glory of the resurrection.
Through Christ our Lord. All: **Amen.**

Dismissal (*See* p. 227)

Second Sunday of Easter
(or OF DIVINE MERCY)

April 12, 2015

Reflection on the Gospel
On Easter evening, the risen Jesus appears and shows the disciples "his hands and his side." It is Jesus who makes the first, convincing move to enable the disciples to believe that he has truly risen from the dead. It is he who wants the disciples to see him, to regain their confidence and peace. He bears the marks of suffering and death. Yet he is risen; he has conquered death. For himself and for all of us.

- *Jesus is here among us . . .*

—Living Liturgy™, *Second Sunday of Easter 2015*

ENTRANCE ANTIPHON (1 Peter 2:2)
Like newborn infants, you must long for the pure, spiritual milk,
that in him you may grow to salvation, alleluia.

Or:

(4 Esdras 2:36-37)
Receive the joy of your glory, giving thanks to God,
who has called you into the heavenly kingdom, alleluia.

COLLECT
God of everlasting mercy,
who in the very recurrence of the paschal feast
kindle the faith of the people you have made your own,
increase, we pray, the grace you have bestowed,
that all may grasp and rightly understand
in what font they have been washed,
by whose Spirit they have been reborn,
by whose Blood they have been redeemed.
Through our Lord Jesus Christ, your Son,
who lives and reigns with you in the unity of the Holy Spirit,
one God, for ever and ever. All: **Amen.**

Reading I (L 44-B) (Acts of the Apostles 4:32-35)
A reading from the Acts of the Apostles

They were of one heart and mind.

**The community of believers was of one heart and mind,
and no one claimed that any of his possessions was his own,
but they had everything in common.
With great power the apostles bore witness
to the resurrection of the Lord Jesus,
and great favor was accorded them all.
There was no needy person among them,
for those who owned property or houses would sell them,
bring the proceeds of the sale,
and put them at the feet of the apostles,
and they were distributed to each according to need.
The word of the Lord.** All: **Thanks be to God.**

Responsorial Psalm 118

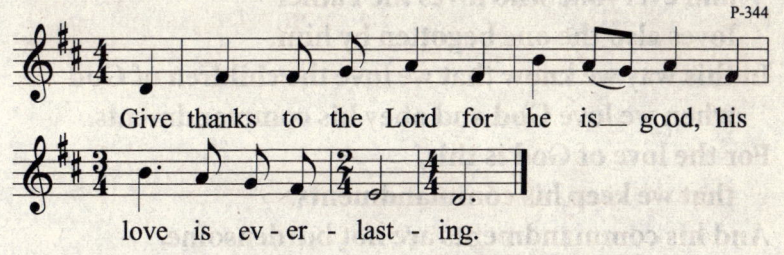

Give thanks to the Lord for he is good, his love is ev-er-last-ing.

Music: Jay F. Hunstiger, © 1990, administered by Liturgical Press. All rights reserved.

Psalm 118:2-4, 13-15, 22-24

℟. (1) **Give thanks to the Lord for he is good, his love is everlasting.** *or:* ℟. **Alleluia.**

Let the house of Israel say,
 "His mercy endures forever."
Let the house of Aaron say,
 "His mercy endures forever."
Let those who fear the Lord say,
 "His mercy endures forever." ℟.

(continued)

I was hard pressed and was falling,
    but the Lord helped me.
My strength and my courage is the Lord,
    and he has been my savior.
The joyful shout of victory
    in the tents of the just. R̸.

The stone which the builders rejected
    has become the cornerstone.
By the Lord has this been done;
    it is wonderful in our eyes.
This is the day the Lord has made;
    let us be glad and rejoice in it. R̸.

Reading II (1 John 5:1-6)

A reading from the first Letter of Saint John

Whoever is begotten by God conquers the world.

Beloved:
Everyone who believes that Jesus is the Christ is begotten by God,
    and everyone who loves the Father
    loves also the one begotten by him.
In this way we know that we love the children of God
    when we love God and obey his commandments.
For the love of God is this,
    that we keep his commandments.
And his commandments are not burdensome,
    for whoever is begotten by God conquers the world.
And the victory that conquers the world is our faith.
Who indeed is the victor over the world
    but the one who believes that Jesus is the Son of God?

This is the one who came through water and blood, Jesus Christ,
    not by water alone, but by water and blood.
The Spirit is the one that testifies,
    and the Spirit is truth.

The word of the Lord. All: **Thanks be to God.**

Gospel (John 20:19-31)
Alleluia (John 20:29)

℣. Alleluia, alleluia. ℟. **Alleluia, alleluia.**
℣. You believe in me, Thomas, because you have seen me,
   says the Lord;
   blessed are those who have not seen me, but still
   believe! ℟.

✢ **A reading from the holy Gospel according to John**

All: **Glory to you, O Lord.**

Eight days later Jesus came and stood in their midst.

**On the evening of that first day of the week,
   when the doors were locked, where the disciples were,
   for fear of the Jews,
   Jesus came and stood in their midst
   and said to them, "Peace be with you."
When he had said this, he showed them his hands and
   his side.
The disciples rejoiced when they saw the Lord.
Jesus said to them again, "Peace be with you.
As the Father has sent me, so I send you."
And when he had said this, he breathed on them and
   said to them,
   "Receive the Holy Spirit.
Whose sins you forgive are forgiven them,
   and whose sins you retain are retained."

Thomas, called Didymus, one of the Twelve,
   was not with them when Jesus came.
So the other disciples said to him, "We have seen the Lord."
But he said to them,
   "Unless I see the mark of the nails in his hands
   and put my finger into the nailmarks
   and put my hand into his side, I will not believe."
Now a week later his disciples were again inside
   and Thomas was with them.**

Jesus came, although the doors were locked,
    and stood in their midst and said, "Peace be with you."
Then he said to Thomas, "Put your finger here and see my hands,
    and bring your hand and put it into my side,
    and do not be unbelieving, but believe."
Thomas answered and said to him, "My Lord and my God!"
Jesus said to him, "Have you come to believe because you have seen me?
Blessed are those who have not seen and have believed."

Now Jesus did many other signs in the presence of his disciples
    that are not written in this book.
But these are written that you may come to believe
    that Jesus is the Christ, the Son of God,
    and that through this belief you may have life in his name.

The Gospel of the Lord. All: **Praise to you, Lord Jesus Christ.**

Prayer over the Offerings
Accept, O Lord, we pray,
the oblations of your people
(and of those you have brought to new birth),
that, renewed by confession of your name and by Baptism,
they may attain unending happiness.
Through Christ our Lord. All: **Amen.**

Communion Antiphon (Cf. John 20:27)
Bring your hand and feel the place of the nails,
and do not be unbelieving but believing, alleluia.

Prayer after Communion
Grant, we pray, almighty God,
that our reception of this paschal Sacrament
may have a continuing effect
in our minds and hearts.
Through Christ our Lord. All: **Amen.**

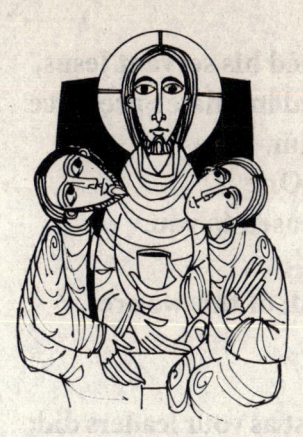

Third Sunday of Easter

April 19, 2015

Reflection on the Gospel

Jesus opened the minds of the disciples to grasp two things written in the Scriptures: that he "would suffer and rise from the dead," and that "repentance, for the forgiveness of sins, would be preached in his name to all the nations." Our repentance—conversion of life—turns us to the God who forgives and who fills us with the new Life of the resurrection. Ultimately, this risen Life within us empowers a way of living that witnesses to God's forgiveness of our sinfulness.

- *Jesus turns us to God, who fills us with new life, and I . . .*

—Living Liturgy™, *Third Sunday of Easter 2015*

ENTRANCE ANTIPHON (Cf. Psalm 66[65]:1-2)
Cry out with joy to God, all the earth;
O sing to the glory of his name.
O render him glorious praise, alleluia.

COLLECT
May your people exult for ever, O God,
in renewed youthfulness of spirit,
so that, rejoicing now in the restored glory of our adoption,
we may look forward in confident hope
to the rejoicing of the day of resurrection.
Through our Lord Jesus Christ, your Son,
who lives and reigns with you in the unity of the Holy Spirit,
one God, for ever and ever. All: **Amen.**

READING I (L 47-B) (Acts of the Apostles 3:13-15, 17-19)
A reading from the Acts of the Apostles

The author of life you put to death, but God raised him from the dead.

Peter said to the people:
"The God of Abraham,
   the God of Isaac, and the God of Jacob,

the God of our fathers, has glorified his servant Jesus,
whom you handed over and denied in Pilate's presence
when he had decided to release him.
You denied the Holy and Righteous One
and asked that a murderer be released to you.
The author of life you put to death,
but God raised him from the dead; of this we are
witnesses.
Now I know, brothers,
that you acted out of ignorance, just as your leaders did;
but God has thus brought to fulfillment
what he had announced beforehand
through the mouth of all the prophets,
that his Christ would suffer.
Repent, therefore, and be converted, that your sins may
be wiped away."

The word of the Lord. All: Thanks be to God.

Responsorial Psalm 4

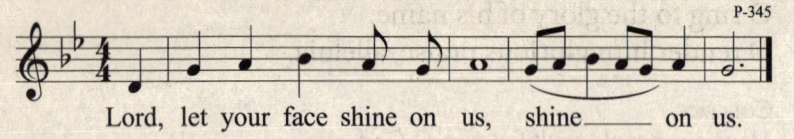

Lord, let your face shine on us, shine on us.

Music: Jay F. Hunstiger, © 1990, administered by Liturgical Press. All rights reserved.

Psalm 4:2, 4, 7-8, 9

℟. (7a) **Lord, let your face shine on us.** *or:* ℟. **Alleluia.**

When I call, answer me, O my just God,
 you who relieve me when I am in distress;
 have pity on me, and hear my prayer! ℟.

Know that the LORD does wonders for his faithful one;
 the LORD will hear me when I call upon him. ℟.

O LORD, let the light of your countenance shine upon us!
 You put gladness into my heart. ℟.

As soon as I lie down, I fall peacefully asleep,
 for you alone, O LORD,
 bring security to my dwelling. ℟.

Reading II (1 John 2:1-5a)

A reading from the first Letter of Saint John

Jesus Christ is expiation not for our sins only but for those of the whole world.

**My children, I am writing this to you
   so that you may not commit sin.
But if anyone does sin, we have an Advocate with the Father,
   Jesus Christ the righteous one.
He is expiation for our sins,
   and not for our sins only but for those of the whole world.
The way we may be sure that we know him is to keep his commandments.
Those who say, "I know him," but do not keep his commandments
   are liars, and the truth is not in them.
But whoever keeps his word,
   the love of God is truly perfected in him.**

The word of the Lord. All: **Thanks be to God.**

Gospel (Luke 24:35-48)
Alleluia (See Luke 24:32)

℣. Alleluia, alleluia. ℟. **Alleluia, alleluia.**
℣. Lord Jesus, open the Scriptures to us;
   make our hearts burn while you speak to us. ℟.

✠ **A reading from the holy Gospel according to Luke**

All: **Glory to you, O Lord.**

Thus it was written that the Christ would suffer and rise from the dead on the third day.

**The two disciples recounted what had taken place on the way,
   and how Jesus was made known to them
   in the breaking of bread.**

While they were still speaking about this,
   he stood in their midst and said to them,
   "Peace be with you."
But they were startled and terrified
   and thought that they were seeing a ghost.
Then he said to them, "Why are you troubled?
And why do questions arise in your hearts?
Look at my hands and my feet, that it is I myself.
Touch me and see, because a ghost does not have flesh
      and bones
   as you can see I have."
And as he said this,
   he showed them his hands and his feet.
While they were still incredulous for joy and were amazed,
   he asked them, "Have you anything here to eat?"
They gave him a piece of baked fish;
   he took it and ate it in front of them.

He said to them,
   "These are my words that I spoke to you while I was
         still with you,
      that everything written about me in the law of Moses
      and in the prophets and psalms must be fulfilled."
Then he opened their minds to understand the Scriptures.
And he said to them,
   "Thus it is written that the Christ would suffer
   and rise from the dead on the third day
   and that repentance, for the forgiveness of sins,
      would be preached in his name
   to all the nations, beginning from Jerusalem.
You are witnesses of these things."

   The Gospel of the Lord. All: **Praise to you, Lord Jesus Christ.**

PRAYER OVER THE OFFERINGS
Receive, O Lord, we pray,
these offerings of your exultant Church,
and, as you have given her cause for such great gladness,

grant also that the gifts we bring
may bear fruit in perpetual happiness.
Through Christ our Lord. All: **Amen.**

Communion Antiphon Year B (Luke 24:46-47)
The Christ had to suffer and on the third day rise from the dead;
in his name repentance and remission of sins
must be preached to all the nations, alleluia.

Prayer after Communion
Look with kindness upon your people, O Lord,
and grant, we pray,
that those you were pleased to renew by eternal mysteries
may attain in their flesh
the incorruptible glory of the resurrection.
Through Christ our Lord. All: **Amen.**

Fourth Sunday of Easter

April 26, 2015

Reflection on the Gospel
In the gospel for this Sunday, Jesus proclaims that "I am the good shepherd" and "I know mine and mine know me." To know Jesus is to be one with him, the Good Shepherd. This means that we are not only sheep who hear our Good Shepherd's voice and come to know him, but we also are to become good shepherds ourselves. Transformed from sheep to shepherd, we take up the life our Good Shepherd has laid down. Jesus requires of us disciples the same mission—to also lay down our lives.

• *To shepherd means I . . .*

—Living Liturgy™, *Fourth Sunday of Easter 2015*

Entrance Antiphon (Cf. Psalm 33[32]:5-6)
The merciful love of the Lord fills the earth;
by the word of the Lord the heavens were made, alleluia.

April 26

Collect

Almighty ever-living God,
lead us to a share in the joys of heaven,
so that the humble flock may reach
where the brave Shepherd has gone before.
Who lives and reigns with you in the unity of the Holy Spirit,
one God, for ever and ever. All: **Amen.**

Reading I (L 50-B) (Acts of the Apostles 4:8-12)

A reading from the Acts of the Apostles

There is no salvation through anyone else.

**Peter, filled with the Holy Spirit, said:
"Leaders of the people and elders:
If we are being examined today
about a good deed done to a cripple,
namely, by what means he was saved,
then all of you and all the people of Israel should know
that it was in the name of Jesus Christ the Nazorean
whom you crucified, whom God raised from the dead;
in his name this man stands before you healed.
He is *the stone rejected by you, the builders,
which has become the cornerstone.*
There is no salvation through anyone else,
nor is there any other name under heaven
given to the human race by which we are to be saved."**

The word of the Lord. All: **Thanks be to God.**

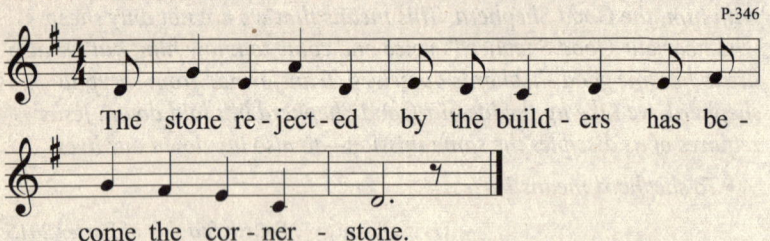

Responsorial Psalm 118

The stone rejected by the builders has become the cornerstone.

Music: Jay F. Hunstiger, © 1990, administered by Liturgical Press. All rights reserved.

Psalm 118:1, 8-9, 21-23, 26, 28, 29

℟. (22) **The stone rejected by the builders has become the cornerstone.** *or:* ℟. **Alleluia.**

> Give thanks to the Lord, for he is good,
>   for his mercy endures forever.
> It is better to take refuge in the Lord
>   than to trust in man.
> It is better to take refuge in the Lord
>   than to trust in princes. ℟.
>
> I will give thanks to you, for you have answered me
>   and have been my savior.
> The stone which the builders rejected
>   has become the cornerstone.
> By the Lord has this been done;
>   it is wonderful in our eyes. ℟.
>
> Blessed is he who comes in the name of the Lord;
>   we bless you from the house of the Lord.
> I will give thanks to you, for you have answered me
>   and have been my savior.
> Give thanks to the Lord, for he is good;
>   for his kindness endures forever. ℟.

Reading II (1 John 3:1-2)
A reading from the first Letter of Saint John

We shall see God as he really is.

Beloved:
See what love the Father has bestowed on us
  that we may be called the children of God.
Yet so we are.
The reason the world does not know us
  is that it did not know him.
Beloved, we are God's children now;
  what we shall be has not yet been revealed.
We do know that when it is revealed we shall be like him,
  for we shall see him as he is.

The word of the Lord. All: **Thanks be to God.**

April 26

Gospel (John 10:11-18)
Alleluia (John 10:14)

℣. Alleluia, alleluia. ℟. **Alleluia, alleluia.**
℣. I am the good shepherd, says the Lord;
I know my sheep, and mine know me. ℟.

☩ **A reading from the holy Gospel according to John**

All: **Glory to you, O Lord.**

The good shepherd lays down his life for the sheep.

Jesus said:
"I am the good shepherd.
A good shepherd lays down his life for the sheep.
A hired man, who is not a shepherd
and whose sheep are not his own,
sees a wolf coming and leaves the sheep and runs away,
and the wolf catches and scatters them.
This is because he works for pay and has no concern for
the sheep.
I am the good shepherd,
and I know mine and mine know me,
just as the Father knows me and I know the Father;
and I will lay down my life for the sheep.
I have other sheep that do not belong to this fold.
These also I must lead, and they will hear my voice,
and there will be one flock, one shepherd.
This is why the Father loves me,
because I lay down my life in order to take it up again.
No one takes it from me, but I lay it down on my own.
I have power to lay it down, and power to take it up again.
This command I have received from my Father."

The Gospel of the Lord. All: **Praise to you, Lord Jesus Christ.**

Prayer over the Offerings
Grant, we pray, O Lord,
that we may always find delight in these paschal mysteries,
so that the renewal constantly at work within us
may be the cause of our unending joy.
Through Christ our Lord. All: **Amen.**

Communion Antiphon
The Good Shepherd has risen,
who laid down his life for his sheep
and willingly died for his flock, alleluia.

Prayer after Communion
Look upon your flock, kind Shepherd,
and be pleased to settle in eternal pastures
the sheep you have redeemed
by the Precious Blood of your Son.
Who lives and reigns for ever and ever. All: **Amen.**

Fifth Sunday of Easter

May 3, 2015

Reflection on the Gospel

The pruning of which Jesus speaks in this gospel is simply a means to an end. The end is the bearing of much fruit. To this end, Jesus' word has a twofold purpose. On the one hand, his word is prophetic and prunes whatever drains life out of his disciples. On the other, his word is the very sap of life that enables disciples to remain in him and bear fruit. True discipleship is to "remain" in Jesus. Only then does his risen Life bloom in us for all to see.

• *Jesus prunes us and we bear fruit because . . .*

—Living Liturgy™, *Fifth Sunday of Easter 2015*

Entrance Antiphon (Cf. Psalm 98[97]:1-2)
O sing a new song to the Lord,
for he has worked wonders;
in the sight of the nations
he has shown his deliverance, alleluia.

Collect

Almighty ever-living God,
constantly accomplish the Paschal Mystery within us,
that those you were pleased to make new in Holy Baptism
may, under your protective care, bear much fruit
and come to the joys of life eternal.
Through our Lord Jesus Christ, your Son,
who lives and reigns with you in the unity of the Holy Spirit,
one God, for ever and ever. All: **Amen.**

Reading I (L 53-B) (Acts of the Apostles 9:26-31)

A reading from the Acts of the Apostles

Barnabas reported to the Apostles how Saul had seen the Lord on the way.

**When Saul arrived in Jerusalem he tried to join the disciples,
but they were all afraid of him,
not believing that he was a disciple.
Then Barnabas took charge of him and brought him to the apostles,
and he reported to them how he had seen the Lord,
and that he had spoken to him,
and how in Damascus he had spoken out boldly in the name of Jesus.
He moved about freely with them in Jerusalem,
and spoke out boldly in the name of the Lord.
He also spoke and debated with the Hellenists,
but they tried to kill him.
And when the brothers learned of this,
they took him down to Caesarea
and sent him on his way to Tarsus.**

**The church throughout all Judea, Galilee, and Samaria was at peace.
It was being built up and walked in the fear of the Lord,
and with the consolation of the Holy Spirit it grew in numbers.**

The word of the Lord. All: **Thanks be to God.**

Responsorial Psalm 22

(musical notation)

I will praise you, Lord, in the as-sem-bly of your peo-ple.

Music: Jay F. Hunstiger, © 1990, administered by Liturgical Press. All rights reserved.

Psalm 22:26-27, 28, 30, 31-32

℟. (26a) **I will praise you, Lord, in the assembly of your people.** *or:* ℟. **Alleluia.**

I will fulfill my vows before those who fear the LORD.
 The lowly shall eat their fill;
they who seek the LORD shall praise him:
 "May your hearts live forever!" ℟.

All the ends of the earth
 shall remember and turn to the LORD;
all the families of the nations
 shall bow down before him. ℟.

To him alone shall bow down
 all who sleep in the earth;
before him shall bend
 all who go down into the dust. ℟.

And to him my soul shall live;
 my descendants shall serve him.
Let the coming generation be told of the LORD
 that they may proclaim to a people yet to be born
 the justice he has shown. ℟.

Reading II (1 John 3:18-24)

A reading from the first Letter of Saint John

This is his commandment: that we may believe and love.

**Children, let us love not in word or speech
 but in deed and truth.**

**Now this is how we shall know that we belong to the truth
 and reassure our hearts before him**

in whatever our hearts condemn,
> for God is greater than our hearts and knows
>> everything.

Beloved, if our hearts do not condemn us,
> we have confidence in God
> and receive from him whatever we ask,
> because we keep his commandments and do what
>> pleases him.

And his commandment is this:
> we should believe in the name of his Son, Jesus Christ,
> and love one another just as he commanded us.

Those who keep his commandments remain in him, and
> he in them,
> and the way we know that he remains in us
> is from the Spirit he gave us.

The word of the Lord. All: Thanks be to God.

GOSPEL (John 15:1-8)

ALLELUIA (John 15:4a, 5b)

℣. Alleluia, alleluia. ℟. **Alleluia, alleluia.**
℣. Remain in me as I remain in you, says the Lord.
Whoever remains in me will bear much fruit. ℟.

✠ **A reading from the holy Gospel according to John**

All: **Glory to you, O Lord.**

Whoever remains in me and I in him will bear much fruit.

Jesus said to his disciples:
> "I am the true vine, and my Father is the vine grower.

He takes away every branch in me that does not bear
> fruit,
> and every one that does he prunes so that it bears
>> more fruit.

You are already pruned because of the word that I spoke
> to you.

Remain in me, as I remain in you.

Just as a branch cannot bear fruit on its own
   unless it remains on the vine,
   so neither can you unless you remain in me.
I am the vine, you are the branches.
Whoever remains in me and I in him will bear much fruit,
   because without me you can do nothing.
Anyone who does not remain in me
   will be thrown out like a branch and wither;
   people will gather them and throw them into a fire
   and they will be burned.
If you remain in me and my words remain in you,
   ask for whatever you want and it will be done for you.
By this is my Father glorified,
   that you bear much fruit and become my disciples."

The Gospel of the Lord. All: **Praise to you, Lord Jesus Christ.**

PRAYER OVER THE OFFERINGS
O God, who by the wonderful exchange effected in this sacrifice
have made us partakers of the one supreme Godhead,
grant, we pray,
that, as we have come to know your truth,
we may make it ours by a worthy way of life.
Through Christ our Lord. All: **Amen.**

COMMUNION ANTIPHON (Cf. John 15:1, 5)
I am the true vine and you are the branches, says the Lord.
Whoever remains in me, and I in him, bears fruit in plenty,
   alleluia.

PRAYER AFTER COMMUNION
Graciously be present to your people, we pray, O Lord,
and lead those you have imbued with heavenly mysteries
to pass from former ways to newness of life.
Through Christ our Lord. All: **Amen.**

Sixth Sunday of Easter

May 10, 2015

Reflection on the Gospel

Immediately after Jesus expresses the desire that his joy become complete in us, he commands us to "love one another." What is his joy? The deep resonance of risen Life that arises from being faithful to the Father's will. What is the love he commands? Laying "down one's life." Joy and love are the Easter mystery made visible. We who remain in Jesus' love and welcome his joy in us embody the Easter mystery, make visible God's saving events.

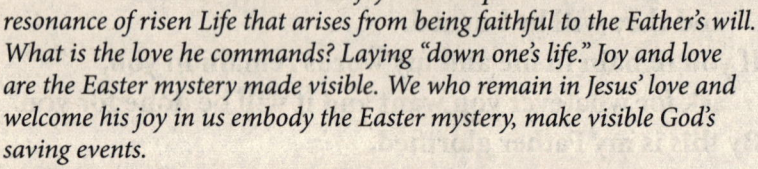

- *Jesus' joy becomes complete when I love another by . . .*

—*Living Liturgy*™, *Sixth Sunday of Easter 2015*

Entrance Antiphon (Cf. Isaiah 48:20)

Proclaim a joyful sound and let it be heard;
proclaim to the ends of the earth:
The Lord has freed his people, alleluia.

Collect

Grant, almighty God,
that we may celebrate with heartfelt devotion these days of joy,
which we keep in honor of the risen Lord,
and that what we relive in remembrance
we may always hold to in what we do.
Through our Lord Jesus Christ, your Son,
who lives and reigns with you in the unity of the Holy Spirit,
one God, for ever and ever. All: **Amen.**

When the Ascension of the Lord is celebrated the following Sunday, the second reading and Gospel from the Seventh Sunday of Easter (*see* nos. 59–61) may be read on the Sixth Sunday of Easter.

Reading I (L 56-B) (Acts of the Apostles 10:25-26, 34-35, 44-48)

A reading from the Acts of the Apostles

The gift of the Holy Spirit was poured out on the Gentiles also.

When Peter entered, Cornelius met him
   and, falling at his feet, paid him homage.
Peter, however, raised him up, saying,
   "Get up. I myself am also a human being."
Then Peter proceeded to speak and said,
   "In truth, I see that God shows no partiality.
Rather, in every nation whoever fears him and acts uprightly
   is acceptable to him."
While Peter was still speaking these things,
   the Holy Spirit fell upon all who were listening to the word.
The circumcised believers who had accompanied Peter
   were astounded that the gift of the Holy Spirit
   should have been poured out on the Gentiles also,
   for they could hear them speaking in tongues and glorifying God.
Then Peter responded,
   "Can anyone withhold the water for baptizing these people,
   who have received the Holy Spirit even as we have?"
He ordered them to be baptized in the name of Jesus Christ.

The word of the Lord. All: Thanks be to God.

RESPONSORIAL PSALM 98

P-348

The Lord has revealed to the nations his saving pow'r.

Music: Jay F. Hunstiger, © 1990, administered by Liturgical Press. All rights reserved.

Psalm 98:1, 2-3, 3-4

℟. (cf. 2b) **The Lord has revealed to the nations his saving power.** *or:* ℟. **Alleluia.**

   Sing to the Lord a new song,
      for he has done wondrous deeds;

(continued)

His right hand has won victory for him,
   his holy arm. ℟.

The Lord has made his salvation known:
   in the sight of the nations he has revealed his justice.
He has remembered his kindness and his faithfulness
   toward the house of Israel. ℟.

All the ends of the earth have seen
   the salvation by our God.
Sing joyfully to the Lord, all you lands;
   break into song; sing praise. ℟.

Reading II (1 John 4:7-10)

A reading from the first Letter of Saint John

God is love.

**Beloved, let us love one another,
   because love is of God;
   everyone who loves is begotten by God and knows God.
Whoever is without love does not know God, for God is love.
In this way the love of God was revealed to us:
   God sent his only Son into the world
   so that we might have life through him.
In this is love:
   not that we have loved God, but that he loved us
   and sent his Son as expiation for our sins.**

The word of the Lord. All: **Thanks be to God.**

Gospel (John 15:9-17)
Alleluia (John 14:23)

℣. Alleluia, alleluia. ℟. **Alleluia, alleluia.**
℣. Whoever loves me will keep my word, says the Lord,
   and my Father will love him and we will come to him. ℟.

☩ **A reading from the holy Gospel according to John**

All: **Glory to you, O Lord.**

No one has greater love than this: to lay down one's life for one's friends.

Jesus said to his disciples:
"As the Father loves me, so I also love you.
Remain in my love.
If you keep my commandments, you will remain in my love,
  just as I have kept my Father's commandments
  and remain in his love.

"I have told you this so that my joy may be in you
  and your joy might be complete.
This is my commandment: love one another as I love you.
No one has greater love than this,
  to lay down one's life for one's friends.
You are my friends if you do what I command you.
I no longer call you slaves,
  because a slave does not know what his master is doing.
I have called you friends,
  because I have told you everything I have heard from my Father.
It was not you who chose me, but I who chose you
  and appointed you to go and bear fruit that will remain,
  so that whatever you ask the Father in my name he may give you.
This I command you: love one another."

The Gospel of the Lord. All: **Praise to you, Lord Jesus Christ.**

Prayer over the Offerings

May our prayers rise up to you, O Lord,
together with the sacrificial offerings,
so that, purified by your graciousness,
we may be conformed to the mysteries of your mighty love.
Through Christ our Lord. All: **Amen.**

Communion Antiphon (John 14:15-16)

If you love me, keep my commandments, says the Lord,
and I will ask the Father and he will send you another Paraclete,
to abide with you for ever, alleluia.

May 10

PRAYER AFTER COMMUNION
Almighty ever-living God,
who restore us to eternal life in the Resurrection of Christ,
increase in us, we pray, the fruits of this paschal Sacrament
and pour into our hearts the strength of this saving food.
Through Christ our Lord. All: **Amen.**

The Ascension of the Lord

AT THE VIGIL MASS

May 13 or 16, 2015

This Mass is used on the evening of the day before the Solemnity, either before or after First Vespers (Evening Prayer I) of the Ascension.

Reflection on the Gospel
As the Jesus of history takes his leave of this world, it is clear that he intends his saving mission to continue. Seemingly without question, fear, or hesitation, the disciples "went forth." But they did not go forth alone: "the Lord worked with them." The mission, the work, and the signs are of the Lord Jesus. This relationship is the guarantee of Jesus' continued mission. So the gospel raises this question for disciples today: Are we of the Lord Jesus?

- *Jesus' saving mission is present in us by . . .*

—Living Liturgy™, *Ascension 2015*

ENTRANCE ANTIPHON (Psalm 68[67]:33, 35)
You kingdoms of the earth, sing to God;
praise the Lord, who ascends above the highest heavens;
his majesty and might are in the skies, alleluia.

COLLECT
O God, whose Son today ascended to the heavens
as the Apostles looked on,
grant, we pray, that, in accordance with his promise,

we may be worthy for him to live with us always on earth,
and we with him in heaven.
Who lives and reigns with you in the unity of the Holy Spirit,
one God, for ever and ever. All: **Amen.**

(Readings are those of the day.)

Prayer over the Offerings
O God, whose Only Begotten Son, our High Priest,
is seated ever-living at your right hand to intercede for us,
grant that we may approach with confidence the throne of grace
and there obtain your mercy.
Through Christ our Lord. All: **Amen.**

Communion Antiphon (Cf. Hebrews 10:12)
Christ, offering a single sacrifice for sins,
is seated for ever at God's right hand, alleluia.

Prayer after Communion
May the gifts we have received from your altar, Lord,
kindle in our hearts a longing for the heavenly homeland
and cause us to press forward, following in the Savior's footsteps,
to the place where for our sake he entered before us.
Who lives and reigns for ever and ever. All: **Amen.**

May 14 or 17

AT THE MASS DURING THE DAY

If the feast of the Ascension is celebrated on the Seventh Sunday of Easter in your diocese, please turn to page 263 for the texts for today.

Entrance Antiphon (Acts of the Apostles 1:11)
Men of Galilee, why gaze in wonder at the heavens?
This Jesus whom you saw ascending into heaven
will return as you saw him go, alleluia.

Collect
Gladden us with holy joys, almighty God,
and make us rejoice with devout thanksgiving,
for the Ascension of Christ your Son
is our exaltation,
and, where the Head has gone before in glory,
the Body is called to follow in hope.
Through our Lord Jesus Christ, your Son,

who lives and reigns with you in the unity of the Holy Spirit,
one God, for ever and ever. All: **Amen.**

Or:

Grant, we pray, almighty God,
that we, who believe that your Only Begotten Son, our Redeemer,
ascended this day to the heavens,
may in spirit dwell already in heavenly realms.
Who lives and reigns with you in the unity of the Holy Spirit,
one God, for ever and ever. All: **Amen.**

READING I (L 58-B) (Acts of the Apostles 1:1-11)

A reading from the beginning of the Acts of the Apostles

As the Apostles were looking on, Jesus was lifted up.

In the first book, Theophilus,
  I dealt with all that Jesus did and taught
  until the day he was taken up,
  after giving instructions through the Holy Spirit
  to the apostles whom he had chosen.
He presented himself alive to them
  by many proofs after he had suffered,
  appearing to them during forty days
  and speaking about the kingdom of God.
While meeting with them,
  he enjoined them not to depart from Jerusalem,
  but to wait for "the promise of the Father
  about which you have heard me speak;
  for John baptized with water,
  but in a few days you will be baptized with the
    Holy Spirit."
When they had gathered together they asked him,
  "Lord, are you at this time going to restore
    the kingdom to Israel?"
He answered them, "It is not for you to know the times
    or seasons
  that the Father has established by his own authority.
But you will receive power when the Holy Spirit comes
    upon you,

and you will be my witnesses in Jerusalem,
> throughout Judea and Samaria,
> and to the ends of the earth."

When he had said this, as they were looking on,
> he was lifted up, and a cloud took him from their sight.

While they were looking intently at the sky as he was going,
> suddenly two men dressed in white garments stood beside them.

They said, "Men of Galilee,
> why are you standing there looking at the sky?

This Jesus who has been taken up from you into heaven
> will return in the same way as you have seen him going into heaven."

The word of the Lord. **All: Thanks be to God.**

Responsorial Psalm 47

P-135

God mounts his throne to shouts of joy, to shouts of joy.

Music: Jay F. Hunstiger, © 1990, administered by Liturgical Press. All rights reserved.

Psalm 47:2-3, 6-7, 8-9

℟. (6) **God mounts his throne to shouts of joy: a blare of trumpets for the Lord.** *or:* ℟. **Alleluia.**

All you peoples, clap your hands,
> shout to God with cries of gladness,

for the Lord, the Most High, the awesome,
> is the great king over all the earth. ℟.

God mounts his throne amid shouts of joy;
> the Lord, amid trumpet blasts.

Sing praise to God, sing praise;
> sing praise to our king, sing praise. ℟.

For king of all the earth is God;
> sing hymns of praise.

God reigns over the nations,
> God sits upon his holy throne. ℟.

May 14 or 17

Reading II

A (Ephesians 1:17-23)

A reading from the Letter of Saint Paul to the Ephesians

God seated Jesus at his right hand in the heavens.

Brothers and sisters:
May the God of our Lord Jesus Christ, the Father of glory,
> **give you a Spirit of wisdom and revelation**
> **resulting in knowledge of him.**
May the eyes of your hearts be enlightened,
> **that you may know what is the hope that belongs to his call,**
> **what are the riches of glory**
> **in his inheritance among the holy ones,**
> **and what is the surpassing greatness of his power**
> **for us who believe,**
> **in accord with the exercise of his great might,**
> **which he worked in Christ,**
> **raising him from the dead**
> **and seating him at his right hand in the heavens,**
> **far above every principality, authority, power, and dominion,**
> **and every name that is named**
> **not only in this age but also in the one to come.**
And he put all things beneath his feet
> **and gave him as head over all things to the church,**
> **which is his body,**
> **the fullness of the one who fills all things in every way.**

The word of the Lord. All: **Thanks be to God.**

Or:

B Longer Form (Ephesians 4:1-13) or *C* Shorter Form [ ] (Ephesians 4:1-7, 11-13)

A reading from the Letter of Saint Paul to the Ephesians

To the extent of the full stature of Christ.

[Brothers and sisters,
I, a prisoner for the Lord,
> urge you to live in a manner worthy of the call
>> you have received,
> with all humility and gentleness, with patience,
> bearing with one another through love,
> striving to preserve the unity of the spirit
> through the bond of peace:
> one body and one Spirit,
> as you were also called to the one hope of your call;
> one Lord, one faith, one baptism;
> one God and Father of all,
> who is over all and through all and in all.

But grace was given to each of us
> according to the measure of Christ's gift.]
Therefore, it says:
> *He ascended on high and took prisoners captive;*
> *he gave gifts to men.*
What does "he ascended" mean except that he also descended
> into the lower regions of the earth?
The one who descended is also the one who ascended
> far above all the heavens,
> that he might fill all things.

[And he gave some as apostles, others as prophets,
> others as evangelists, others as pastors and teachers,
> to equip the holy ones for the work of ministry,
> for building up the body of Christ,
> until we all attain to the unity of faith
> and knowledge of the Son of God, to mature to manhood,
> to the extent of the full stature of Christ.]

The word of the Lord. All: Thanks be to God.

Gospel (Mark 16:15-20)
Alleluia (Matthew 28:19a, 20b)

℣. Alleluia, alleluia. ℟. **Alleluia, alleluia.**
℣. Go and teach all nations, says the Lord;
I am with you always, until the end of the world. ℟.

✠ **A reading from the conclusion of the holy Gospel according to Mark**

All: **Glory to you, O Lord.**

The Lord Jesus was taken up into heaven and took his seat at the right hand of God.

Jesus said to his disciples:
   "Go into the whole world
   and proclaim the gospel to every creature.
Whoever believes and is baptized will be saved;
   whoever does not believe will be condemned.
These signs will accompany those who believe:
   in my name they will drive out demons,
   they will speak new languages.
They will pick up serpents with their hands,
   and if they drink any deadly thing, it will not harm them.
They will lay hands on the sick, and they will recover."

So then the Lord Jesus, after he spoke to them,
   was taken up into heaven
   and took his seat at the right hand of God.
But they went forth and preached everywhere,
   while the Lord worked with them
   and confirmed the word through accompanying signs.

The Gospel of the Lord. All: **Praise to you, Lord Jesus Christ.**

Prayer over the Offerings

We offer sacrifice now in supplication, O Lord,
to honor the wondrous Ascension of your Son:
grant, we pray,
that through this most holy exchange
we, too, may rise up to the heavenly realms.
Through Christ our Lord. All: **Amen.**

Communion Antiphon (Matthew 28:20)
Behold, I am with you always,
even to the end of the age, alleluia.

Prayer after Communion
Almighty ever-living God,
who allow those on earth to celebrate divine mysteries,
grant, we pray,
that Christian hope may draw us onward
to where our nature is united with you.
Through Christ our Lord. All: **Amen.**

Seventh Sunday of Easter

May 17, 2015

Reflection on the Gospel
Jesus is not naive about sending out disciples. His lengthy prayer for them (and us) recognizes that there will be resistance ("the world hated them") to the word of truth. Nevertheless, Jesus' prayer assures us that we are never alone. We are one with each other in the Body of Christ. And one with Christ, his Father, and their Spirit. In spite of the hard work of proclaiming the Gospel and meeting resistance, disciples experience joy because their relationship with God is secure.

- *Jesus the proclamation of the Gospel that gives us great joy . . .*

—*Living Liturgy*™, *Seventh Sunday of Easter 2015*

Entrance Antiphon (Cf. Psalm 27[26]:7-9)
O Lord, hear my voice, for I have called to you;
of you my heart has spoken: Seek his face;
hide not your face from me, alleluia.

Collect

Graciously hear our supplications, O Lord,
so that we, who believe that the Savior of the human race
is with you in your glory,
may experience, as he promised,
until the end of the world,
his abiding presence among us.
Who lives and reigns with you in the unity of the Holy Spirit,
one God, for ever and ever. **All: Amen.**

In those places where the solemnity of the Ascension of the Lord has been transferred to the Seventh Sunday of Easter, the Mass and readings of the Ascension are used. See page 257.

Reading I (L 60-B) (Acts of the Apostles 1:15-17, 20a, 20c-26)

A reading from the Acts of the Apostles

It is necessary that one of the men who accompanied us become with us a witness to the resurrection.

Peter stood up in the midst of the brothers
   —there was a group of about one hundred and twenty persons
in the one place—.
He said, "My brothers,
   the Scripture had to be fulfilled
   which the Holy Spirit spoke beforehand
   through the mouth of David, concerning Judas,
   who was the guide for those who arrested Jesus.
He was numbered among us
   and was allotted a share in this ministry.

"For it is written in the Book of Psalms:
   May another take his office.

"Therefore, it is necessary that one of the men
   who accompanied us the whole time
   the Lord Jesus came and went among us,
   beginning from the baptism of John
   until the day on which he was taken up from us,
   become with us a witness to his resurrection."
So they proposed two, Judas called Barsabbas,
   who was also known as Justus, and Matthias.

Then they prayed,
> "You, Lord, who know the hearts of all,
> show which one of these two you have chosen
> to take the place in this apostolic ministry
> from which Judas turned away to go to his own place."

Then they gave lots to them, and the lot fell upon
> Matthias,
> and he was counted with the eleven apostles.

The word of the Lord. All: Thanks be to God.

Responsorial Psalm 103

The Lord has set his throne in heav-en.

Music: Jay F. Hunstiger, © 1990, administered by Liturgical Press. All rights reserved.

Psalm 103:1-2, 11-12, 19-20

℟. (19a) **The Lord has set his throne in heaven.**
  or: ℟. **Alleluia.**

Bless the LORD, O my soul;
  and all my being, bless his holy name.
Bless the LORD, O my soul,
  and forget not all his benefits. ℟.

For as the heavens are high above the earth,
  so surpassing is his kindness toward those who fear him.
As far as the east is from the west,
  so far has he put our transgressions from us. ℟.

The LORD has established his throne in heaven,
  and his kingdom rules over all.
Bless the LORD, all you his angels,
  you mighty in strength, who do his bidding. ℟.

Reading II (1 John 4:11-16)

A reading from the first Letter of Saint John

Whoever remains in love, remains in God, and God in them.

Beloved, if God so loved us,
  we also must love one another.
No one has ever seen God.
Yet, if we love one another, God remains in us,
  and his love is brought to perfection in us.

This is how we know that we remain in him and he in us,
  that he has given us of his Spirit.
Moreover, we have seen and testify
  that the Father sent his Son as savior of the world.
Whoever acknowledges that Jesus is the Son of God,
  God remains in him and he in God.
We have come to know and to believe in the love God
    has for us.
God is love, and whoever remains in love
  remains in God and God in him.

The word of the Lord. All: **Thanks be to God.**

Gospel (John 17:11b-19)
Alleluia (*See* John 14:18)
℣. Alleluia, alleluia. ℟. **Alleluia, alleluia.**
℣. I will not leave you orphans, says the Lord.
  I will come back to you, and your hearts will rejoice. ℟.

✠ A reading from the holy Gospel according to John

All: **Glory to you, O Lord.**

That they may be one just as we are one!

Lifting up his eyes to heaven, Jesus prayed, saying:
  "Holy Father, keep them in your name that you have
      given me,
  so that they may be one just as we are one.
When I was with them I protected them in your name
      that you gave me,
  and I guarded them, and none of them was lost
  except the son of destruction,
  in order that the Scripture might be fulfilled.
But now I am coming to you.

I speak this in the world
   so that they may share my joy completely.
I gave them your word, and the world hated them,
   because they do not belong to the world
   any more than I belong to the world.
I do not ask that you take them out of the world
   but that you keep them from the evil one.
They do not belong to the world
   any more than I belong to the world.
Consecrate them in the truth. Your word is truth.
As you sent me into the world,
   so I sent them into the world.
And I consecrate myself for them,
   so that they also may be consecrated in truth."
The Gospel of the Lord. All: **Praise to you, Lord Jesus Christ.**

Prayer over the Offerings
Accept, O Lord, the prayers of your faithful
with the sacrificial offerings,
that through these acts of devotedness
we may pass over to the glory of heaven.
Through Christ our Lord. All: **Amen.**

Communion Antiphon (John 17:22)
Father, I pray that they may be one
as we also are one, alleluia.

Prayer after Communion
Hear us, O God our Savior,
and grant us confidence,
that through these sacred mysteries
there will be accomplished in the body of the whole Church
what has already come to pass in Christ her Head.
Who lives and reigns for ever and ever. All: **Amen.**

Pentecost Sunday

VIGIL MASS Simple Form

May 23, 2015

The Mass of the Vigil of Pentecost is used on Saturday evening in those places where the Sunday obligation may be fulfilled on Saturday evening.

Entrance Antiphon (Romans 5:5; cf. 8:11)
The love of God has been poured into our hearts
through the Spirit of God dwelling within us, alleluia.

Collect
Almighty ever-living God,
who willed the Paschal Mystery
to be encompassed as a sign in fifty days,
grant that from out of the scattered nations
the confusion of many tongues
may be gathered by heavenly grace
into one great confession of your name.
Through our Lord Jesus Christ, your Son,
who lives and reigns with you in the unity of the Holy Spirit,
one God, for ever and ever. All: **Amen.**

Or:

Grant, we pray, almighty God,
that the splendor of your glory
may shine forth upon us
and that, by the bright rays of the Holy Spirit,
the light of your light may confirm the hearts
of those born again by your grace.
Through our Lord Jesus Christ, your Son,
who lives and reigns with you in the unity of the Holy Spirit,
one God, for ever and ever. All: **Amen.**

These readings are used at Saturday Evening Mass celebrated either before or after Evening Prayer I of Pentecost Sunday. The first of four options for the First Reading for this Mass is given here. Please see the others in the lectionary: Exodus 19:3-8a, 16-20b; Ezekiel 37:1-14; or Joel 3:1-5.

Reading I (L 62) A (Genesis 11:1-9)
A reading from the Book of Genesis

It was called Babel because there the Lord confused the speech of all the world.

The whole world spoke the same language, using the
 same words.
While the people were migrating in the east,
 they came upon a valley in the land of Shinar and
 settled there.
They said to one another,
 "Come, let us mold bricks and harden them with fire."
They used bricks for stone, and bitumen for mortar.
Then they said, "Come, let us build ourselves a city
 and a tower with its top in the sky,
 and so make a name for ourselves;
 otherwise we shall be scattered all over the earth."

The Lord came down to see the city and the tower
 that the people had built.
Then the Lord said: "If now, while they are one people,
 all speaking the same language,
 they have started to do this,
 nothing will later stop them from doing whatever they
 presume to do.
Let us then go down there and confuse their language,
 so that one will not understand what another says."
Thus the Lord scattered them from there all over the earth,
 and they stopped building the city.
That is why it was called Babel,
 because there the Lord confused the speech of all the
 world.
It was from that place that he scattered them all over the
 earth.

The word of the Lord. All: **Thanks be to God.**

Responsorial Psalm 104

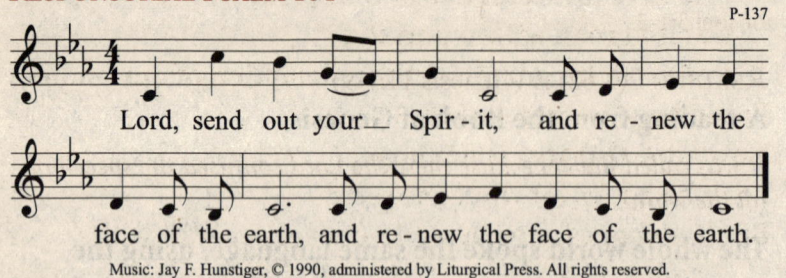

Lord, send out your Spirit, and renew the face of the earth, and renew the face of the earth.

Music: Jay F. Hunstiger, © 1990, administered by Liturgical Press. All rights reserved.

Psalm 104:1-2, 24, 35, 27-28, 29, 30

℟. *(See 30)* **Lord, send out your Spirit, and renew the face of the earth.** *or:* ℟. **Alleluia.**

Bless the LORD, O my soul!
    O LORD, my God, you are great indeed!
You are clothed with majesty and glory,
    robed in light as with a cloak. ℟.

How manifold are your works, O LORD!
    In wisdom you have wrought them all—
the earth is full of your creatures;
    bless the LORD, O my soul! Alleluia. ℟.

Creatures all look to you
    to give them food in due time.
When you give it to them, they gather it;
    when you open your hand, they are filled with good
        things. ℟.

If you take away their breath, they perish
    and return to their dust.
When you send forth your spirit, they are created,
    and you renew the face of the earth. ℟.

Reading II (Romans 8:22-27)

A reading from the Letter of Saint Paul to the Romans

The Spirit intercedes with inexpressible groanings.

Brothers and sisters:
We know that all creation is groaning in labor pains
    even until now;
    and not only that, but we ourselves,

> who have the firstfruits of the Spirit,
> we also groan within ourselves
> as we wait for adoption, the redemption of our bodies.
> For in hope we were saved.
> Now hope that sees is not hope.
> For who hopes for what one sees?
> But if we hope for what we do not see, we wait with endurance.
>
> In the same way, the Spirit too comes to the aid of our weakness;
> for we do not know how to pray as we ought,
> but the Spirit himself intercedes with inexpressible groanings.
> And the one who searches hearts
> knows what is the intention of the Spirit,
> because he intercedes for the holy ones
> according to God's will.

The word of the Lord. All: **Thanks be to God.**

Gospel (John 7:37-39)
Alleluia
℣. Alleluia, alleluia. ℟. **Alleluia, alleluia.**
℣. Come, Holy Spirit, fill the hearts of the faithful
and kindle in them the fire of your love. ℟.

✠ **A reading from the holy Gospel according to John**

All: **Glory to you, O Lord.**

Rivers of living water will flow.

On the last and greatest day of the feast,
   Jesus stood up and exclaimed,
   "Let anyone who thirsts come to me and drink.
As Scripture says:
   ***Rivers of living water will flow from within him** who
       believes in me."*
He said this in reference to the Spirit
   that those who came to believe in him were to receive.

There was, of course, no Spirit yet,
   because Jesus had not yet been glorified.

The Gospel of the Lord. All: **Praise to you, Lord Jesus Christ.**

PRAYER OVER THE OFFERINGS
Pour out upon these gifts the blessing of your Spirit,
we pray, O Lord,
so that through them your Church may be imbued with such love
that the truth of your saving mystery
may shine forth for the whole world.
Through Christ our Lord. All: **Amen.**

COMMUNION ANTIPHON (John 7:37)
On the last day of the festival, Jesus stood and cried out:
If anyone is thirsty, let him come to me and drink, alleluia.

PRAYER AFTER COMMUNION
May these gifts we have consumed
benefit us, O Lord,
that we may always be aflame with the same Spirit,
whom you wondrously poured out on your Apostles.
Through Christ our Lord. All: **Amen.**

DISMISSAL
To dismiss the people the Deacon or, if there is no Deacon, the Priest himself sings or says:

Go forth, the Mass is ended, alleluia, alleluia.

Or:

Go in peace, alleluia, alleluia.
All reply: **Thanks be to God, alleluia, alleluia.**

May 24

MASS DURING THE DAY

Reflection on the Gospel

We celebrate this Sunday a wondrous and unprecedented gift of God—"the Spirit of truth" given to us. This Spirit of truth changes us—through the Spirit we share a common identity as the Body of Christ and take up a common mission to proclaim the Gospel. The Spirit propels us to engage with the world in a new way: we testify to the mighty acts of God through the very way that we live. The truth God gives transforms us and, through us, transforms the world.

- The Spirit inspires us to . . .

—*Living Liturgy*™, *Pentecost 2015*

ENTRANCE ANTIPHON (Wisdom 1:7)
The Spirit of the Lord has filled the whole world
and that which contains all things
understands what is said, alleluia.

Or:

(Romans 5:5; cf. 8:11)
The love of God has been poured into our hearts
through the Spirit of God dwelling within us, alleluia.

COLLECT
O God, who by the mystery of today's great feast
sanctify your whole Church in every people and nation,
pour out, we pray, the gifts of the Holy Spirit
across the face of the earth
and, with the divine grace that was at work
when the Gospel was first proclaimed,
fill now once more the hearts of believers.
Through our Lord Jesus Christ, your Son,
who lives and reigns with you in the unity of the Holy Spirit,
one God, for ever and ever. **All: Amen.**

READING I (L 63) (Acts of the Apostles 2:1-11)
A reading from the Acts of the Apostles

They were all filled with the Holy Spirit and began to speak.

**When the time for Pentecost was fulfilled,
   they were all in one place together.
And suddenly there came from the sky
   a noise like a strong driving wind,
   and it filled the entire house in which they were.
Then there appeared to them tongues as of fire,
   which parted and came to rest on each one of them.
And they were all filled with the Holy Spirit
   and began to speak in different tongues,
   as the Spirit enabled them to proclaim.**

**Now there were devout Jews from every nation under
heaven staying in Jerusalem.
At this sound, they gathered in a large crowd,
but they were confused
because each one heard them speaking in his own
language.
They were astounded, and in amazement they asked,
"Are not all these people who are speaking Galileans?
Then how does each of us hear them in his native language?
We are Parthians, Medes, and Elamites,
inhabitants of Mesopotamia, Judea and Cappadocia,
Pontus and Asia, Phrygia and Pamphylia,
Egypt and the districts of Libya near Cyrene,
as well as travelers from Rome,
both Jews and converts to Judaism, Cretans and Arabs,
yet we hear them speaking in our own tongues
of the mighty acts of God."

The word of the Lord. All: Thanks be to God.**

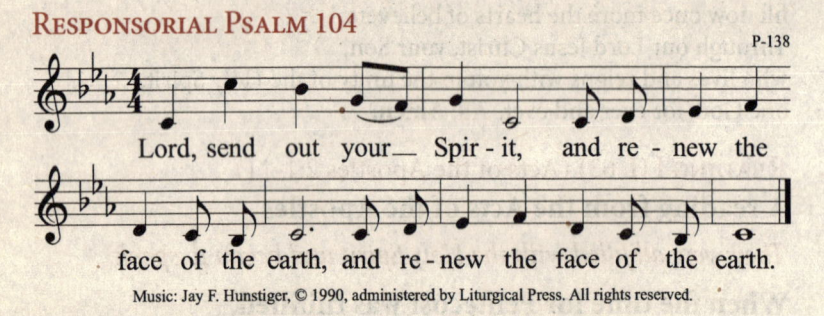

Responsorial Psalm 104

Lord, send out your Spirit, and renew the face of the earth, and renew the face of the earth.

Music: Jay F. Hunstiger, © 1990, administered by Liturgical Press. All rights reserved.

Psalm 104:1, 24, 29-30, 31, 34

℟. (*See* 30) **Lord, send out your Spirit, and renew the face of the earth.** *or:* ℟. **Alleluia.**

Bless the LORD, O my soul!
　O LORD, my God, you are great indeed!
How manifold are your works, O LORD!
　The earth is full of your creatures. ℟.

If you take away their breath, they perish
　and return to their dust.

When you send forth your spirit, they are created,
> and you renew the face of the earth. ℟.

May the glory of the Lord endure forever;
> may the Lord be glad in his works!

Pleasing to him be my theme;
> I will be glad in the Lord. ℟.

Reading II

A (1 Corinthians 12:3b-7, 12-13)

A reading from the first Letter of Saint Paul to the Corinthians

In one Spirit we were all baptized into one body.

Brothers and sisters:
No one can say, "Jesus is Lord," except by the Holy Spirit.

There are different kinds of spiritual gifts but the same Spirit;
> **there are different forms of service but the same Lord;**
> **there are different workings but the same God**
> **who produces all of them in everyone.**

To each individual the manifestation of the Spirit
> **is given for some benefit.**

As a body is one though it has many parts,
> **and all the parts of the body, though many, are one body,**
> **so also Christ.**

For in one Spirit we were all baptized into one body,
> **whether Jews or Greeks, slaves or free persons,**
> **and we were all given to drink of one Spirit.**

The word of the Lord. All: **Thanks be to God.**

Or:

B (Galatians 5:16-25)

A reading from the Letter of Saint Paul to the Galatians

The fruit of the Spirit.

Brothers and sisters, live by the Spirit
> **and you will certainly not gratify the desire of the flesh.**

For the flesh has desires against the Spirit,
 and the Spirit against the flesh;
 these are opposed to each other,
 so that you may not do what you want.
But if you are guided by the Spirit, you are not under the law.
Now the works of the flesh are obvious:
 immorality, impurity, lust, idolatry,
 sorcery, hatreds, rivalry, jealousy,
 outbursts of fury, acts of selfishness,
 dissensions, factions, occasions of envy,
 drinking bouts, orgies, and the like.
I warn you, as I warned you before,
 that those who do such things will not inherit the kingdom of God.
In contrast, the fruit of the Spirit is love, joy, peace,
 patience, kindness, generosity,
 faithfulness, gentleness, self-control.
Against such there is no law.
Now those who belong to Christ Jesus have crucified their flesh
 with its passions and desires.
If we live in the Spirit, let us also follow the Spirit.

The word of the Lord. All: Thanks be to God.

Sequence
Veni, Sancte Spiritus

Come, Holy Spirit, come!
And from your celestial home
 Shed a ray of light divine!
Come, Father of the poor!
Come, source of all our store!
 Come, within our bosoms shine.
You, of comforters the best;
You, the soul's most welcome guest;
 Sweet refreshment here below;

In our labor, rest most sweet;
Grateful coolness in the heat;
   Solace in the midst of woe.
O most blessed Light divine,
Shine within these hearts of yours,
   And our inmost being fill!
Where you are not, we have naught,
Nothing good in deed or thought,
   Nothing free from taint of ill.
Heal our wounds, our strength renew;
On our dryness pour your dew;
   Wash the stains of guilt away:
Bend the stubborn heart and will;
Melt the frozen, warm the chill;
   Guide the steps that go astray.
On the faithful, who adore
And confess you, evermore
   In your sevenfold gift descend;
Give them virtue's sure reward;
Give them your salvation, Lord;
   Give them joys that never end. Amen.
   Alleluia.

Gospel
Alleluia
℣. Alleluia, alleluia. ℟. **Alleluia, alleluia.**
℣. Come, Holy Spirit, fill the hearts of your faithful and kindle in them the fire of your love. ℟.

A (John 20:19-23)

✠ **A reading from the holy Gospel according to John**

All: **Glory to you, O Lord.**

As the Father sent me, so I send you: Receive the Holy Spirit.

On the evening of that first day of the week,
   when the doors were locked, where the disciples were,
   for fear of the Jews,

Jesus came and stood in their midst
and said to them, "Peace be with you."
When he had said this, he showed them his hands and
his side.
The disciples rejoiced when they saw the Lord.
Jesus said to them again, "Peace be with you.
As the Father has sent me, so I send you."
And when he had said this, he breathed on them and
said to them,
"Receive the Holy Spirit.
Whose sins you forgive are forgiven them,
and whose sins you retain are retained."

The Gospel of the Lord. All: **Praise to you, Lord Jesus Christ.**

Or:

B (John 15:26-27; 16:12-15)

☩ **A reading from the holy Gospel according to John**

All: **Glory to you, O Lord.**

The Spirit of truth will guide you to all the truth.

Jesus said to his disciples:
"When the Advocate comes whom I will send you
from the Father,
the Spirit of truth that proceeds from the Father,
he will testify to me.
And you also testify,
because you have been with me from the beginning.

"I have much more to tell you, but you cannot bear it now.
But when he comes, the Spirit of truth,
he will guide you to all truth.
He will not speak on his own,
but he will speak what he hears,
and will declare to you the things that are coming.
He will glorify me,
because he will take from what is mine and declare it
to you.

Everything that the Father has is mine;
> for this reason I told you that he will take from what is mine
> and declare it to you."

The Gospel of the Lord. All: **Praise to you, Lord Jesus Christ.**

If it is customary or obligatory for the faithful to attend Mass on the Monday or even the Tuesday after Pentecost, the readings from the Mass of Pentecost Sunday may be repeated or the readings of the Ritual Mass for Confirmation, nos. 764–768, may be used in its place.

Prayer over the Offerings
Grant, we pray, O Lord,
that, as promised by your Son,
the Holy Spirit may reveal to us more abundantly
the hidden mystery of this sacrifice
and graciously lead us into all truth.
Through Christ our Lord. All: **Amen.**

Communion Antiphon (Acts of the Apostles 2:4, 11)
They were all filled with the Holy Spirit
and spoke of the marvels of God, alleluia.

Prayer after Communion
O God, who bestow heavenly gifts upon your Church,
safeguard, we pray, the grace you have given,
that the gift of the Holy Spirit poured out upon her
may retain all its force
and that this spiritual food
may gain her abundance of eternal redemption.
Through Christ our Lord. All: **Amen.**

Dismissal
To dismiss the people the Deacon or, if there is no Deacon, the Priest himself sings or says:

Go forth, the Mass is ended, alleluia, alleluia.

Or:

Go in peace, alleluia, alleluia.
All reply: **Thanks be to God, alleluia, alleluia.**

The Most Holy Trinity

May 31, 2015

Reflection on the Gospel

In this gospel passage for the solemnity of the Most Holy Trinity, Jesus commands the disciples to baptize "in the name of the Father, and of the Son, and of the Holy Spirit." Jesus reveals his undivided, divine relationship with the Father when he declares, "All power in heaven and on earth has been given to me." Baptism professes our faith in the Holy Trinity and celebrates our insertion into the intimate, relational life of Father, Son, and Holy Spirit.

- *When I . . . I profess my faith in the Holy Trinity.*

—*Living Liturgy™, Trinity Sunday 2015*

ENTRANCE ANTIPHON

Blest be God the Father,
and the Only Begotten Son of God,
and also the Holy Spirit,
for he has shown us his merciful love.

COLLECT

God our Father, who by sending into the world
the Word of truth and the Spirit of sanctification
made known to the human race your wondrous mystery,
grant us, we pray, that in professing the true faith,
we may acknowledge the Trinity of eternal glory
and adore your Unity, powerful in majesty.
Through our Lord Jesus Christ, your Son,
who lives and reigns with you in the unity of the Holy Spirit,
one God, for ever and ever. All: **Amen.**

READING I (L 165-B) (Deuteronomy 4:32-34, 39-40)

A reading from the Book of Deuteronomy

The Lord is God in the heavens above and on earth below and there is no other.

Moses said to the people:
"Ask now of the days of old, before your time,
ever since God created man upon the earth;
ask from one end of the sky to the other:
Did anything so great ever happen before?
Was it ever heard of?
Did a people ever hear the voice of God
speaking from the midst of fire, as you did, and live?
Or did any god venture to go and take a nation for himself
from the midst of another nation,
by testings, by signs and wonders, by war,
with strong hand and outstretched arm, and by great terrors,
all of which the Lord, your God,
did for you in Egypt before your very eyes?
This is why you must now know,
and fix in your heart, that the Lord is God
in the heavens above and on earth below,
and that there is no other.
You must keep his statutes and commandments that I enjoin on you today,
that you and your children after you may prosper,
and that you may have long life on the land
which the Lord, your God, is giving you forever."

The word of the Lord. **All:** Thanks be to God.

RESPONSIVE PSALM 33

Blessed the people the Lord has chosen to be his own.

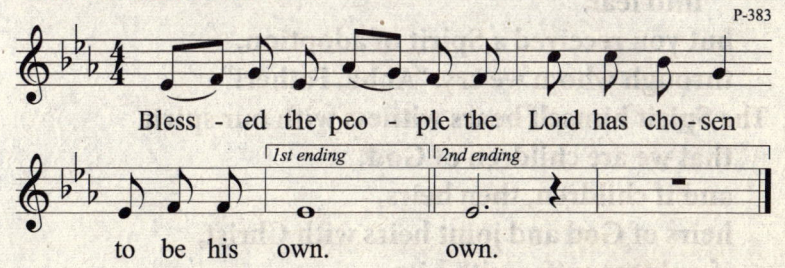

Music: Jay F. Hunstiger, © 1991, administered by Liturgical Press. All rights reserved.

Psalm 33:4-5, 6, 9, 18-19, 20, 22

℟. (12b) **Blessed the people the Lord has chosen to be his own.**

Upright is the word of the Lord,
 and all his works are trustworthy.
He loves justice and right;
 of the kindness of the Lord the earth is full. ℟.

By the word of the Lord the heavens were made;
 by the breath of his mouth all their host.
For he spoke, and it was made;
 he commanded, and it stood forth. ℟.

See, the eyes of the Lord are upon those who fear him,
 upon those who hope for his kindness,
to deliver them from death
 and preserve them in spite of famine. ℟.

Our soul waits for the Lord,
 who is our help and our shield.
May your kindness, O Lord, be upon us
 who have put our hope in you. ℟.

Reading II (Romans 8:14-17)

A reading from the Letter of Saint Paul to the Romans

You received a Spirit of adoption, through whom we cry, "Abba, Father!"

**Brothers and sisters:
Those who are led by the Spirit of God are sons of God.
For you did not receive a spirit of slavery to fall back into fear,
 but you received a Spirit of adoption,
 through whom we cry, "Abba, Father!"
The Spirit himself bears witness with our spirit
 that we are children of God,
 and if children, then heirs,
 heirs of God and joint heirs with Christ,
 if only we suffer with him
 so that we may also be glorified with him.

The word of the Lord.** All: **Thanks be to God.**

Gospel (Matthew 28:16-20)
Alleluia (Revelation 1:8)
℣. Alleluia, alleluia. ℟. **Alleluia, alleluia.**
℣. Glory to the Father, the Son, and the Holy Spirit;
to God who is, who was, and who is to come. ℟.

✠ **A reading from the holy Gospel according to Matthew**

All: **Glory to you, O Lord.**

Baptizing them in the name of the Father, and of the Son, and of the Holy Spirit.

The eleven disciples went to Galilee,
  to the mountain to which Jesus had ordered them.
When they all saw him, they worshiped, but they doubted.
Then Jesus approached and said to them,
  "All power in heaven and on earth has been given to me.
Go, therefore, and make disciples of all nations,
  baptizing them in the name of the Father,
  and of the Son, and of the Holy Spirit,
  teaching them to observe all that I have commanded
    you.
And behold, I am with you always, until the end of the age."
The Gospel of the Lord. All: **Praise to you, Lord Jesus Christ.**

Prayer over the Offerings
Sanctify by the invocation of your name,
we pray, O Lord our God,
this oblation of our service,
and by it make of us an eternal offering to you.
Through Christ our Lord. All: **Amen.**

Communion Antiphon (Galatians 4:6)
Since you are children of God,
God has sent into your hearts the Spirit of his Son,
the Spirit who cries out: Abba, Father.

Prayer after Communion
May receiving this Sacrament, O Lord our God,
bring us health of body and soul,
as we confess your eternal holy Trinity and undivided Unity.
Through Christ our Lord. All: **Amen.**

The Most Holy Body and Blood of Christ

June 7, 2015

Reflection on the Gospel

The annual Passover meal celebrates the Jewish people "passing over" from lives of slavery and drudgery in Egypt to lives of freedom and abundance in the Promised Land. This meal portends another passover—Jesus' own passing over from suffering and death to risen Life. And yet another passover: our passing over from old self to new self, from life of sin to life of grace. Each Eucharist, each time we eat and drink the Body and Blood of Christ, we embrace anew our passing over to new Life in Christ.

- *Each time I eat and drink the Body and Blood of Christ, I . . .*

—Living Liturgy™, *Body and Blood of Christ 2015*

ENTRANCE ANTIPHON (Cf. Psalm 81[80]:17)

He fed them with the finest wheat
and satisfied them with honey from the rock.

COLLECT

O God, who in this wonderful Sacrament
have left us a memorial of your Passion,
grant us, we pray,
so to revere the sacred mysteries of your Body and Blood
that we may always experience in ourselves
the fruits of your redemption.
Who live and reign with God the Father
in the unity of the Holy Spirit,
one God, for ever and ever. All: **Amen.**

READING I (L 168-B) (Exodus 24:3-8)

A reading from the Book of Exodus

This is the blood of the covenant that the Lord has made with you.

**When Moses came to the people
and related all the words and ordinances of the L**ORD**,**

they all answered with one voice,
"We will do everything that the Lord has told us."
Moses then wrote down all the words of the Lord and,
rising early the next day,
he erected at the foot of the mountain an altar
and twelve pillars for the twelve tribes of Israel.
Then, having sent certain young men of the Israelites
to offer holocausts and sacrifice young bulls
as peace offerings to the Lord,
Moses took half of the blood and put it in large bowls;
the other half he splashed on the altar.
Taking the book of the covenant, he read it aloud to the people,
who answered, "All that the Lord has said, we will heed and do."
Then he took the blood and sprinkled it on the people, saying,
"This is the blood of the covenant
that the Lord has made with you
in accordance with all these words of his."

The word of the Lord. All: Thanks be to God.

Responsorial Psalm 116

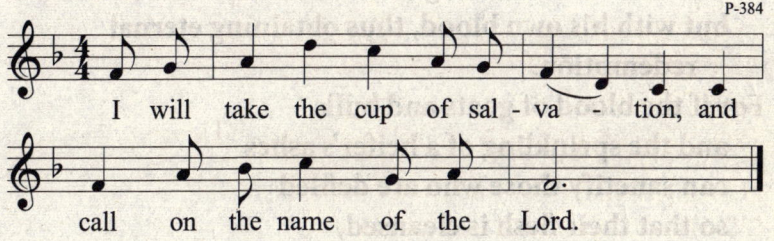

I will take the cup of sal-va-tion, and call on the name of the Lord.

Music: Jay F. Hunstiger, © 1990, administered by Liturgical Press. All rights reserved.

Psalm 116:12-13, 15-16, 17-18

℟. (13) **I will take the cup of salvation, and call on the name of the Lord.** *or:* ℟. **Alleluia.**

How shall I make a return to the Lord
for all the good he has done for me?

(continued)

The cup of salvation I will take up,
  and I will call upon the name of the Lord. ℟.

Precious in the eyes of the Lord
  is the death of his faithful ones.
I am your servant, the son of your handmaid;
  you have loosed my bonds. ℟.

To you will I offer sacrifice of thanksgiving,
  and I will call upon the name of the Lord.
My vows to the Lord I will pay
  in the presence of all his people. ℟.

Reading II (Hebrews 9:11-15)

A reading from the Letter to the Hebrews

The blood of Christ will cleanse our consciences.

**Brothers and sisters:
When Christ came as high priest
  of the good things that have come to be,
    passing through the greater and more perfect
      tabernacle
    not made by hands, that is, not belonging to this
      creation,
  he entered once for all into the sanctuary,
  not with the blood of goats and calves
  but with his own blood, thus obtaining eternal
    redemption.
For if the blood of goats and bulls
  and the sprinkling of a heifer's ashes
  can sanctify those who are defiled
  so that their flesh is cleansed,
  how much more will the blood of Christ,
  who through the eternal Spirit offered himself
    unblemished to God,
  cleanse our consciences from dead works
  to worship the living God.
For this reason he is mediator of a new covenant:
  since a death has taken place for deliverance**

from transgressions under the first covenant,
those who are called may receive the promised eternal inheritance.

The word of the Lord. **All:** Thanks be to God.

Sequence
Lauda Sion

The sequence *Laud, O Zion (Lauda Sion)*, or the shorter form beginning with the verse *Lo! the angel's food is given*, may be sung optionally before the Alleluia.

Laud, O Zion, your salvation,
Laud with hymns of exultation,
    Christ, your king and shepherd true:

Bring him all the praise you know,
He is more than you bestow.
    Never can you reach his due.

Special theme for glad thanksgiving
Is the quick'ning and the living
    Bread today before you set:

From his hands of old partaken,
As we know, by faith unshaken,
    Where the Twelve at supper met.

Full and clear ring out your chanting,
Joy nor sweetest grace be wanting,
    From your heart let praises burst:

For today the feast is holden,
When the institution olden
    Of that supper was rehearsed.

Here the new law's new oblation,
By the new king's revelation,
    Ends the form of ancient rite:

Now the new the old effaces,
Truth away the shadow chases,
    Light dispels the gloom of night.

What he did at supper seated,
Christ ordained to be repeated,
   His memorial ne'er to cease:

And his rule for guidance taking,
Bread and wine we hallow, making
   Thus our sacrifice of peace.

This the truth each Christian learns,
Bread into his flesh he turns,
   To his precious blood the wine:

Sight has fail'd, nor thought conceives,
But a dauntless faith believes,
   Resting on a pow'r divine.

Here beneath these signs are hidden
Priceless things to sense forbidden;
   Signs, not things are all we see:

Blood is poured and flesh is broken,
Yet in either wondrous token
   Christ entire we know to be.

Whoso of this food partakes,
Does not rend the Lord nor breaks;
   Christ is whole to all that taste:

Thousands are, as one, receivers,
One, as thousands of believers,
   Eats of him who cannot waste.

Bad and good the feast are sharing,
Of what divers dooms preparing,
   Endless death, or endless life.

Life to these, to those damnation,
See how like participation
   Is with unlike issues rife.

When the sacrament is broken,
Doubt not, but believe 'tis spoken,
   That each sever'd outward token
     doth the very whole contain.

Nought the precious gift divides,
Breaking but the sign betides
   Jesus still the same abides,
      still unbroken does remain.

The shorter form of the sequence begins here.

Lo! the angel's food is given
To the pilgrim who has striven;
   See the children's bread from heaven,
      which on dogs may not be spent.

Truth the ancient types fulfilling,
Isaac bound, a victim willing,
   Paschal lamb, its lifeblood spilling,
      manna to the fathers sent.

Very bread, good shepherd, tend us,
Jesu, of your love befriend us,
   You refresh us, you defend us,
   Your eternal goodness send us
In the land of life to see.

You who all things can and know,
Who on earth such food bestow,
   Grant us with your saints, though lowest,
   Where the heav'nly feast you show,
Fellow heirs and guests to be. Amen. Alleluia.

GOSPEL (Mark 14:12-16, 22-26)
ALLELUIA (John 6:51)
℣. Alleluia, alleluia.   ℟. **Alleluia, alleluia.**
℣. I am the living bread that came down from heaven,
    says the Lord;
  whoever eats this bread will live forever. ℟.

✠ A reading from the holy Gospel according to Mark

All: **Glory to you, O Lord.**

This is my body. This is my blood.

On the first day of the Feast of Unleavened Bread,
   when they sacrificed the Passover lamb,

Jesus' disciples said to him,
"Where do you want us to go
and prepare for you to eat the Passover?"
He sent two of his disciples and said to them,
"Go into the city and a man will meet you,
carrying a jar of water.
Follow him.
Wherever he enters, say to the master of the house,
'The Teacher says, "Where is my guest room
where I may eat the Passover with my disciples?"'
Then he will show you a large upper room furnished and
ready.
Make the preparations for us there."
The disciples then went off, entered the city,
and found it just as he had told them;
and they prepared the Passover.

While they were eating,
he took bread, said the blessing,
broke it, gave it to them, and said,
"Take it; this is my body."
Then he took a cup, gave thanks, and gave it to them,
and they all drank from it.
He said to them,
"This is my blood of the covenant,
which will be shed for many.
Amen, I say to you,
I shall not drink again the fruit of the vine
until the day when I drink it new in the kingdom of
God."
Then, after singing a hymn,
they went out to the Mount of Olives.

The Gospel of the Lord. All: **Praise to you, Lord Jesus Christ.**

Prayer over the Offerings
Grant your Church, O Lord, we pray,
the gifts of unity and peace,

whose signs are to be seen in mystery
in the offerings we here present.
Through Christ our Lord. All: **Amen.**

Communion Antiphon (John 6:57)
Whoever eats my flesh and drinks my blood
remains in me and I in him, says the Lord.

Prayer after Communion
Grant, O Lord, we pray,
that we may delight for all eternity
in that share in your divine life,
which is foreshadowed in the present age
by our reception of your precious Body and Blood.
Who live and reign for ever and ever. All: **Amen.**

Eleventh Sunday in Ordinary Time

June 14, 2015

Reflection on the Gospel

In this gospel both the land and the mustard seed actualize their potential—they do what by nature they are created to do. The "kingdom of God" is visible when we, like the land and mustard seed, actualize our own potential and do what we are called to do as Jesus' disciples. What are we to do? Hear God's word, nurture it in the fertile soil of our hearts, and let it sprout good works. In this way we become living parables doing what God created us to do.

• *The Kingdom of God lives . . .*

—Living Liturgy™, *Eleventh Sunday in Ordinary Time 2015*

Entrance Antiphon (Cf. Ps 27[26]:7, 9)
O Lord, hear my voice, for I have called to you; be my help.
Do not abandon or forsake me, O God, my Savior!

Collect

O God, strength of those who hope in you,
graciously hear our pleas,
and, since without you mortal frailty can do nothing,
grant us always the help of your grace,
that in following your commands
we may please you by our resolve and our deeds.
Through our Lord Jesus Christ, your Son,
who lives and reigns with you in the unity of the Holy Spirit,
one God, for ever and ever. All: **Amen.**

Reading I (L 92-B) (Ezekiel 17:22-24)

A reading from the Book of the Prophet Ezekiel

I have lifted high the lowly tree.

Thus says the Lord God:
   I, too, will take from the crest of the cedar,
      from its topmost branches tear off a tender shoot,
and plant it on a high and lofty mountain;
      on the mountain heights of Israel I will plant it.
It shall put forth branches and bear fruit,
      and become a majestic cedar.
Birds of every kind shall dwell beneath it,
      every winged thing in the shade of its boughs.
And all the trees of the field shall know
      that I, the Lord,
bring low the high tree,
      lift high the lowly tree,
wither up the green tree,
      and make the withered tree bloom.
As I, the Lord, have spoken, so will I do.

The word of the Lord. All: **Thanks be to God.**

Responsorial Psalm 92

Lord, it is good to give thanks to you.

Music: Jay F. Hunstiger, © 1990, administered by Liturgical Press. All rights reserved.

Psalm 92:2-3, 13-14, 15-16

℟. (See 2a) **Lord, it is good to give thanks to you.**

> It is good to give thanks to the Lord,
>> to sing praise to your name, Most High,
>
> To proclaim your kindness at dawn
>> and your faithfulness throughout the night. ℟.
>
> The just one shall flourish like the palm tree,
>> like a cedar of Lebanon shall he grow.
>
> They that are planted in the house of the Lord
>> shall flourish in the courts of our God. ℟.
>
> They shall bear fruit even in old age;
>> vigorous and sturdy shall they be,
>
> Declaring how just is the Lord,
>> my rock, in whom there is no wrong. ℟.

Reading II (2 Corinthians 5:6-10)

A reading from the second Letter of Saint Paul to the Corinthians

Whether we are at home or away, we aspire to please the Lord.

Brothers and sisters:
We are always courageous,
> **although we know that while we are at home in the body**
> **we are away from the Lord,**
> **for we walk by faith, not by sight.**

Yet we are courageous,
> **and we would rather leave the body and go home to the Lord.**

Therefore, we aspire to please him,
> **whether we are at home or away.**

For we must all appear before the judgment seat of Christ,
> **so that each may receive recompense,**
>> **according to what he did in the body, whether good or evil.**

The word of the Lord. All: **Thanks be to God.**

Gospel (Mark 4:26-34)

Alleluia

℣. Alleluia, alleluia. ℟. **Alleluia, alleluia.**
℣. The seed is the word of God, Christ is the sower.
All who come to him will live for ever. ℟.

☩ A reading from the holy Gospel according to Mark

All: **Glory to you, O Lord.**

It is the smallest of all seeds, and becomes the largest of plants.

Jesus said to the crowds:
"This is how it is with the kingdom of God;
it is as if a man were to scatter seed on the land
and would sleep and rise night and day
and through it all the seed would sprout and grow,
he knows not how.
Of its own accord the land yields fruit,
first the blade, then the ear, then the full grain in the ear.
And when the grain is ripe, he wields the sickle at once,
for the harvest has come."

He said,
"To what shall we compare the kingdom of God,
or what parable can we use for it?
It is like a mustard seed that, when it is sown in the ground,
is the smallest of all the seeds on the earth.
But once it is sown, it springs up and becomes the largest of plants
and puts forth large branches,
so that the birds of the sky can dwell in its shade."
With many such parables
he spoke the word to them as they were able to understand it.
Without parables he did not speak to them,
but to his own disciples he explained everything in private.

The Gospel of the Lord. All: **Praise to you, Lord Jesus Christ.**

Prayer over the Offerings
O God, who in the offerings presented here
provide for the twofold needs of human nature,
nourishing us with food
and renewing us with your Sacrament,
grant, we pray,
that the sustenance they provide
may not fail us in body or in spirit.
Through Christ our Lord. All: **Amen.**

Communion Antiphon (Psalm 27[26]:4)
There is one thing I ask of the Lord, only this do I seek:
to live in the house of the Lord all the days of my life.

Or:

(John 17:11)
Holy Father, keep in your name those you have given me,
that they may be one as we are one, says the Lord.

Prayer after Communion
As this reception of your Holy Communion, O Lord,
foreshadows the union of the faithful in you,
so may it bring about unity in your Church.
Through Christ our Lord. All: **Amen.**

Twelfth Sunday in Ordinary Time

June 21, 2015

Reflection on the Gospel

At the end of a day of preaching and healing, Jesus was no doubt tired. The disciples took him in the boat "just as he was." So, Jesus fell fast asleep. When a "violent squall" arose, the disciples thought that Jesus didn't care that they were "perishing." But Jesus did care; he came precisely to save humanity from perishing. The disciples' faith is weak because the disciples do not yet know who Jesus is and why he came. We, however, do. So how strong is our faith?

- *Faith in Jesus saves me by . . .*

—Living Liturgy™, *Twelfth Sunday in Ordinary Time 2015*

ENTRANCE ANTIPHON (Cf. Psalm 28[27]:8-9)
The Lord is the strength of his people,
a saving refuge for the one he has anointed.
Save your people, Lord, and bless your heritage,
and govern them for ever.

COLLECT
Grant, O Lord,
that we may always revere and love your holy name,
for you never deprive of your guidance
those you set firm on the foundation of your love.
Through our Lord Jesus Christ, your Son,
who lives and reigns with you in the unity of the Holy Spirit,
one God, for ever and ever. All: **Amen.**

READING I (L 95-B) (Job 38:1, 8-11)
A reading from the Book of Job

Here shall your proud waves be stilled!

**The Lord addressed Job out of the storm and said:
Who shut within doors the sea,
    when it burst forth from the womb;**

when I made the clouds its garment
   and thick darkness its swaddling bands?
When I set limits for it
   and fastened the bar of its door,
and said: Thus far shall you come but no farther,
   and here shall your proud waves be stilled!

The word of the Lord. All: Thanks be to God.

Responsorial Psalm 107

Give thanks to the Lord, his love is ev-er-last-ing.

Music: Jay F. Hunstiger, © 1990, administered by Liturgical Press. All rights reserved.

Psalm 107:23-24, 25-26, 28-29, 30-31

℟. (1b) **Give thanks to the Lord, his love is everlasting.**
   or: ℟. **Alleluia.**

They who sailed the sea in ships,
   trading on the deep waters,
these saw the works of the Lord
   and his wonders in the abyss. ℟.

His command raised up a storm wind
   which tossed its waves on high.
They mounted up to heaven; they sank to the depths;
   their hearts melted away in their plight. ℟.

They cried to the Lord in their distress;
   from their straits he rescued them,
He hushed the storm to a gentle breeze,
   and the billows of the sea were stilled. ℟.

They rejoiced that they were calmed,
   and he brought them to their desired haven.
Let them give thanks to the Lord for his kindness
   and his wondrous deeds to the children of men. ℟.

Reading II (2 Corinthians 5:14-17)
A reading from the second Letter of Saint Paul to the Corinthians

Behold, new things have come.

Brothers and sisters:
The love of Christ impels us,
>   **once we have come to the conviction that one died for all;**
>   **therefore, all have died.**

He indeed died for all,
>   **so that those who live might no longer live for themselves**
>   **but for him who for their sake died and was raised.**

Consequently, from now on we regard no one according to the flesh;
>   **even if we once knew Christ according to the flesh,**
>   **yet now we know him so no longer.**

So whoever is in Christ is a new creation:
>   **the old things have passed away;**
>   **behold, new things have come.**

The word of the Lord. All: **Thanks be to God.**

Gospel (Mark 4:35-41)
Alleluia (Luke 7:16)
℣. Alleluia, alleluia. ℟. **Alleluia, alleluia.**
℣. A great prophet has risen in our midst
   God has visited his people. ℟.

✚ **A reading from the holy Gospel according to Mark**

All: **Glory to you, O Lord.**

Who is this whom even wind and sea obey?

On that day, as evening drew on, Jesus said to his disciples:
>   **"Let us cross to the other side."**
Leaving the crowd, they took Jesus with them in the boat
>   **just as he was.**
And other boats were with him.

A violent squall came up and waves were breaking over
    the boat,
  so that it was already filling up.
Jesus was in the stern, asleep on a cushion.
They woke him and said to him,
  "Teacher, do you not care that we are perishing?"
He woke up,
    rebuked the wind, and said to the sea, "Quiet! Be still!"
The wind ceased and there was great calm.
Then he asked them, "Why are you terrified?
Do you not yet have faith?"
They were filled with great awe and said to one another,
  "Who then is this whom even wind and sea obey?"

The Gospel of the Lord. All: **Praise to you, Lord Jesus Christ.**

Prayer over the Offerings
Receive, O Lord, the sacrifice of conciliation and praise
and grant that, cleansed by its action,
we may make offering of a heart pleasing to you.
Through Christ our Lord. All: **Amen.**

Communion Antiphon (Psalm 145[144]:15)
The eyes of all look to you, Lord,
and you give them their food in due season.

Or:

(John 10:11, 15)
I am the Good Shepherd,
and I lay down my life for my sheep, says the Lord.

Prayer after Communion
Renewed and nourished
by the Sacred Body and Precious Blood of your Son,
we ask of your mercy, O Lord,
that what we celebrate with constant devotion
may be our sure pledge of redemption.
Through Christ our Lord. All: **Amen.**

The Nativity of St. John the Baptist

AT THE VIGIL MASS

Tuesday Evening
June 23, 2015

Reflection on the Gospel

Elizabeth and Zechariah carried out God's will when they named their newborn son John as the angel commanded. John, too, carried out God's will when he heralded the coming of the Messiah. So do we carry out God's will when we herald the presence of Jesus, call others to repentance as did John, and faithfully bear the name bestowed on us by our baptism: Christ. Identified with Christ at baptism and carrying his name, we are most ourselves when we also are obedient to God's will.

• *I herald the Kingdom of God by . . .*

—Living Liturgy™, *Nativity of John the Baptist 2015*

Entrance Antiphon (Luke 1:15, 14)
He will be great in the sight of the Lord
and will be filled with the Holy Spirit,
even from his mother's womb;
and many will rejoice at his birth.

Collect
Grant, we pray, almighty God,
that your family may walk in the way of salvation
and, attentive to what Saint John the Precursor urged,
may come safely to the One he foretold,
our Lord Jesus Christ.
Who lives and reigns with you in the unity of the Holy Spirit,
one God, for ever and ever. All: **Amen.**

Reading I (L 586) (Jeremiah 1:4-10)
A reading from the Book of the Prophet Jeremiah

Before I formed you in the womb I knew you.

In the days of King Josiah, the word of the LORD came to me, saying:

**Before I formed you in the womb I knew you,
before you were born I dedicated you,
a prophet to the nations I appointed you.**

**"Ah, Lord GOD!" I said,
"I know not how to speak; I am too young."
But the LORD answered me,
Say not, "I am too young."
To whomever I send you, you shall go;
whatever I command you, you shall speak.
Have no fear before them,
because I am with you to deliver you, says the LORD.**

Then the LORD extended his hand and touched my mouth, saying,

**See, I place my words in your mouth!
This day I set you
over nations and over kingdoms,
to root up and to tear down,
to destroy and to demolish,
to build and to plant.**

The word of the Lord. All: **Thanks be to God.**

RESPONSORIAL PSALM 71

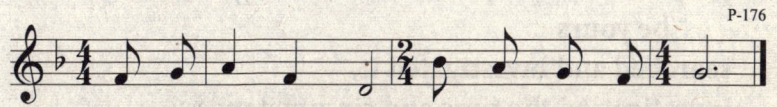

Since my mo-ther's womb, you have been my strength.

Music: Jay F. Hunstiger, © 2004, administered by Liturgical Press. All rights reserved.

Psalm 71:1-2, 3-4a, 5-6ab, 15ab and 17

℟. (6) **Since my mother's womb, you have been my strength.**

In you, O LORD, I take refuge;
let me never be put to shame.
In your justice rescue me, and deliver me;
incline your ear to me, and save me. ℟.

(continued)

Be my rock of refuge,
   a stronghold to give me safety,
   for you are my rock and my fortress.
O my God, rescue me from the hand of the wicked. R℣.

For you are my hope, O Lord;
   my trust, O Lord, from my youth.
On you I depend from birth;
   from my mother's womb you are my strength. R℣.

My mouth shall declare your justice,
   day by day your salvation.
O God, you have taught me from my youth,
   and till the present I proclaim your wondrous deeds. R℣.

Reading II (1 Peter 1:8-12)
A reading from the first Letter of Saint Peter

The prophets who prophesied about the grace that was to be yours searched and investigated it.

Beloved:
Although you have not seen Jesus Christ you love him;
   even though you do not see him now yet believe in him,
   you rejoice with an indescribable and glorious joy,
   as you attain the goal of your faith, the salvation of
      your souls.

Concerning this salvation,
   prophets who prophesied about the grace that was to
      be yours
   searched and investigated it,
   investigating the time and circumstances
   that the Spirit of Christ within them indicated
   when he testified in advance
   to the sufferings destined for Christ
   and the glories to follow them.
It was revealed to them that they were serving not
      themselves but you
   with regard to the things that have now been
      announced to you

by those who preached the good news to you
through the Holy Spirit sent from heaven,
things into which angels longed to look.

The word of the Lord. All: Thanks be to God.

Gospel (Luke 1:5-17)
Alleluia (See John 1:7; Luke 1:17)
℣. Alleluia, alleluia. ℟. **Alleluia, alleluia.**
℣. He came to testify to the light,
to prepare a people fit for the Lord. ℟.

✠ A reading from the holy Gospel according to Luke

All: **Glory to you, O Lord.**

Your wife Elizabeth will bear you a son and you shall name him John.

In the days of Herod, King of Judea,
there was a priest named Zechariah
of the priestly division of Abijah;
his wife was from the daughters of Aaron,
and her name was Elizabeth.
Both were righteous in the eyes of God,
observing all the commandments
and ordinances of the Lord blamelessly.
But they had no child, because Elizabeth was barren
and both were advanced in years.
Once when he was serving
as priest in his division's turn before God,
according to the practice of the priestly service,
he was chosen by lot
to enter the sanctuary of the Lord to burn incense.
Then, when the whole assembly of the people was
praying outside
at the hour of the incense offering,
the angel of the Lord appeared to him,
standing at the right of the altar of incense.
Zechariah was troubled by what he saw, and fear came
upon him.

But the angel said to him, "Do not be afraid, Zechariah,
   because your prayer has been heard.
Your wife Elizabeth will bear you a son,
   and you shall name him John.
And you will have joy and gladness,
   and many will rejoice at his birth,
   for he will be great in the sight of the Lord.
John will drink neither wine nor strong drink.
He will be filled with the Holy Spirit even from his
      mother's womb,
   and he will turn many of the children of Israel
   to the Lord their God.
He will go before him in the spirit and power of Elijah
   to turn their hearts toward their children
   and the disobedient to the understanding of the
      righteous,
   to prepare a people fit for the Lord."
The Gospel of the Lord. All: **Praise to you, Lord Jesus Christ.**

Prayer over the Offerings
Look with favor, O Lord,
upon the offerings made by your people
on the Solemnity of Saint John the Baptist,
and grant that what we celebrate in mystery
we may follow with deeds of devoted service.
Through Christ our Lord. All: **Amen.**

Communion Antiphon (Luke 1:68)
Blessed be the Lord, the God of Israel!
He has visited his people and redeemed them.

Prayer after Communion
May the marvelous prayer of Saint John the Baptist
accompany us who have eaten our fill
at this sacrificial feast, O Lord,
and, since Saint John proclaimed your Son
to be the Lamb who would take away our sins,
may he implore now for us your favor.
Through Christ our Lord. All: **Amen.**

Wednesday, June 24

AT THE MASS DURING THE DAY

Entrance Antiphon (John 1:6-7; Luke 1:17)
A man was sent from God, whose name was John.
He came to testify to the light,
to prepare a people fit for the Lord.

Collect
O God, who raised up Saint John the Baptist
to make ready a nation fit for Christ the Lord,
give your people, we pray,
the grace of spiritual joys
and direct the hearts of all the faithful
into the way of salvation and peace.
Through our Lord Jesus Christ, your Son,
who lives and reigns with you in the unity of the Holy Spirit,
one God, for ever and ever. All: **Amen.**

Reading I (L 587) (Isaiah 49:1-6)
A reading from the Book of the Prophet Isaiah

I will make you a light to the nations.

> Hear me, O coastlands,
>   listen, O distant peoples.
> The Lord called me from birth,
>   from my mother's womb he gave me my name.
> He made of me a sharp-edged sword
>   and concealed me in the shadow of his arm.
> He made me a polished arrow,
>   in his quiver he hid me.
> You are my servant, he said to me,
>   Israel, through whom I show my glory.
>
> Though I thought I had toiled in vain,
>   and for nothing, uselessly, spent my strength,
> yet my reward is with the Lord,
>   my recompense is with my God.
> For now the Lord has spoken
>   who formed me as his servant from the womb,

**that Jacob may be brought back to him
 and Israel gathered to him;
and I am made glorious in the sight of the LORD,
 and my God is now my strength!
It is too little, he says, for you to be my servant,
 to raise up the tribes of Jacob,
 and restore the survivors of Israel;
I will make you a light to the nations,
 that my salvation may reach to the ends of the earth.**

The word of the Lord. All: Thanks be to God.

RESPONSORIAL PSALM 139

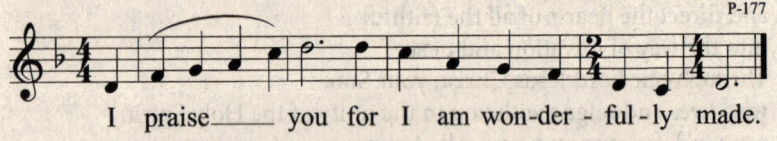

I praise you for I am won-der-ful-ly made.

Music: Jay F. Hunstiger, © 2004, administered by Liturgical Press. All rights reserved.

Psalm 139:1b-3, 13-14ab, 14c-15

℟. (14) **I praise you, for I am wonderfully made.**

O LORD, you have probed me, you know me;
 you know when I sit and when I stand;
 you understand my thoughts from afar.
My journeys and my rest you scrutinize,
 with all my ways you are familiar. ℟.

Truly you have formed my inmost being;
 you knit me in my mother's womb.
I give you thanks that I am fearfully, wonderfully made;
 wonderful are your works. ℟.

My soul also you knew full well;
 nor was my frame unknown to you
When I was made in secret,
 when I was fashioned in the depths of the earth. ℟.

READING II (Acts of the Apostles 13:22-26)

A reading from the Acts of the Apostles

John heralded his coming by proclaiming a baptism of repentance.

In those days, Paul said:
"God raised up David as king;
   of him God testified,
     I have found David, son of Jesse, a man after my own heart;
     he will carry out my every wish.
From this man's descendants God, according to his promise,
   has brought to Israel a savior, Jesus.
John heralded his coming by proclaiming a baptism of repentance
   to all the people of Israel;
   and as John was completing his course, he would say,
   'What do you suppose that I am? I am not he.
Behold, one is coming after me;
   I am not worthy to unfasten the sandals of his feet.'

"My brothers, sons of the family of Abraham,
   and those others among you who are God-fearing,
   to us this word of salvation has been sent."

The word of the Lord. All: **Thanks be to God.**

Gospel (Luke 1:57-66, 80)

Alleluia (Luke 1:76)

℣. Alleluia, alleluia. ℟. **Alleluia, alleluia.**
℣. You, child, will be called prophet of the Most High,
for you will go before the Lord to prepare his way. ℟.

✠ **A reading from the holy Gospel according to Luke**

All: **Glory to you, O Lord.**

John is his name.

When the time arrived for Elizabeth to have her child
   she gave birth to a son.
Her neighbors and relatives heard
   that the Lord had shown his great mercy toward her,
   and they rejoiced with her.

When they came on the eighth day to circumcise the child,
    they were going to call him Zechariah after his father,
    but his mother said in reply,
    "No. He will be called John."
But they answered her,
    "There is no one among your relatives who has this
        name."
So they made signs, asking his father what he wished
    him to be called.
He asked for a tablet and wrote, "John is his name,"
    and all were amazed.
Immediately his mouth was opened, his tongue freed,
    and he spoke blessing God.
Then fear came upon all their neighbors,
    and all these matters were discussed
        throughout the hill country of Judea.
All who heard these things took them to heart, saying,
    "What, then, will this child be?"
For surely the hand of the Lord was with him.

The child grew and became strong in spirit,
    and he was in the desert until the day
        of his manifestation to Israel.

The Gospel of the Lord. All: **Praise to you, Lord Jesus Christ.**

Prayer over the Offerings
We place these offerings on your altar, O Lord,
to celebrate with fitting honor the nativity of him
who both foretold the coming of the world's Savior
and pointed him out when he came.
Who lives and reigns for ever and ever. All: **Amen.**

Communion Antiphon (Cf. Luke 1:78)
Through the tender mercy of our God,
the Dawn from on high will visit us.

Prayer after Communion
Having feasted at the banquet of the heavenly Lamb,
we pray, O Lord,
that, finding joy in the nativity of Saint John the Baptist,

your Church may know as the author of her rebirth
the Christ whose coming John foretold.
Who lives and reigns for ever and ever. All: **Amen.**

Thirteenth Sunday in Ordinary Time

June 28, 2015

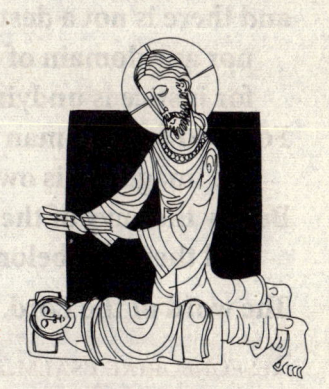

Reflection on the Gospel

Faith in who Jesus is and what he can do brings us to act. Jairus approaches Jesus directly, kneels before him, and asks for healing for his daughter. The "woman afflicted with hemorrhages" dares not approach Jesus directly; she simply wishes to "touch his clothes" to be cured. In both cases their faith gave them the courage to approach Jesus and raised their expectation that he had the power to heal. Our faith, too, gives us courage and expectation. What do we do with it?

- *With faith, touch the hem of his garment and . . .*

—Living Liturgy™, *Thirteenth Sunday in Ordinary Time 2015*

Entrance Antiphon (Psalm 47[46]:2)

All peoples, clap your hands.
Cry to God with shouts of joy!

Collect

O God, who through the grace of adoption
chose us to be children of light,
grant, we pray,
that we may not be wrapped in the darkness of error
but always be seen to stand in the bright light of truth.
Through our Lord Jesus Christ, your Son,
who lives and reigns with you in the unity of the Holy Spirit,
one God, for ever and ever. All: **Amen.**

Reading I (L 98-B) (Wisdom 1:13-15; 2:23-24)

A reading from the Book of Wisdom

By the envy of the devil, death entered the world.

God did not make death,
>   nor does he rejoice in the destruction of the living.
> For he fashioned all things that they might have being;
>   and the creatures of the world are wholesome,
> and there is not a destructive drug among them
>   nor any domain of the netherworld on earth,
>   for justice is undying.
> For God formed man to be imperishable;
>   the image of his own nature he made him.
> But by the envy of the devil, death entered the world,
>   and they who belong to his company experience it.

The word of the Lord. All: Thanks be to God.

Responsorial Psalm 30

I will praise you, Lord, for you have rescued me.

Music: Jay F. Hunstiger, © 1990, administered by Liturgical Press. All rights reserved.

Psalm 30:2, 4, 5-6, 11, 12, 13

℟. (2a) **I will praise you, Lord, for you have rescued me.**

> I will extol you, O Lord, for you drew me clear
>   and did not let my enemies rejoice over me.
> O Lord, you brought me up from the netherworld;
>   you preserved me from among those going down into
>   the pit. ℟.

> Sing praise to the Lord, you his faithful ones,
>   and give thanks to his holy name.
> For his anger lasts but a moment;
>   a lifetime, his good will.
> At nightfall, weeping enters in,
>   but with the dawn, rejoicing. ℟.

> Hear, O Lord, and have pity on me;
>   O Lord, be my helper.
> You changed my mourning into dancing;
>   O Lord, my God, forever will I give you thanks. ℟.

READING II (2 Corinthians 8:7, 9; 13-15)
A reading from the second Letter of Saint Paul to the Corinthians

Your abundance should supply the needs of the poor.

Brothers and sisters:
As you excel in every respect, in faith, discourse,
    knowledge, all earnestness, and in the love we have
        for you,
    may you excel in this gracious act also.

For you know the gracious act of our Lord Jesus Christ,
    that though he was rich, for your sake he became poor,
    so that by his poverty you might become rich.
Not that others should have relief while you are burdened,
    but that as a matter of equality
        your abundance at the present time should supply
            their needs,
    so that their abundance may also supply your needs,
    that there may be equality.
As it is written:
    Whoever had much did not have more,
        and whoever had little did not have less.

The word of the Lord. All: **Thanks be to God.**

GOSPEL (Mark 5:21-43) *or* Shorter Form [ ] (Mark 5:21-24, 35b-43)

ALLELUIA (*See* 2 Timothy 1:10)
℣. Alleluia, alleluia.   ℟. **Alleluia, alleluia.**
℣. Our Savior Jesus Christ destroyed death
    and brought life to light through the Gospel. ℟.

✠ **A reading from the holy Gospel according to Mark**

All: **Glory to you, O Lord.**

Little girl, I say to you, arise!

[When Jesus had crossed again in the boat
    to the other side,
    a large crowd gathered around him, and he stayed
        close to the sea.

One of the synagogue officials, named Jairus, came
 forward.
Seeing him he fell at his feet and pleaded earnestly with
 him, saying,
 "My daughter is at the point of death.
Please, come lay your hands on her
 that she may get well and live."
He went off with him,
 and a large crowd followed him and pressed upon
 him.]
There was a woman afflicted with hemorrhages for
 twelve years.
She had suffered greatly at the hands of many doctors
 and had spent all that she had.
Yet she was not helped but only grew worse.
She had heard about Jesus and came up behind him in
 the crowd
 and touched his cloak.
She said, "If I but touch his clothes, I shall be cured."
Immediately her flow of blood dried up.
She felt in her body that she was healed of her affliction.
Jesus, aware at once that power had gone out from him,
 turned around in the crowd and asked, "Who has
 touched my clothes?"
But his disciples said to Jesus,
 "You see how the crowd is pressing upon you,
 and yet you ask, 'Who touched me?'"
And he looked around to see who had done it.
The woman, realizing what had happened to her,
 approached in fear and trembling.
She fell down before Jesus and told him the whole truth.
He said to her, "Daughter, your faith has saved you.
Go in peace and be cured of your affliction."

[While he was still speaking,
>people from the synagogue official's house arrived
>>and said,
>"Your daughter has died; why trouble the teacher any
>>longer?"
Disregarding the message that was reported,
>Jesus said to the synagogue official,
>"Do not be afraid; just have faith."
He did not allow anyone to accompany him inside
>except Peter, James, and John, the brother of James.
When they arrived at the house of the synagogue official,
>he caught sight of a commotion,
>people weeping and wailing loudly.
So he went in and said to them,
>"Why this commotion and weeping?
The child is not dead but asleep."
And they ridiculed him.
Then he put them all out.
He took along the child's father and mother
>and those who were with him
>and entered the room where the child was.
He took the child by the hand and said to her, "*Talitha
>koum*,"
>which means, "Little girl, I say to you, arise!"
The girl, a child of twelve, arose immediately and walked
>around.
At that they were utterly astounded.
He gave strict orders that no one should know this
>and said that she should be given something to eat.]

The Gospel of the Lord. All: **Praise to you, Lord Jesus Christ.**

PRAYER OVER THE OFFERINGS
O God, who graciously accomplish
the effects of your mysteries,
grant, we pray,
that the deeds by which we serve you
may be worthy of these sacred gifts.
Through Christ our Lord. All: **Amen.**

COMMUNION ANTIPHON (Cf. Psalm 103[102]:1)
Bless the Lord, O my soul,
and all within me, his holy name.

Or:

(John 17:20-21)
O Father, I pray for them, that they may be one in us,
that the world may believe that you have sent me,
 says the Lord.

PRAYER AFTER COMMUNION
May this divine sacrifice we have offered and received
fill us with life, O Lord, we pray,
so that, bound to you in lasting charity,
we may bear fruit that lasts for ever.
Through Christ our Lord. All: **Amen.**

Fourteenth Sunday in Ordinary Time

July 5, 2015

Reflection on the Gospel

The limited expectations of those in Jesus' "native place" blocked their ability to see in faith who Jesus really was. In response to Jesus' teaching and wisdom, mighty deeds and healings, "they took offense." Their limited expectations limited Jesus' own ability to show that a new in-breaking of God was among them. This gospel challenges us to examine the limits of our own expectations about who Jesus is and what he can do for us.

• *We may think we really know Jesus but . . .*

—Living Liturgy™, *Fourteenth Sunday in Ordinary Time 2015*

Entrance Antiphon (Cf. Psalm 48[47]:10-11)
Your merciful love, O God,
we have received in the midst of your temple.
Your praise, O God, like your name,
reaches the ends of the earth;
your right hand is filled with saving justice.

Collect
O God, who in the abasement of your Son
have raised up a fallen world,
fill your faithful with holy joy,
for on those you have rescued from slavery to sin
you bestow eternal gladness.
Through our Lord Jesus Christ, your Son,
who lives and reigns with you in the unity of the Holy Spirit,
one God, for ever and ever. All: **Amen.**

Reading I (L 101-B) (Ezekiel 2:2-5)
A reading from the Book of the Prophet Ezekiel
They are a rebellious house but shall know that a prophet has been among them.

**As the Lord spoke to me, the spirit entered into me
and set me on my feet,
and I heard the one who was speaking say to me:
Son of man, I am sending you to the Israelites,
rebels who have rebelled against me;
they and their ancestors have revolted against me to this very day.
Hard of face and obstinate of heart
are they to whom I am sending you.
But you shall say to them: Thus says the Lord God!
And whether they heed or resist—for they are a rebellious house—
they shall know that a prophet has been among them.**

The word of the Lord. All: **Thanks be to God.**

Responsorial Psalm 123

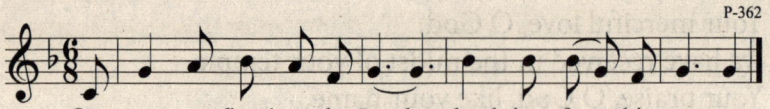

Our eyes are fixed on the Lord,— plead-ing for— his mer-cy.

Music: Jay F. Hunstiger, © 1990, administered by Liturgical Press. All rights reserved.

Psalm 123:1-2, 2, 3-4

℟. (2cd) **Our eyes are fixed on the Lord, pleading for his mercy.**

To you I lift up my eyes
 who are enthroned in heaven—
As the eyes of servants
 are on the hands of their masters. ℟.

As the eyes of a maid
 are on the hands of her mistress,
So are our eyes on the L{\sc ord}, our God,
 till he have pity on us. ℟.

Have pity on us, O L{\sc ord}, have pity on us,
 for we are more than sated with contempt;
our souls are more than sated
 with the mockery of the arrogant,
 with the contempt of the proud. ℟.

Reading II (2 Corinthians 12:7-10)

A reading from the second Letter of Saint Paul to the Corinthians

I will boast in my weaknesses, in order that the power of Christ may dwell in me.

Brothers and sisters:
That I, Paul, might not become too elated,
 because of the abundance of the revelations,
 a thorn in the flesh was given to me, an angel of Satan,
 to beat me, to keep me from being too elated.
Three times I begged the Lord about this, that it might leave me,
 but he said to me, "My grace is sufficient for you,
 for power is made perfect in weakness."

I will rather boast most gladly of my weaknesses,
   in order that the power of Christ may dwell with me.
Therefore, I am content with weaknesses, insults,
   hardships, persecutions, and constraints,
      for the sake of Christ;
      for when I am weak, then I am strong.

The word of the Lord. All: Thanks be to God.

GOSPEL (Mark 6:1-6)
ALLELUIA (See Luke 4:18)
℣. Alleluia, alleluia. ℟. **Alleluia, alleluia.**
℣. The Spirit of the Lord is upon me,
   for he sent me to bring glad tidings to the poor. ℟.

✢ **A reading from the holy Gospel according to Mark**

All: **Glory to you, O Lord.**

A prophet is not without honor except in his native place.

**Jesus departed from there and came to his native place,
      accompanied by his disciples.
When the sabbath came he began to teach in the
      synagogue,
   and many who heard him were astonished.
They said, "Where did this man get all this?
What kind of wisdom has been given him?
What mighty deeds are wrought by his hands!
Is he not the carpenter, the son of Mary,
   and the brother of James and Joses and Judas and
      Simon?
And are not his sisters here with us?"
And they took offense at him.
Jesus said to them,
   "A prophet is not without honor except in his native
      place
   and among his own kin and in his own house."**

So he was not able to perform any mighty deed there, apart from curing a few sick people by laying his hands on them.
He was amazed at their lack of faith.

The Gospel of the Lord. All: **Praise to you, Lord Jesus Christ.**

Prayer over the Offerings
May this oblation dedicated to your name
purify us, O Lord,
and day by day bring our conduct
closer to the life of heaven.
Through Christ our Lord. All: **Amen.**

Communion Antiphon (Psalm 34[33]:9)
Taste and see that the Lord is good;
blessed the man who seeks refuge in him.

Or:

(Matthew 11:28)
Come to me, all who labor and are burdened,
and I will refresh you, says the Lord.

Prayer After Communion
Grant, we pray, O Lord,
that, having been replenished by such great gifts,
we may gain the prize of salvation
and never cease to praise you.
Through Christ our Lord. All: **Amen.**

Fifteenth Sunday in Ordinary Time

July 12, 2015

Reflection on the Gospel

"Jesus summoned the Twelve." "Summoned" is a significant word here. This is a call that cannot be ignored because the mission is so urgent: to preach repentance. The mission is so urgent that the Twelve are not even to burden themselves with seeming necessities of life. The mission is so urgent that the Twelve are given Jesus' own authority to expel demons and cure illnesses. The mission is so urgent that we ourselves must respond faithfully as did the Twelve.

- *Having been summoned by Jesus, my response must be . . .*

—*Living Liturgy*™, *Fifteenth Sunday in Ordinary Time 2015*

Entrance Antiphon (Cf. Psalm 17[16]:15)

As for me, in justice I shall behold your face;
I shall be filled with the vision of your glory.

Collect

O God, who show the light of your truth
to those who go astray,
so that they may return to the right path,
give all who for the faith they profess
are accounted Christians
the grace to reject whatever is contrary to the name of Christ
and to strive after all that does it honor.
Through our Lord Jesus Christ, your Son,
who lives and reigns with you in the unity of the Holy Spirit,
one God, for ever and ever. All: **Amen.**

Reading I (L 104-B) (Amos 7:12-15)

A reading from the Book of the Prophet Amos

Go, prophesy to my people.

Amaziah, priest of Bethel, said to Amos,
   "Off with you, visionary, flee to the land of Judah!
There earn your bread by prophesying,
   but never again prophesy in Bethel;
   for it is the king's sanctuary and a royal temple."
Amos answered Amaziah, "I was no prophet,
   nor have I belonged to a company of prophets;
   I was a shepherd and a dresser of sycamores.
The LORD took me from following the flock, and said to me,
   Go, prophesy to my people Israel."

The word of the Lord. All: Thanks be to God.

RESPONSORIAL PSALM 85

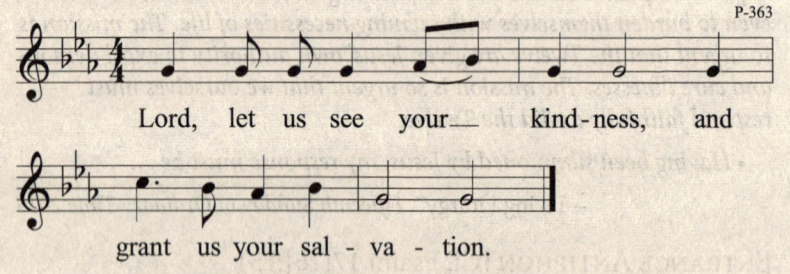

Lord, let us see your kindness, and grant us your salvation.

Music: Jay F. Hunstiger, © 1993, administered by Liturgical Press. All rights reserved.

Psalm 85:9-10, 11-12, 13-14

℟. (8) **Lord, let us see your kindness, and grant us your salvation.**

I will hear what God proclaims;
   the LORD—for he proclaims peace.
Near indeed is his salvation to those who fear him,
   glory dwelling in our land. ℟.

Kindness and truth shall meet;
   justice and peace shall kiss.
Truth shall spring out of the earth,
   and justice shall look down from heaven. ℟.

The LORD himself will give his benefits;
   our land shall yield its increase.
Justice shall walk before him,
   and prepare the way of his steps. ℟.

READING II A (Ephesians 1:3-14) *or* Shorter Form [ ]
(Ephesians 1:3-10)

A reading from the Letter of Saint Paul to the Ephesians

God chose us in Christ, before the foundation of the world.

[Blessed be the God and Father of our Lord Jesus Christ,
    who has blessed us in Christ
    with every spiritual blessing in the heavens,
    as he chose us in him, before the foundation of the
        world,
    to be holy and without blemish before him.
In love he destined us for adoption to himself through
        Jesus Christ,
    in accord with the favor of his will,
    for the praise of the glory of his grace
    that he granted us in the beloved.
In him we have redemption by his blood,
    the forgiveness of transgressions,
    in accord with the riches of his grace that he lavished
        upon us.
In all wisdom and insight, he has made known to us
    the mystery of his will in accord with his favor
    that he set forth in him as a plan for the fullness of
        times,
    to sum up all things in Christ, in heaven and on
        earth.]
In him we were also chosen,
    destined in accord with the purpose of the One
    who accomplishes all things according to the
        intention of his will,
    so that we might exist for the praise of his glory,
    we who first hoped in Christ.
In him you also, who have heard the word of truth,
    the gospel of your salvation, and have believed in him,
    were sealed with the promised holy Spirit,
    which is the first installment of our inheritance

toward redemption as God's possession, to the praise
  of his glory.

The word of the Lord. All: Thanks be to God.

GOSPEL (Mark 6:7-13)
ALLELUIA (*See* Ephesians 1:17-18)
℣. Alleluia, alleluia. ℟. **Alleluia, alleluia.**
℣. May the Father of our Lord Jesus Christ
  enlighten the eyes of our hearts,
  that we may know what is the hope that
  belongs to our call. ℟.

✠ A reading from the holy Gospel according to Mark

All: **Glory to you, O Lord.**

He began to send them out.

Jesus summoned the Twelve and began to send them out
  two by two
  and gave them authority over unclean spirits.
He instructed them to take nothing for the journey
  but a walking stick—
  no food, no sack, no money in their belts.
They were, however, to wear sandals
  but not a second tunic.
He said to them,
  "Wherever you enter a house, stay there until you
    leave.
Whatever place does not welcome you or listen to you,
  leave there and shake the dust off your feet
  in testimony against them."
So they went off and preached repentance.
The Twelve drove out many demons,
  and they anointed with oil many who were sick and
    cured them.

The Gospel of the Lord. All: **Praise to you, Lord Jesus Christ.**

Prayer over the Offerings

Look upon the offerings of the Church, O Lord,
as she makes her prayer to you,
and grant that, when consumed by those who believe,
they may bring ever greater holiness.
Through Christ our Lord. All: **Amen.**

Communion Antiphon (Cf. Psalm 84[83]:4-5)

The sparrow finds a home,
and the swallow a nest for her young:
by your altars, O Lord of hosts, my King and my God.
Blessed are they who dwell in your house,
for ever singing your praise.

Or:

(John 6:57)

Whoever eats my flesh and drinks my blood
remains in me and I in him, says the Lord.

Prayer after Communion

Having consumed these gifts, we pray, O Lord,
that, by our participation in this mystery,
its saving effects upon us may grow.
Through Christ our Lord. All: **Amen.**

Sixteenth Sunday in Ordinary Time

July 19, 2015

Reflection on the Gospel

Jesus, the true shepherd of God, always responds to the needs of others. How does Jesus respond when the apostles return from their mission and report to him? He invites them to come away and rest. How does Jesus respond when the crowd persists in hastening to him? He teaches them. In fact, he shepherds both the apostles and the crowd. Jesus shepherds everyone toward fuller life through both the re-creating power of rest and the transforming possibilities of new teaching.

- *The Good Shepherd transforms . . .*

—Living Liturgy™, *Sixteenth Sunday in Ordinary Time 2015*

ENTRANCE ANTIPHON (Psalm 54[53]:6, 8)

See, I have God for my help.
The Lord sustains my soul.
I will sacrifice to you with willing heart,
and praise your name, O Lord, for it is good.

COLLECT

Show favor, O Lord, to your servants
and mercifully increase the gifts of your grace,
that, made fervent in hope, faith and charity,
they may be ever watchful in keeping your commands.
Through our Lord Jesus Christ, your Son,
who lives and reigns with you in the unity of the Holy Spirit,
one God, for ever and ever. All: **Amen.**

READING I (L 107-B) (Jeremiah 23:1-6)

A reading from the Book of the Prophet Jeremiah

I will gather the remnant of my flock and appoint shepherds for them.

**Woe to the shepherds
   who mislead and scatter the flock of my pasture,
      says the LORD.**

Therefore, thus says the Lord, the God of Israel,
> against the shepherds who shepherd my people:
> You have scattered my sheep and driven them away.

You have not cared for them,
> but I will take care to punish your evil deeds.

I myself will gather the remnant of my flock
> from all the lands to which I have driven them
> and bring them back to their meadow;
> there they shall increase and multiply.

I will appoint shepherds for them who will shepherd them
> so that they need no longer fear and tremble;
> and none shall be missing, says the Lord.

Behold, the days are coming, says the Lord,
> when I will raise up a righteous shoot to David;
> as king he shall reign and govern wisely,
> he shall do what is just and right in the land.

In his days Judah shall be saved,
> Israel shall dwell in security.

This is the name they give him:
> "The Lord our justice."

The word of the Lord. **All:** Thanks be to God.

Responsional Psalm 23

The Lord is my shep-herd; there is noth-ing I shall want.

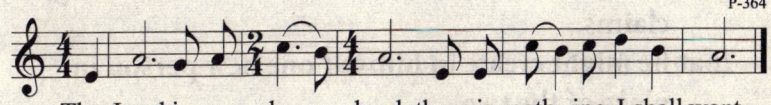

Music: Jay F. Hunstiger, © 1990, administered by Liturgical Press. All rights reserved.

Psalm 23:1-3, 3-4, 5, 6

℟. (1) **The Lord is my shepherd; there is nothing I shall want.**

The Lord is my shepherd; I shall not want.
> In verdant pastures he gives me repose;
beside restful waters he leads me;
> he refreshes my soul. ℟.

He guides me in right paths
> for his name's sake.

(continued)

Even though I walk in the dark valley
   I fear no evil; for you are at my side
with your rod and your staff
   that give me courage. ℟.

You spread the table before me
   in the sight of my foes;
you anoint my head with oil;
   my cup overflows. ℟.

Only goodness and kindness follow me
   all the days of my life;
and I shall dwell in the house of the Lord
   for years to come. ℟.

Reading II (Ephesians 2:13-18)
A reading from the Letter of Saint Paul to the Ephesians

Christ is our peace who made both one.

Brothers and sisters:
In Christ Jesus you who once were far off
   have become near by the blood of Christ.

For he is our peace, he who made both one
   and broke down the dividing wall of enmity, through his flesh,
   abolishing the law with its commandments and legal claims,
   that he might create in himself one new person in place of the two,
   thus establishing peace,
   and might reconcile both with God,
   in one body, through the cross,
   putting that enmity to death by it.
He came and preached peace to you who were far off
   and peace to those who were near,
   for through him we both have access in one Spirit to the Father.

The word of the Lord. All: **Thanks be to God.**

Gospel (Mark 6:30-34)
Alleluia (John 10:27)
℣. Alleluia, alleluia. ℟. **Alleluia, alleluia.**
℣. My sheep hear my voice, says the Lord;
I know them, and they follow me. ℟.

✠ **A reading from the holy Gospel according to Mark**

All: **Glory to you, O Lord.**

They were like sheep without a shepherd.

**The apostles gathered together with Jesus
and reported all they had done and taught.
He said to them,
"Come away by yourselves to a deserted place and rest a while."
People were coming and going in great numbers,
and they had no opportunity even to eat.
So they went off in the boat by themselves to a deserted place.
People saw them leaving and many came to know about it.
They hastened there on foot from all the towns
and arrived at the place before them.**

**When he disembarked and saw the vast crowd,
his heart was moved with pity for them,
for they were like sheep without a shepherd;
and he began to teach them many things.**

The Gospel of the Lord. All: **Praise to you, Lord Jesus Christ.**

Prayer over the Offerings
O God, who in the one perfect sacrifice
brought to completion varied offerings of the law,
accept, we pray, this sacrifice from your faithful servants
and make it holy, as you blessed the gifts of Abel,
so that what each has offered to the honor of your majesty
may benefit the salvation of all.
Through Christ our Lord. All: **Amen.**

Communion Antiphon (Psalm 111[110]:4-5)

The Lord, the gracious, the merciful,
has made a memorial of his wonders;
he gives food to those who fear him.

Or:

(Revelation 3:20)
Behold, I stand at the door and knock, says the Lord.
If anyone hears my voice and opens the door to me,
I will enter his house and dine with him, and he with me.

Prayer after Communion

Graciously be present to your people, we pray, O Lord,
and lead those you have imbued with heavenly mysteries
to pass from former ways to newness of life.
Through Christ our Lord. All: **Amen.**

Seventeenth Sunday in Ordinary Time

July 26, 2015

Reflection on the Gospel

Let's let a miracle be a miracle! Jesus tested Philip, who failed the test because he fixated on calculating the amount of food needed to feed the hungry crowd and its cost. Jesus "knew what he was going to do"—he gave the crowd "as much . . . as they wanted." Amazingly, the miracle of giving them "as much . . . as they wanted" was still less than the other miracle Jesus gave them: "the sign" of the fullness of messianic Life. So much Life—even "twelve wicker baskets" more than they wanted.

- *Let the miracle begin by . . .*

—Living Liturgy™, *Seventeenth Sunday in Ordinary Time 2015*

Entrance Antiphon (Cf. Psalm 68[67]:6-7, 36)
God is in his holy place,
God who unites those who dwell in his house;
he himself gives might and strength to his people.

Collect
O God, protector of those who hope in you,
without whom nothing has firm foundation, nothing is holy,
bestow in abundance your mercy upon us
and grant that, with you as our ruler and guide,
we may use the good things that pass
in such a way as to hold fast even now
to those that ever endure.
Through our Lord Jesus Christ, your Son,
who lives and reigns with you in the unity of the Holy Spirit,
one God, for ever and ever. **All: Amen.**

Reading I (L 110-B) (2 Kings 4:42-44)
A reading from the second Book of Kings

They shall eat and there shall be some left over.

A man came from Baal-shalishah bringing to Elisha, the man of God,
twenty barley loaves made from the firstfruits,
and fresh grain in the ear.
Elisha said, "Give it to the people to eat."
But his servant objected,
"How can I set this before a hundred people?"
Elisha insisted, "Give it to the people to eat.
For thus says the Lord,
'They shall eat and there shall be some left over.'"
And when they had eaten, there was some left over,
as the Lord had said.

The word of the Lord. All: Thanks be to God.

Responsorial Psalm 145

The hand of the Lord feeds us; he answers all our needs.

Music: Jay F. Hunstiger, © 1993, administered by Liturgical Press. All rights reserved.

Psalm 145:10-11, 15-16, 17-18

℟. (See 16) **The hand of the Lord feeds us; he answers all our needs.**

Let all your works give you thanks, O Lord,
 and let your faithful ones bless you.
Let them discourse of the glory of your kingdom
 and speak of your might. ℟.

The eyes of all look hopefully to you,
 and you give them their food in due season;
you open your hand
 and satisfy the desire of every living thing. ℟.

The Lord is just in all his ways
 and holy in all his works.
The Lord is near to all who call upon him,
 to all who call upon him in truth. ℟.

Reading II (Ephesians 4:1-6)

A reading from the Letter of Saint Paul to the Ephesians

One body, one Lord, one faith, one baptism.

**Brothers and sisters:
I, a prisoner for the Lord,
 urge you to live in a manner worthy of the call you
  have received,
 with all humility and gentleness, with patience,
 bearing with one another through love,
 striving to preserve the unity of the spirit through the
  bond of peace:**

one body and one Spirit,
as you were also called to the one hope of your call;
one Lord, one faith, one baptism;
one God and Father of all,
who is over all and through all and in all.

The word of the Lord. All: **Thanks be to God.**

GOSPEL (John 6:1-15)
ALLELUIA (Luke 7:16)

℣. Alleluia, alleluia.   ℟. **Alleluia, alleluia.**
℣. A great prophet has risen in our midst.
God has visited his people. ℟.

✠ **A reading from the holy Gospel according to John**

All: **Glory to you, O Lord.**

He distributed as much as they wanted to those who were reclining.

Jesus went across the Sea of Galilee.
A large crowd followed him,
   because they saw the signs he was performing on the sick.
Jesus went up on the mountain,
   and there he sat down with his disciples.
The Jewish feast of Passover was near.
When Jesus raised his eyes
   and saw that a large crowd was coming to him,
   he said to Philip,
   "Where can we buy enough food for them to eat?"
He said this to test him,
   because he himself knew what he was going to do.
Philip answered him,
   "Two hundred days' wages worth of food would not be enough
   for each of them to have a little."
One of his disciples,
   Andrew, the brother of Simon Peter, said to him,

"There is a boy here who has five barley loaves and
>   two fish;
> but what good are these for so many?"
Jesus said, "Have the people recline."
Now there was a great deal of grass in that place.
So the men reclined, about five thousand in number.
Then Jesus took the loaves, gave thanks,
>   and distributed them to those who were reclining,
>   and also as much of the fish as they wanted.
When they had had their fill, he said to his disciples,
>   "Gather the fragments left over,
>   so that nothing will be wasted."
So they collected them,
>   and filled twelve wicker baskets with fragments
>   from the five barley loaves
>   that had been more than they could eat.
When the people saw the sign he had done, they said,
>   "This is truly the Prophet, the one who is to come into
>   the world."
Since Jesus knew that they were going to come and carry
>   him off
>   to make him king,
>   he withdrew again to the mountain alone.

The Gospel of the Lord. All: Praise to you, Lord Jesus Christ.

Prayer over the Offerings

Accept, O Lord, we pray, the offerings
which we bring from the abundance of your gifts,
that through the powerful working of your grace
these most sacred mysteries may sanctify our present way of life
and lead us to eternal gladness.
Through Christ our Lord. All: **Amen.**

Communion Antiphon (Psalm 103[102]:2)

Bless the Lord, O my soul,
and never forget all his benefits.

Or:

(Matthew 5:7-8)
Blessed are the merciful, for they shall receive mercy.
Blessed are the clean of heart, for they shall see God.

Prayer after Communion
We have consumed, O Lord, this divine Sacrament,
the perpetual memorial of the Passion of your Son;
grant, we pray, that this gift,
which he himself gave us with love beyond all telling,
may profit us for salvation.
Through Christ our Lord. All: **Amen.**

Eighteenth Sunday in Ordinary Time

August 2, 2015

Reflection on the Gospel

The bread the crowd seeks is perishable. They eat this bread but become hungry again. The bread Jesus offers is eternal. Those who eat this bread will never hunger again. They cannot procure this bread because it is the Father's gift: the "true bread from heaven" that is Jesus himself. There is a tension—a grave misunderstanding—between what the crowd seeks and what Jesus offers. What do we seek? Do we seek only nourishment? Or do we seek the Bread only God can give—Bread that is abundant and Life-giving?

• Lord, "the true bread from heaven" give us life, ...

—Living Liturgy™, *Eighteenth Sunday in Ordinary Time 2015*

Entrance Antiphon (Psalm 70[69]:2, 6)
O God, come to my assistance;
O Lord, make haste to help me!
You are my rescuer, my help;
O Lord, do not delay.

Collect

Draw near to your servants, O Lord,
and answer their prayers with unceasing kindness,
that, for those who glory in you as their Creator and guide,
you may restore what you have created
and keep safe what you have restored.
Through our Lord Jesus Christ, your Son,
who lives and reigns with you in the unity of the Holy Spirit,
one God, for ever and ever. All: **Amen.**

Reading I (L 113-B) (Exodus 16:2-4, 12-15)

A reading from the Book of Exodus

I will rain down bread from heaven for you.

The whole Israelite community grumbled against Moses and Aaron.
The Israelites said to them,
"Would that we had died at the Lord's hand in the land of Egypt,
as we sat by our fleshpots and ate our fill of bread!
But you had to lead us into this desert
to make the whole community die of famine!"

Then the Lord said to Moses,
"I will now rain down bread from heaven for you.
Each day the people are to go out and gather their daily portion;
thus will I test them,
to see whether they follow my instructions or not.

"I have heard the grumbling of the Israelites.
Tell them: In the evening twilight you shall eat flesh,
and in the morning you shall have your fill of bread,
so that you may know that I, the Lord, am your God."

In the evening quail came up and covered the camp.
In the morning a dew lay all about the camp,
and when the dew evaporated, there on the surface of the desert
were fine flakes like hoarfrost on the ground.

On seeing it, the Israelites asked one another, "What is
   this?"
   for they did not know what it was.
But Moses told them,
   "This is the bread that the LORD has given you to eat."
The word of the Lord. **All:** Thanks be to God.

RESPONSORIAL PSALM 78

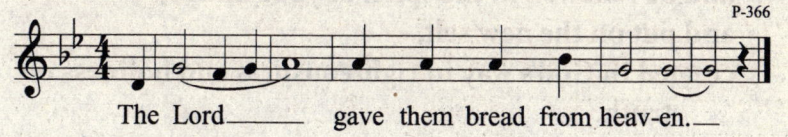

The Lord gave them bread from heav-en.

Music: Jay F. Hunstiger, © 1990, administered by Liturgical Press. All rights reserved.

Psalm 78:3-4, 23-24, 25, 54

℟. (24b) **The Lord gave them bread from heaven.**

What we have heard and know,
   and what our fathers have declared to us,
We will declare to the generation to come
   the glorious deeds of the Lord and his strength
   and the wonders that he wrought. ℟.

He commanded the skies above
   and opened the doors of heaven;
he rained manna upon them for food
   and gave them heavenly bread. ℟.

Man ate the bread of angels,
   food he sent them in abundance.
And he brought them to his holy land,
   to the mountains his right hand had won. ℟.

READING II (Ephesians 4:17, 20-24)

A reading from the Letter of Saint Paul to the Ephesians

Put on the new self that has been created in God's way.

Brothers and sisters:
I declare and testify in the Lord
   that you must no longer live as the Gentiles do,
   in the futility of their minds;

that is not how you learned Christ,
assuming that you have heard of him and were taught in him,
as truth is in Jesus,
that you should put away the old self of your former way of life,
corrupted through deceitful desires,
and be renewed in the spirit of your minds,
and put on the new self,
created in God's way in righteousness and holiness of truth.

The word of the Lord. All: **Thanks be to God.**

Gospel (John 6:24-35)
Alleluia (Matthew 4:4b)
℣. Alleluia, alleluia. ℟. **Alleluia, alleluia.**
℣. One does not live on bread alone, but by every word that comes forth from the mouth of God. ℟.

✠ **A reading from the holy Gospel according to John**

All: **Glory to you, O Lord.**

Whoever comes to me will never hunger, and whoever believes in me will never thirst.

**When the crowd saw that neither Jesus nor his disciples were there,
they themselves got into boats
and came to Capernaum looking for Jesus.
And when they found him across the sea they said to him,
"Rabbi, when did you get here?"
Jesus answered them and said,
"Amen, amen, I say to you,
you are looking for me not because you saw signs
but because you ate the loaves and were filled.
Do not work for food that perishes
but for the food that endures for eternal life,
which the Son of Man will give you.
For on him the Father, God, has set his seal."**

So they said to him,
"What can we do to accomplish the works of God?"
Jesus answered and said to them,
"This is the work of God, that you believe in the one
he sent."
So they said to him,
"What sign can you do, that we may see and believe in
you?
What can you do?
Our ancestors ate manna in the desert, as it is written:
He gave them bread from heaven to eat.
So Jesus said to them,
"Amen, amen, I say to you,
it was not Moses who gave the bread from heaven;
my Father gives you the true bread from heaven.
For the bread of God is that which comes down from
heaven
and gives life to the world."
So they said to him,
"Sir, give us this bread always."
Jesus said to them,
"I am the bread of life;
whoever comes to me will never hunger,
and whoever believes in me will never thirst."

The Gospel of the Lord. **All:** **Praise to you, Lord Jesus Christ.**

Prayer over the Offerings
Graciously sanctify these gifts, O Lord, we pray,
and, accepting the oblation of this spiritual sacrifice,
make of us an eternal offering to you.
Through Christ our Lord. **All:** **Amen.**

Communion Antiphon (Wisdom 16:20)
You have given us, O Lord, bread from heaven,
endowed with all delights and sweetness in every taste.

Or:

(John 6:35)
I am the bread of life, says the Lord;
whoever comes to me will not hunger
and whoever believes in me will not thirst.

Prayer after Communion
Accompany with constant protection, O Lord,
those you renew with these heavenly gifts
and, in your never-failing care for them,
make them worthy of eternal redemption.
Through Christ our Lord. **All: Amen.**

Nineteenth Sunday in Ordinary Time

August 9, 2015

Reflection on the Gospel
"The Jews murmured" because they could not get beyond their limited perception of who they thought Jesus was to the mystery about himself he reveals: "I am the bread of life," the Bread "come down from heaven," the Bread to whom we must come, the Bread who gives us a share in his "eternal life," the Bread in whom we must believe, the Bread who gives Self "for the life of the world." Jesus persists in revealing himself as the Bread sent by God to nourish the crowd (and us) for the journey to eternal Life.

• *The life of the world, the Bread come down from heaven . . .*

—Living Liturgy™, *Nineteenth Sunday in Ordinary Time 2015*

Entrance Antiphon (Cf. Ps 74[73]:20, 19, 22, 23)
Look to your covenant, O Lord,
and forget not the life of your poor ones for ever.
Arise, O God, and defend your cause,
and forget not the cries of those who seek you.

August 9

Collect

Almighty ever-living God,
whom, taught by the Holy Spirit,
we dare to call our Father,
bring, we pray, to perfection in our hearts
the spirit of adoption as your sons and daughters,
that we may merit to enter into the inheritance
which you have promised.
Through our Lord Jesus Christ, your Son,
who lives and reigns with you in the unity of the Holy Spirit,
one God, for ever and ever. All: **Amen.**

Reading I (L 116-B) (1 Kings 19:4-8)

A reading from the first Book of Kings

Strengthened by that food, he walked to the mountain of God.

**Elijah went a day's journey into the desert,
  until he came to a broom tree and sat beneath it.
He prayed for death, saying:
  "This is enough, O Lord!
Take my life, for I am no better than my fathers."
He lay down and fell asleep under the broom tree,
  but then an angel touched him and ordered him to
    get up and eat.
Elijah looked and there at his head was a hearth cake
  and a jug of water.
After he ate and drank, he lay down again,
  but the angel of the Lord came back a second time,
  touched him, and ordered,
  "Get up and eat, else the journey will be too long for
    you!"
He got up, ate, and drank;
  then strengthened by that food,
  he walked forty days and forty nights to the mountain
    of God, Horeb.**

The word of the Lord. All: **Thanks be to God.**

Responsorial Psalm 34

Taste and see the good-ness of the Lord, taste and see the good-ness of the Lord.

Music: Jay F. Hunstiger, © 1990, administered by Liturgical Press. All rights reserved.

Psalm 34:2-3, 4-5, 6-7, 8-9

℟. (9a) **Taste and see the goodness of the Lord.**

> I will bless the LORD at all times;
> > his praise shall be ever in my mouth.
> Let my soul glory in the LORD;
> > the lowly will hear me and be glad. ℟.

> Glorify the LORD with me,
> > let us together extol his name.
> I sought the LORD, and he answered me
> > and delivered me from all my fears. ℟.

> Look to him that you may be radiant with joy,
> > and your faces may not blush with shame.
> When the afflicted man called out, the LORD heard,
> > and from all his distress he saved him. ℟.

> The angel of the LORD encamps
> > around those who fear him and delivers them.
> Taste and see how good the LORD is;
> > blessed the man who takes refuge in him. ℟.

Reading II (Ephesians 4:30—5:2)

A reading from the Letter of Saint Paul to the Ephesians

Walk in love, just like Christ.

Brothers and sisters:
Do not grieve the Holy Spirit of God,
> **with which you were sealed for the day of redemption.**
All bitterness, fury, anger, shouting, and reviling
> **must be removed from you, along with all malice.**

And be kind to one another, compassionate,
> forgiving one another as God has forgiven you in Christ.

So be imitators of God, as beloved children, and live in love,
> as Christ loved us and handed himself over for us
> as a sacrificial offering to God for a fragrant aroma.

The word of the Lord. All: Thanks be to God.

GOSPEL (John 6:41-51)
ALLELUIA (John 6:51)
℣. Alleluia, alleluia. ℟. **Alleluia, alleluia.**
℣. I am the living bread that came down from heaven, says the Lord;
> whoever eats this bread will live forever. ℟.

☩ A reading from the holy Gospel according to John

All: **Glory to you, O Lord.**

I am the living bread that came down from heaven.

The Jews murmured about Jesus because he said,
> "I am the bread that came down from heaven,"
> and they said,
> "Is this not Jesus, the son of Joseph?
Do we not know his father and mother?
Then how can he say,
> 'I have come down from heaven'?"
Jesus answered and said to them,
> "Stop murmuring among yourselves.
No one can come to me unless the Father who sent me draw him,
> and I will raise him on the last day.
It is written in the prophets:
> *They shall all be taught by God.*
Everyone who listens to my Father and learns from him comes to me.

Not that anyone has seen the Father
   except the one who is from God;
   he has seen the Father.
Amen, amen, I say to you,
   whoever believes has eternal life.
I am the bread of life.
Your ancestors ate the manna in the desert, but they died;
   this is the bread that comes down from heaven
   so that one may eat it and not die.
I am the living bread that came down from heaven;
   whoever eats this bread will live forever;
      and the bread that I will give is my flesh for the life of
         the world."
The Gospel of the Lord. All: **Praise to you, Lord Jesus Christ.**

Prayer over the Offerings
Be pleased, O Lord, to accept the offerings of your Church,
for in your mercy you have given them to be offered
and by your power you transform them
into the mystery of our salvation.
Through Christ our Lord. All: **Amen.**

Communion Antiphon (Psalm 147:12, 14)
O Jerusalem, glorify the Lord,
who gives you your fill of finest wheat.

Or:

(Cf. John 6:51)
The bread that I will give, says the Lord,
is my flesh for the life of the world.

Prayer after Communion
May the communion in your Sacrament
that we have consumed, save us, O Lord,
and confirm us in the light of your truth.
Through Christ our Lord. All: **Amen.**

The Assumption of the Blessed Virgin Mary

AT THE VIGIL MASS

August 14, 2015

The Mass of the Vigil of the Assumption is to be used at evening Masses.

Reflection on the Gospel

"Mary set out." Her journey extended far beyond traveling to Elizabeth to help her in her need. Her journey's duration was actually Mary's lifelong journey of praising God, of allowing God to do great things through her, of being an instrument for God to keep the divine promise of salvation. This day we celebrate the completion of Mary's journey, when she "returned to her home," being taken body and soul into heaven to be forever with her Lord whom she bore in her womb.

- Mary, the Mother of God and our mother, is our model . . .

—*Living Liturgy*™, *Assumption 2015*

Entrance Antiphon
Glorious things are spoken of you, O Mary,
who today were exalted above the choirs of Angels
into eternal triumph with Christ.

Collect
O God, who, looking on the lowliness of the Blessed Virgin Mary,
raised her to this grace,
that your Only Begotten Son was born of her according to the flesh
and that she was crowned this day with surpassing glory,
grant through her prayers,
that, saved by the mystery of your redemption,
we may merit to be exalted by you on high.
Through our Lord Jesus Christ, your Son,
who lives and reigns with you in the unity of the Holy Spirit,
one God, for ever and ever. **All: Amen.**

Reading I (L 621) (1 Chronicles 15:3-4, 15-16; 16:1-2)
A reading from the first Book of Chronicles

They brought in the ark of God and set it within the tent which David had pitched for it.

David assembled all Israel in Jerusalem to bring the ark of the Lord
   to the place which he had prepared for it.
David also called together the sons of Aaron and the Levites.

The Levites bore the ark of God on their shoulders with poles,
   as Moses had ordained according to the word of the Lord.

David commanded the chiefs of the Levites
   to appoint their kinsmen as chanters,
   to play on musical instruments, harps, lyres, and cymbals,
   to make a loud sound of rejoicing.

They brought in the ark of God and set it within the tent which David had pitched for it.
Then they offered up burnt offerings and peace offerings to God.
When David had finished offering up the burnt offerings and peace offerings,
   he blessed the people in the name of the Lord.

The word of the Lord. **All:** Thanks be to God.

Responsorial Psalm 132

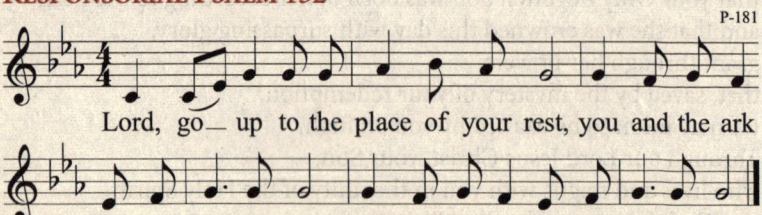

Lord, go up to the place of your rest, you and the ark of your ho-li-ness, you and the ark of your ho-li-ness.

Music: Jay F. Hunsfiger, © 1990, administered by Liturgical Press. All rights reserved.

Psalm 132:6-7, 9-10, 13-14

℟. (8) **Lord, go up to the place of your rest, you and the ark of your holiness.**

Behold, we heard of it in Ephrathah;
  we found it in the fields of Jaar.
Let us enter into his dwelling,
  let us worship at his footstool. ℟.

May your priests be clothed with justice;
  let your faithful ones shout merrily for joy.
For the sake of David your servant,
  reject not the plea of your anointed. ℟.

For the LORD has chosen Zion;
  he prefers her for his dwelling.
"Zion is my resting place forever;
  in her will I dwell, for I prefer her." ℟.

READING II (1 Corinthians 15:54b-57)

A reading from the first Letter of Saint Paul to the Corinthians

God gave us victory through Jesus Christ.

Brothers and sisters:
When that which is mortal clothes itself with immortality, then the word that is written shall come about:

> *Death is swallowed up in victory.*
> *Where, O death, is your victory?*
> *Where, O death, is your sting?*

The sting of death is sin,
  and the power of sin is the law.
But thanks be to God who gives us the victory
  through our Lord Jesus Christ.

The word of the Lord. All: **Thanks be to God.**

GOSPEL (Luke 11:27-28)
ALLELUIA (Luke 11:28)

℣. Alleluia, alleluia. ℟. **Alleluia, alleluia.**
℣. Blessed are they who hear the word of God
  and observe it. ℟.

✠ **A reading from the holy Gospel according to Luke**

All: **Glory to you, O Lord.**

Blessed is the womb that carried you!

While Jesus was speaking,
   a woman from the crowd called out and said to him,
   "Blessed is the womb that carried you
   and the breasts at which you nursed."
He replied,
   "Rather, blessed are those
   who hear the word of God and observe it."

The Gospel of the Lord. All: **Praise to you, Lord Jesus Christ.**

Prayer over the Offerings
Receive, we pray, O Lord,
the sacrifice of conciliation and praise,
which we celebrate on the Assumption of the holy Mother of God,
that it may lead us to your pardon
and confirm us in perpetual thanksgiving.
Through Christ our Lord. All: **Amen.**

Communion Antiphon (Cf. Luke 11:27)
Blessed is the womb of the Virgin Mary,
which bore the Son of the eternal Father.

Prayer after Communion
Having partaken of this heavenly table,
we beseech your mercy, Lord our God,
that we, who honor the Assumption of the Mother of God,
may be freed from every threat of harm.
Through Christ our Lord. All: **Amen.**

August 15

AT THE MASS DURING THE DAY

Entrance Antiphon (Cf. Revelation 12:1)
A great sign appeared in heaven:
a woman clothed with the sun, and the moon beneath her feet,
and on her head a crown of twelve stars.

Or:

Let us all rejoice in the Lord,
as we celebrate the feast day in honor of the Virgin Mary,
at whose Assumption the Angels rejoice
and praise the Son of God.

Collect
Almighty ever-living God,
who assumed the Immaculate Virgin Mary, the Mother of your Son,
body and soul into heavenly glory,
grant, we pray,
that, always attentive to the things that are above,
we may merit to be sharers of her glory.
Through our Lord Jesus Christ, your Son,
who lives and reigns with you in the unity of the Holy Spirit,
one God, for ever and ever. All: **Amen.**

Reading I (L 622) (Revelation 11:19a; 12:1-6a, 10ab)
A reading from the Book of Revelation

A woman clothed with the sun, with the moon beneath her feet.

God's temple in heaven was opened,
   and the ark of his covenant could be seen in the temple.
A great sign appeared in the sky, a woman clothed with the sun,
   with the moon under her feet,
   and on her head a crown of twelve stars.
She was with child and wailed aloud in pain as she labored to give birth.
Then another sign appeared in the sky;
   it was a huge red dragon, with seven heads and ten horns,
   and on its heads were seven diadems.
Its tail swept away a third of the stars in the sky
   and hurled them down to the earth.
Then the dragon stood before the woman about to give birth,
   to devour her child when she gave birth.

She gave birth to a son, a male child,
  destined to rule all the nations with an iron rod.
Her child was caught up to God and his throne.
The woman herself fled into the desert
  where she had a place prepared by God.

Then I heard a loud voice in heaven say:
  "Now have salvation and power come,
    and the Kingdom of our God
    and the authority of his Anointed One."

The word of the Lord. All: **Thanks be to God.**

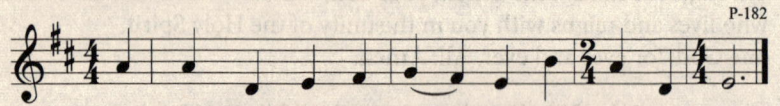

Responsorial Psalm 45

The queen stands at your right hand, arrayed in gold.

Music: Jay F. Hunstiger, © 1990, administered by Liturgical Press. All rights reserved.

Psalm 45:10bc, 11, 12ab, 16

℟. (10bc) **The queen stands at your right hand, arrayed in gold.**

The queen takes her place at your right hand in gold of Ophir. ℟.

Hear, O daughter, and see; turn your ear,
  forget your people and your father's house. ℟.

So shall the king desire your beauty;
  for he is your lord. ℟.

They are borne in with gladness and joy;
  they enter the palace of the king. ℟.

Reading II (1 Corinthians 15:20-27)

A reading from the first Letter of Saint Paul to the Corinthians

Christ, the firstfruits; then those who belong to him.

Brothers and sisters:
Christ has been raised from the dead,
  the firstfruits of those who have fallen asleep.

For since death came through man,
> the resurrection of the dead came also through man.

For just as in Adam all die,
> so too in Christ shall all be brought to life,
> but each one in proper order:
> Christ the firstfruits;
> then, at his coming, those who belong to Christ;
> then comes the end,
> when he hands over the Kingdom to his God and Father,
> when he has destroyed every sovereignty
> and every authority and power.

For he must reign until he has put all his enemies under his feet.

The last enemy to be destroyed is death,
> for "he subjected everything under his feet."

The word of the Lord. All: **Thanks be to God.**

Gospel (Luke 1:39-56)

Alleluia

℣. Alleluia, alleluia.   ℟. **Alleluia, alleluia.**
℣. Mary is taken up to heaven;
> a chorus of angels exults. ℟.

✚ **A reading from the holy Gospel according to Luke**

All: **Glory to you, O Lord.**

The Almighty has done great things for me; he has raised up the lowly.

**Mary set out
> and traveled to the hill country in haste
> to a town of Judah,
> where she entered the house of Zechariah
> and greeted Elizabeth.
When Elizabeth heard Mary's greeting,
> the infant leaped in her womb,
> and Elizabeth, filled with the Holy Spirit,
> cried out in a loud voice and said,**

"Blessed are you among women,
   and blessed is the fruit of your womb.
And how does this happen to me,
   that the mother of my Lord should come to me?
For at the moment the sound of your greeting reached my ears,
   the infant in my womb leaped for joy.
Blessed are you who believed
   that what was spoken to you by the Lord
   would be fulfilled."

And Mary said:
   "My soul proclaims the greatness of the Lord;
      my spirit rejoices in God my Savior
      for he has looked with favor on his lowly servant.
   From this day all generations will call me blessed:
      the Almighty has done great things for me
      and holy is his Name.
   He has mercy on those who fear him
      in every generation.
   He has shown the strength of his arm,
      and has scattered the proud in their conceit.
   He has cast down the mighty from their thrones,
      and has lifted up the lowly.
   He has filled the hungry with good things,
      and the rich he has sent away empty.
   He has come to the help of his servant Israel
      for he has remembered his promise of mercy,
      the promise he made to our fathers,
      to Abraham and his children forever."

Mary remained with her about three months
   and then returned to her home.

The Gospel of the Lord. All: **Praise to you, Lord Jesus Christ.**

Prayer over the Offerings

May this oblation, our tribute of homage,
rise up to you, O Lord,

and, through the intercession of the most Blessed Virgin Mary,
whom you assumed into heaven,
may our hearts, aflame with the fire of love,
constantly long for you.
Through Christ our Lord. **All: Amen.**

COMMUNION ANTIPHON (Luke 1:48-49)
All generations will call me blessed,
for he who is mighty has done great things for me.

PRAYER AFTER COMMUNION
Having received the Sacrament of salvation,
we ask you to grant, O Lord,
that, through the intercession of the Blessed Virgin Mary,
whom you assumed into heaven,
we may be brought to the glory of the resurrection.
Through Christ our Lord. **All: Amen.**

Twentieth Sunday in Ordinary Time

August 16, 2015

Reflection on the Gospel

Who is "this man"? Jesus declares that he is "living bread" sent by his "living Father"; he shares divine Life with the Father. When we eat his flesh and drink his blood, we partake in this same divine Life. And so, like the risen Christ, we will be the Presence of God incarnated in human flesh. What a mystery! Its depth challenges us no less than the Jews of Jesus' time. We, too, are faced with the question, Who is "this man"?

- *Sharing in the flesh and blood of Jesus, the "living bread" sent by the Father, we . . .*

—Living Liturgy™, *Twentieth Sunday in Ordinary Time 2015*

ENTRANCE ANTIPHON (Psalm 84[83]:10-11)
Turn your eyes, O God, our shield;
and look on the face of your anointed one;

one day within your courts
is better than a thousand elsewhere.

Collect

O God, who have prepared for those who love you
good things which no eye can see,
fill our hearts, we pray, with the warmth of your love,
so that, loving you in all things and above all things,
we may attain your promises,
which surpass every human desire.
Through our Lord Jesus Christ, your Son,
who lives and reigns with you in the unity of the Holy Spirit,
one God, for ever and ever. **All: Amen.**

Reading I (L 119-B) (Proverbs 9:1-6)

A reading from the Book of Proverbs

Come, eat of my food and drink of the wine I have mixed.

**Wisdom has built her house,
    she has set up her seven columns;
she has dressed her meat, mixed her wine,
    yes, she has spread her table.
She has sent out her maidens; she calls
    from the heights out over the city:
"Let whoever is simple turn in here";
    To the one who lacks understanding, she says,
"Come, eat of my food,
    and drink of the wine I have mixed!
Forsake foolishness that you may live;
    advance in the way of understanding."

The word of the Lord. All: Thanks be to God.**

Responsorial Psalm 34

Taste and see the good-ness of the Lord,
taste and see the good-ness of the Lord.

Music: Jay F. Hunstiger, © 1990, administered by Liturgical Press. All rights reserved.

Psalm 34:2-3, 4-5, 6-7

℟. (9a) **Taste and see the goodness of the Lord.**

I will bless the Lord at all times;
>his praise shall be ever in my mouth.
Let my soul glory in the Lord;
>the lowly will hear me and be glad. ℟.

Glorify the Lord with me,
>let us together extol his name.
I sought the Lord, and he answered me
>and delivered me from all my fears. ℟.

Look to him that you may be radiant with joy,
>and your faces may not blush with shame.
When the poor one called out, the Lord heard,
>and from all his distress he saved him. ℟.

Reading II (Ephesians 5:15-20)

A reading from the Letter of Saint Paul to the Ephesians

Understand what is the will of the Lord.

Brothers and sisters:
Watch carefully how you live,
>**not as foolish persons but as wise,**
>**making the most of the opportunity,**
>**because the days are evil.**
Therefore, do not continue in ignorance,
>**but try to understand what is the will of the Lord.**
And do not get drunk on wine, in which lies debauchery,
>**but be filled with the Spirit,**
>>**addressing one another in psalms and hymns and spiritual songs,**
>**singing and playing to the Lord in your hearts,**
>**giving thanks always and for everything**
>>**in the name of our Lord Jesus Christ to God the Father.**

The word of the Lord. All: **Thanks be to God.**

Gospel (John 6:51-58)
Alleluia (John 6:56)
℣. Alleluia, alleluia. ℟. **Alleluia, alleluia.**
℣. Whoever eats my flesh and drinks my blood
remains in me and I in him, says the Lord. ℟.

✣ A reading from the holy Gospel according to John

All: **Glory to you, O Lord.**

My flesh is true food and my blood is true drink.

Jesus said to the crowds:
  "I am the living bread that came down from heaven;
  whoever eats this bread will live forever;
  and the bread that I will give
  is my flesh for the life of the world."
The Jews quarreled among themselves, saying,
  "How can this man give us his flesh to eat?"
Jesus said to them,
  "Amen, amen, I say to you,
  unless you eat the flesh of the Son of Man and drink
    his blood,
  you do not have life within you.
Whoever eats my flesh and drinks my blood
  has eternal life,
  and I will raise him on the last day.
For my flesh is true food,
  and my blood is true drink.
Whoever eats my flesh and drinks my blood
  remains in me and I in him.
Just as the living Father sent me
  and I have life because of the Father,
  so also the one who feeds on me
  will have life because of me.
This is the bread that came down from heaven.
Unlike your ancestors who ate and still died,
  whoever eats this bread will live forever."

The Gospel of the Lord. All: **Praise to you, Lord Jesus Christ.**

Prayer over the Offerings
Receive our oblation, O Lord,
by which is brought about a glorious exchange,
that, by offering what you have given,
we may merit to receive your very self.
Through Christ our Lord. All: **Amen.**

Communion Antiphon (Psalm 130[129]:7)
With the Lord there is mercy;
in him is plentiful redemption.

Or:

(John 6:51-52)
I am the living bread that came down from heaven,
  says the Lord.
Whoever eats of this bread will live for ever.

Prayer after Communion
Made partakers of Christ through these Sacraments,
we humbly implore your mercy, Lord,
that, conformed to his image on earth,
we may merit also to be his coheirs in heaven.
Who lives and reigns for ever and ever. All: **Amen.**

Twenty-First Sunday in Ordinary Time

August 23, 2015

Reflection on the Gospel

The choice Jesus sets before the disciples in this gospel is deeper than simply "Do you also want to leave?" Jesus is inviting them to come to believe in who he is ("the Holy One of God" given as Bread from heaven) and what he offers (his own Body and Blood for eternal Life). Believing must become the lived conviction of choosing to stay with and in the risen Christ. Choosing to stay with Jesus is a way of living modeled on Jesus' own way of self-giving living.

- *To whom Lord shall we go, you have the words of eternal life . . .*

—Living Liturgy™, *Twenty-First Sunday in Ordinary Time 2015*

Entrance Antiphon (Cf. Psalm 86[85]:1-3)

Turn your ear, O Lord, and answer me;
save the servant who trusts in you, my God.
Have mercy on me, O Lord, for I cry to you all the day long.

Collect

O God, who cause the minds of the faithful
to unite in a single purpose,
grant your people to love what you command
and to desire what you promise,
that, amid the uncertainties of this world,
our hearts may be fixed on that place
where true gladness is found.
Through our Lord Jesus Christ, your Son,
who lives and reigns with you in the unity of the Holy Spirit,
one God, for ever and ever. All: **Amen.**

Reading I (L 122-B) (Joshua 24:1-2a, 15-17, 18b)

A reading from the Book of Joshua

We will serve the Lord, for he is our God.

Joshua gathered together all the tribes of Israel at Shechem, summoning their elders, their leaders, their judges, and their officers.

When they stood in ranks before God,
> Joshua addressed all the people:
> "If it does not please you to serve the Lord,
> decide today whom you will serve,
> the gods your fathers served beyond the River
> or the gods of the Amorites in whose country you are now dwelling.

As for me and my household, we will serve the Lord."

But the people answered,
> "Far be it from us to forsake the Lord
> for the service of other gods.

For it was the Lord, our God,
> who brought us and our fathers up out of the land of Egypt,
> out of a state of slavery.

He performed those great miracles before our very eyes
> and protected us along our entire journey
> and among the peoples through whom we passed.

Therefore we also will serve the Lord, for he is our God."

The word of the Lord. All: **Thanks be to God.**

Responsorial Psalm 34

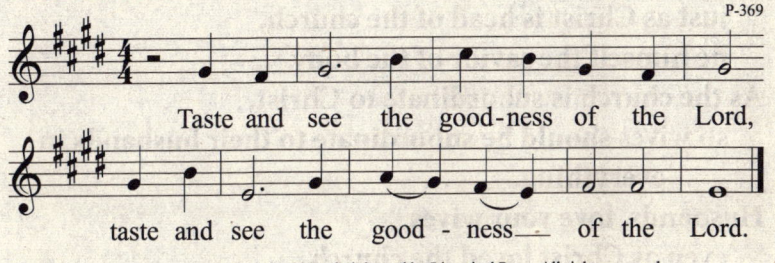

Taste and see the good-ness of the Lord, taste and see the good-ness of the Lord.

Music: Jay F. Hunstiger, © 1990, administered by Liturgical Press. All rights reserved.

Psalm 34:2-3, 16-17, 18-19, 20-21

℟. (9a) **Taste and see the goodness of the Lord.**

> I will bless the Lord at all times;
> > his praise shall be ever in my mouth.
> Let my soul glory in the Lord;
> > the lowly will hear me and be glad. ℟.

(continued)

> The Lord has eyes for the just,
>> and ears for their cry.
> The Lord confronts the evildoers,
>> to destroy remembrance of them from the earth. ℟.
>
> When the just cry out, the Lord hears them,
>> and from all their distress he rescues them.
> The Lord is close to the brokenhearted;
>> and those who are crushed in spirit he saves. ℟.
>
> Many are the troubles of the just one,
>> but out of them all the Lord delivers him;
> he watches over all his bones;
>> not one of them shall be broken. ℟.

Reading II

A Longer Form (Ephesians 5:21-32)

A reading from the Letter of Saint Paul to the Ephesians

This is a great mystery, regarding Christ and the Church.

Brothers and sisters:
Be subordinate to one another out of reverence for Christ.
Wives should be subordinate to their husbands as to
   the Lord.
For the husband is head of his wife
   just as Christ is head of the church,
   he himself the savior of the body.
As the church is subordinate to Christ,
   so wives should be subordinate to their husbands in
      everything.
Husbands, love your wives,
   even as Christ loved the church
   and handed himself over for her to sanctify her,
   cleansing her by the bath of water with the word,
   that he might present to himself the church in splendor,
   without spot or wrinkle or any such thing,
   that she might be holy and without blemish.
So also husbands should love their wives as their own
   bodies.

He who loves his wife loves himself.
For no one hates his own flesh
   but rather nourishes and cherishes it,
   even as Christ does the church,
   because we are members of his body.
For this reason a man shall leave his father and his mother
   and be joined to his wife,
   and the two shall become one flesh.
This is a great mystery,
   but I speak in reference to Christ and the church.

The word of the Lord. All: Thanks be to God.

Or:

B Shorter Form (Ephesians 5:2a, 25-32)
A reading from the Letter of Saint Paul to the Ephesians
This is a great mystery, regarding Christ and the Church.

Brothers and sisters:
Live in love, as Christ loved us.
Husbands, love your wives,
   even as Christ loved the church
   and handed himself over for her to sanctify her,
   cleansing her by the bath of water with the word,
   that he might present to himself the church in splendor,
   without spot or wrinkle or any such thing,
   that she might be holy and without blemish.
So also husbands should love their wives as their own
   bodies.
He who loves his wife loves himself.
For no one hates his own flesh
   but rather nourishes and cherishes it,
   even as Christ does the church,
   because we are members of his body.
For this reason a man shall leave his father and his mother
   and be joined to his wife,
   and the two shall become one flesh.

This is a great mystery,
>   but I speak in reference to Christ and the church.

The word of the Lord. **All:** Thanks be to God.

Gospel (John 6:60-69)
Alleluia (John 6:63c, 68c)
℣. Alleluia, alleluia. ℟. **Alleluia, alleluia.**
℣. Your words, Lord, are Spirit and life;
you have the words of everlasting life. ℟.

✠ A reading from the holy Gospel according to John

All: Glory to you, O Lord.

To whom shall we go? You have the words of eternal life.

Many of Jesus' disciples who were listening said,
>   **"This saying is hard; who can accept it?"**
> **Since Jesus knew that his disciples were murmuring about this,**
>   **he said to them, "Does this shock you?**
> **What if you were to see the Son of Man ascending**
>   **to where he was before?**
> **It is the spirit that gives life,**
>   **while the flesh is of no avail.**
> **The words I have spoken to you are Spirit and life.**
> **But there are some of you who do not believe."**
> **Jesus knew from the beginning the ones who would not believe**
>   **and the one who would betray him.**
> **And he said,**
>   **"For this reason I have told you that no one can come to me**
>   **unless it is granted him by my Father."**
> **As a result of this,**
>   **many of his disciples returned to their former way of life**
>   **and no longer accompanied him.**
> **Jesus then said to the Twelve, "Do you also want to leave?"**

Simon Peter answered him, "Master, to whom shall we go?
You have the words of eternal life.
We have come to believe
   and are convinced that you are the Holy One of God."

The Gospel of the Lord. **All: Praise to you, Lord Jesus Christ.**

Prayer over the Offerings
O Lord, who gained for yourself a people by adoption
through the one sacrifice offered once for all,
bestow graciously on us, we pray,
the gifts of unity and peace in your Church.
Through Christ our Lord. **All: Amen.**

Communion Antiphon (Cf. Psalm 104[103]:13-15)
The earth is replete with the fruits of your work, O Lord;
you bring forth bread from the earth
and wine to cheer the heart.

Or:

(Cf. John 6:54)
Whoever eats my flesh and drinks my blood
has eternal life, says the Lord,
and I will raise him up on the last day.

Prayer after Communion
Complete within us, O Lord, we pray,
the healing work of your mercy
and graciously perfect and sustain us,
so that in all things we may please you.
Through Christ our Lord. **All: Amen.**

Twenty-Second Sunday in Ordinary Time

August 30, 2015

Reflection on the Gospel

In the gospel it appears that "the Pharisees with some scribes" are judging Jesus and his disciples for how they fail to keep the Jewish traditions. In fact, Jesus is passing judgment on the Pharisees and scribes by facing them with their own self-righteousness. The Pharisees fixate on keeping human traditions; Jesus frees people from rigid adherence to human traditions. At stake is right covenantal relationship with God and others in the community. Law is about right relationships, not about self-righteousness.

• *Lord, help us to be in right relationship with you and . . .*

—*Living Liturgy™, Twenty-Second Sunday in Ordinary Time 2015*

ENTRANCE ANTIPHON (Cf. Psalm 86[85]:3, 5)

Have mercy on me, O Lord, for I cry to you all the day long.
O Lord, you are good and forgiving,
full of mercy to all who call to you.

COLLECT

God of might, giver of every good gift,
put into our hearts the love of your name,
so that, by deepening our sense of reverence,
you may nurture in us what is good
and, by your watchful care,
keep safe what you have nurtured.
Through our Lord Jesus Christ, your Son,
who lives and reigns with you in the unity of the Holy Spirit,
one God, for ever and ever. All: **Amen.**

READING I (L 125-B) (Deuteronomy 4:1-2, 6-8)

A reading from the Book of Deuteronomy

You shall not add to what I command you . . . keep the commands of the Lord.

Moses said to the people:
  "Now, Israel, hear the statutes and decrees
  which I am teaching you to observe,
  that you may live, and may enter in and take
      possession of the land
  which the Lord, the God of your fathers, is giving you.
In your observance of the commandments of the Lord,
    your God,
  which I enjoin upon you,
  you shall not add to what I command you nor subtract
      from it.
Observe them carefully,
  for thus will you give evidence
  of your wisdom and intelligence to the nations,
  who will hear of all these statutes and say,
  'This great nation is truly a wise and intelligent people.'
For what great nation is there
  that has gods so close to it as the Lord, our God, is to
      us
  whenever we call upon him?
Or what great nation has statutes and decrees
  that are as just as this whole law
  which I am setting before you today?"

The word of the Lord. **All:** Thanks be to God.

Responsorial Psalm 15

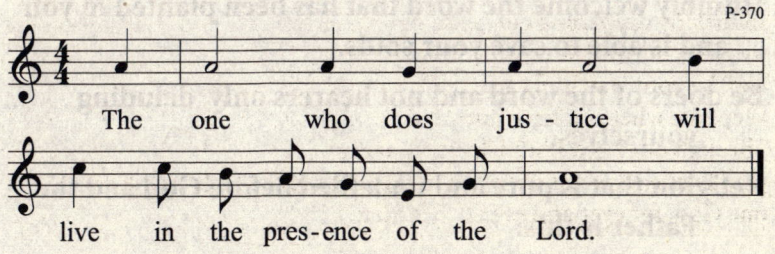

The one who does jus-tice will live in the pres-ence of the Lord.

Music: Jay F. Hunstiger, © 1990, administered by Liturgical Press. All rights reserved.

Psalm 15:2-3, 3-4, 4-5

℟. (1a) **The one who does justice will live in the presence of the Lord.**

Whoever walks blamelessly and does justice;
    who thinks the truth in his heart
    and slanders not with his tongue. ℟.

Who harms not his fellow man,
    nor takes up a reproach against his neighbor;
by whom the reprobate is despised,
    while he honors those who fear the Lord. ℟.

Who lends not his money at usury
    and accepts no bribe against the innocent.
Whoever does these things
    shall never be disturbed. ℟.

Reading II (James 1:17-18, 21b-22, 27)

A reading from the Letter of Saint James

Be doers of the word.

Dearest brothers and sisters:
All good giving and every perfect gift is from above,
    coming down from the Father of lights,
        with whom there is no alteration or shadow caused by change.
He willed to give us birth by the word of truth
    that we may be a kind of firstfruits of his creatures.

Humbly welcome the word that has been planted in you
    and is able to save your souls.

Be doers of the word and not hearers only, deluding yourselves.

Religion that is pure and undefiled before God and the Father is this:
    to care for orphans and widows in their affliction
    and to keep oneself unstained by the world.

The word of the Lord. All: **Thanks be to God.**

G ospel (Mark 7:1-8, 14-15, 21-23)
A lleluia (James 1:18)

℣. Alleluia, alleluia.   ℟. **Alleluia, alleluia.**
℣. The Father willed to give us birth by the word of truth
   that we may be a kind of firstfruits of his creatures. ℟.

✢ A reading from the holy Gospel according to Mark

All: **Glory to you, O Lord.**

You disregard God's commandment but cling to human tradition.

**When the Pharisees with some scribes who had come
      from Jerusalem
   gathered around Jesus,
      they observed that some of his disciples ate their meals
         with unclean, that is, unwashed, hands.
—For the Pharisees and, in fact, all Jews,
   do not eat without carefully washing their hands,
   keeping the tradition of the elders.
And on coming from the marketplace
   they do not eat without purifying themselves.
And there are many other things that they have
      traditionally observed,
   the purification of cups and jugs and kettles and beds.—
So the Pharisees and scribes questioned him,
   "Why do your disciples not follow the tradition of the
         elders
   but instead eat a meal with unclean hands?"
He responded,
   "Well did Isaiah prophesy about you hypocrites, as it
         is written:**
      *This people honors me with their lips,
         but their hearts are far from me;
      in vain do they worship me,
         teaching as doctrines human precepts.*
**You disregard God's commandment but cling to human
      tradition."**

He summoned the crowd again and said to them,
  "Hear me, all of you, and understand.
Nothing that enters one from outside can defile that person;
  but the things that come out from within are what defile.

"From within people, from their hearts,
  come evil thoughts, unchastity, theft, murder,
  adultery, greed, malice, deceit,
  licentiousness, envy, blasphemy, arrogance, folly.
All these evils come from within and they defile."

The Gospel of the Lord. All: **Praise to you, Lord Jesus Christ.**

Prayer over the Offerings
May this sacred offering, O Lord,
confer on us always the blessing of salvation,
that what it celebrates in mystery
it may accomplish in power.
Through Christ our Lord. All: **Amen.**

Communion Antiphon (Psalm 31[30]:20)
How great is the goodness, Lord,
that you keep for those who fear you.

Or:

(Matthew 5:9-10)
Blessed are the peacemakers,
for they shall be called children of God.
Blessed are they who are persecuted for the sake of righteousness,
for theirs is the kingdom of heaven.

Prayer after Communion
Renewed by this bread from the heavenly table,
we beseech you, Lord,
that, being the food of charity,
it may confirm our hearts
and stir us to serve you in our neighbor.
Through Christ our Lord. All: **Amen.**

Twenty-Third Sunday in Ordinary Time

September 6, 2015

Reflection on the Gospel
In this gospel Jesus opens the ears and loosens the tongue of the deaf-mute. Both he and the crowd cannot contain themselves, but proclaim what Jesus has done. What has Jesus really done? The miracles Jesus performs reveal his own divine power, his own compassion for the human condition, his own mission. Jesus cares for each of us, cares enough to reach out and touch us! Faced with this revelation, no one can keep silent. The Word grants the power of word.

- *Come see the power of the Word as he . . .*

—Living Liturgy™, *Twenty-Third Sunday in Ordinary Time 2015*

Entrance Antiphon (Psalm 119[118]:137, 124)
You are just, O Lord, and your judgment is right;
treat your servant in accord with your merciful love.

Collect
O God, by whom we are redeemed and receive adoption,
look graciously upon your beloved sons and daughters,
that those who believe in Christ
may receive true freedom
and an everlasting inheritance.
Through our Lord Jesus Christ, your Son,
who lives and reigns with you in the unity of the Holy Spirit,
one God, for ever and ever. All: **Amen.**

Reading I (L 128-B) (Isaiah 35:4-7a)
A reading from the Book of the Prophet Isaiah

The ears of those who are deaf will be cleared; and the tongue of those who are mute will sing.

Thus says the Lord:
 Say to those whose hearts are frightened:
  Be strong, fear not!

Here is your God,
   he comes with vindication;
with divine recompense
   he comes to save you.
Then will the eyes of the blind be opened,
   the ears of the deaf be cleared;
then will the lame leap like a stag,
   then the tongue of the mute will sing.
Streams will burst forth in the desert,
   and rivers in the steppe.
The burning sands will become pools,
   and the thirsty ground, springs of water.

The word of the Lord. All: **Thanks be to God.**

Responsorial Psalm 146

Praise the Lord, my soul! Al-le-lu-ia.

Music: Jay F. Hunstiger, © 1990, administered by Liturgical Press. All rights reserved.

Psalm 146:7, 8-9a, 9bc-10

℟. (1b) **Praise the Lord, my soul!** *or:* ℟. **Alleluia.**

The God of Jacob keeps faith forever,
   secures justice for the oppressed,
   gives food to the hungry.
The Lord sets captives free. ℟.

The Lord gives sight to the blind;
   the Lord raises up those who were bowed down.
The Lord loves the just;
   the Lord protects strangers. ℟.

The fatherless and the widow the Lord sustains,
   but the way of the wicked he thwarts.
The Lord shall reign forever;
   your God, O Zion, through all generations. Alleluia. ℟.

Reading II (James 2:1-5)

A reading from the Letter of Saint James

Did not God choose the poor to be heirs of the kingdom?

**My brothers and sisters, show no partiality
as you adhere to the faith in our glorious Lord Jesus Christ.
For if a man with gold rings and fine clothes
comes into your assembly,
and a poor person in shabby clothes also comes in,
and you pay attention to the one wearing the fine clothes
and say, "Sit here, please,"
while you say to the poor one, "Stand there," or "Sit at my feet,"
have you not made distinctions among yourselves
and become judges with evil designs?
Listen, my beloved brothers and sisters.
Did not God choose those who are poor in the world
to be rich in faith and heirs of the kingdom
that he promised to those who love him?**

The word of the Lord. All: **Thanks be to God.**

Gospel (Mark 7:31-37)

Alleluia (*See* Matthew 4:23)

℣. Alleluia, alleluia. ℟. **Alleluia, alleluia.**
℣. Jesus proclaimed the Gospel of the kingdom
and cured every disease among the people. ℟.

✠ **A reading from the holy Gospel according to Mark**

All: **Glory to you, O Lord.**

He makes the deaf hear and the mute speak.

**Again Jesus left the district of Tyre
and went by way of Sidon to the Sea of Galilee,
into the district of the Decapolis.
And people brought to him a deaf man who had a speech impediment
and begged him to lay his hand on him.**

He took him off by himself away from the crowd.
He put his finger into the man's ears
 and, spitting, touched his tongue;
  then he looked up to heaven and groaned, and said to him,
   "Ephphatha!"—that is, "Be opened!"—
And immediately the man's ears were opened,
 his speech impediment was removed,
 and he spoke plainly.
He ordered them not to tell anyone.
But the more he ordered them not to,
 the more they proclaimed it.
They were exceedingly astonished and they said,
 "He has done all things well.
He makes the deaf hear and the mute speak."

The Gospel of the Lord. All: **Praise to you, Lord Jesus Christ.**

Prayer over the Offerings
O God, who give us the gift of true prayer and of peace,
graciously grant that, through this offering,
we may do fitting homage to your divine majesty
and, by partaking of the sacred mystery,
we may be faithfully united in mind and heart.
Through Christ our Lord. All: **Amen.**

Communion Antiphon (Cf. Psalm 42[41]:2-3)
Like the deer that yearns for running streams,
so my soul is yearning for you, my God;
my soul is thirsting for God, the living God.

Or:

(John 8:12)
I am the light of the world, says the Lord;
whoever follows me will not walk in darkness,
but will have the light of life.

Prayer after Communion
Grant that your faithful, O Lord,
whom you nourish and endow with life
through the food of your Word and heavenly Sacrament,

may so benefit from your beloved Son's great gifts
that we may merit an eternal share in his life.
Who lives and reigns for ever and ever. All: **Amen.**

Twenty-Fourth Sunday in Ordinary Time

September 13, 2015

Reflection on the Gospel

Jesus is called "the Christ"—Peter is called Satan. Salvation confronts human resistance. Peter had a certain image, belief, expectation of what "the Christ" was to be, to do. Suffering, rejection, and being killed had nothing to do with Peter's Christ. But they have everything to do with the Christ of God. Without a right understanding of "the Christ," we cannot, with him, rise to new Life. We take up our own cross daily because this is the way to a share in risen Life.

- *Lord, help me to take up my cross daily by . . .*

—Living Liturgy™, *Twenty-Fourth Sunday in Ordinary Time 2015*

Entrance Antiphon (Cf. Sirach 36:18)

Give peace, O Lord, to those who wait for you,
that your prophets be found true.
Hear the prayers of your servant,
and of your people Israel.

Collect

Look upon us, O God,
Creator and ruler of all things,
and, that we may feel the working of your mercy,
grant that we may serve you with all our heart.
Through our Lord Jesus Christ, your Son,
who lives and reigns with you in the unity of the Holy Spirit,
one God, for ever and ever. All: **Amen.**

Reading I (L 131-B) (Isaiah 50:4c-9a)
A reading from the Book of the Prophet Isaiah

I gave my back to those who beat me.

> The Lord God opens my ear that I may hear;
> and I have not rebelled,
>> have not turned back.
> I gave my back to those who beat me,
>> my cheeks to those who plucked my beard;
> my face I did not shield
>> from buffets and spitting.
>
> The Lord God is my help,
>> therefore I am not disgraced;
> I have set my face like flint,
>> knowing that I shall not be put to shame.
> He is near who upholds my right;
>> if anyone wishes to oppose me,
>> let us appear together.
> Who disputes my right?
>> Let that man confront me.
> See, the Lord God is my help;
>> who will prove me wrong?

The word of the Lord. **All:** Thanks be to God.

Responsorial Psalm 116

I will walk in the presence of the Lord, in the land of the living.

Music: Jay F. Hunstiger, © 1990, administered by Liturgical Press. All rights reserved.

Psalm 116:1-2, 3-4, 5-6, 8-9

℟. (9) **I will walk before the Lord, in the land of the living.** *or:* ℟. **Alleluia.**

I love the Lord because he has heard
 my voice in supplication,
because he has inclined his ear to me
 the day I called. ℟.

The cords of death encompassed me;
 the snares of the netherworld seized upon me;
 I fell into distress and sorrow,
and I called upon the name of the Lord,
 "O Lord, save my life!" ℟.

Gracious is the Lord and just;
 yes, our God is merciful.
The Lord keeps the little ones;
 I was brought low, and he saved me. ℟.

For he has freed my soul from death,
 my eyes from tears, my feet from stumbling.
I shall walk before the Lord
 in the land of the living. ℟.

Reading II (James 2:14-18)

A reading from the Letter of Saint James

Faith, if it does not have works, is dead.

What good is it, my brothers and sisters,
 if someone says he has faith but does not have works?
Can that faith save him?
If a brother or sister has nothing to wear
 and has no food for the day,
 and one of you says to them,
 "Go in peace, keep warm, and eat well,"
 but you do not give them the necessities of the body,
 what good is it?
So also faith of itself,
 if it does not have works, is dead.

Indeed someone might say,
  "You have faith and I have works."
Demonstrate your faith to me without works,
  and I will demonstrate my faith to you from my works.

The word of the Lord. All: **Thanks be to God.**

GOSPEL (Mark 8:27-35)
ALLELUIA (Galatians 6:14)
℣. Alleluia, alleluia. ℟. **Alleluia, alleluia.**
℣. May I never boast except in the cross of our Lord
  through which the world has been crucified to me and I to the world. ℟.

☩ **A reading from the holy Gospel according to Mark**

All: **Glory to you, O Lord.**

You are the Christ . . . the Son of Man must suffer greatly.

Jesus and his disciples set out
  for the villages of Caesarea Philippi.
Along the way he asked his disciples,
  "Who do people say that I am?"
They said in reply,
  "John the Baptist, others Elijah,
  still others one of the prophets."
And he asked them,
  "But who do you say that I am?"
Peter said to him in reply,
  "You are the Christ."
Then he warned them not to tell anyone about him.
He began to teach them
  that the Son of Man must suffer greatly
  and be rejected by the elders, the chief priests, and the scribes,
  and be killed, and rise after three days.
He spoke this openly.
Then Peter took him aside and began to rebuke him.

At this he turned around and, looking at his disciples,
rebuked Peter and said, "Get behind me, Satan.
You are thinking not as God does, but as human beings
do."

He summoned the crowd with his disciples and said to
them,
"Whoever wishes to come after me must deny himself,
take up his cross, and follow me.
For whoever wishes to save his life will lose it,
but whoever loses his life for my sake
and that of the gospel will save it."

The Gospel of the Lord. All: **Praise to you, Lord Jesus Christ.**

Prayer over the Offerings
Look with favor on our supplications, O Lord,
and in your kindness accept these, your servants' offerings,
that what each has offered to the honor of your name
may serve the salvation of all.
Through Christ our Lord. All: **Amen.**

Communion Antiphon (Cf. Psalm 36[35]:8)
How precious is your mercy, O God!
The children of men seek shelter in the shadow of your
    wings.

Or:

(Cf 1 Corinthians 10:16)
The chalice of blessing that we bless
is a communion in the Blood of Christ;
and the bread that we break
is a sharing in the Body of the Lord.

Prayer after Communion
May the working of this heavenly gift, O Lord, we pray,
take possession of our minds and bodies,
so that its effects, and not our own desires,
may always prevail in us.
Through Christ our Lord. All: **Amen.**

Twenty-Fifth Sunday in Ordinary Time

September 20, 2015

Reflection on the Gospel

The scandal of this gospel is that Jesus, the leader and teacher of the disciples, will be reduced to the least when he is handed over and dies. How do the disciples react to this scandalous teaching? They argue among themselves about who is the greatest! The disciples do not understand greatest and least, first and last, servant of all. They do not understand that Jesus' own death is a call to die to self, to choose to become the greatest by being the least.

- *Lord, help me to die to self and answer your call to serve . . .*

—Living Liturgy™, *Twenty-Fifth Sunday in Ordinary Time 2015*

Entrance Antiphon
I am the salvation of the people, says the Lord.
Should they cry to me in any distress,
I will hear them, and I will be their Lord for ever.

Collect
O God, who founded all the commands of your sacred Law
upon love of you and of our neighbor,
grant that, by keeping your precepts,
we may merit to attain eternal life.
Through our Lord Jesus Christ, your Son,
who lives and reigns with you in the unity of the Holy Spirit,
one God, for ever and ever. All: **Amen.**

Reading I (L 134-B) (Wisdom 2:12, 17-20)
A reading from the Book of Wisdom

Let us condemn him to a shameful death.

The wicked say:
    Let us beset the just one, because he is obnoxious to us;
        he sets himself against our doings,

reproaches us for transgressions of the law
>and charges us with violations of our training.

Let us see whether his words be true;
>let us find out what will happen to him.

For if the just one be the son of God, God will defend him
>and deliver him from the hand of his foes.

With revilement and torture let us put the just one to the test
>that we may have proof of his gentleness
>and try his patience.

Let us condemn him to a shameful death;
>for according to his own words, God will take care of him.

The word of the Lord. All: **Thanks be to God.**

Responsorial Psalm 54

The Lord upholds my life.

Music: Jay F. Hunstiger, © 1990, administered by Liturgical Press. All rights reserved.

Psalm 54:3-4, 5, 6-8

℟. (6b) **The Lord upholds my life.**

O God, by your name save me,
>and by your might defend my cause.
O God, hear my prayer;
>hearken to the words of my mouth. ℟.

For the haughty have risen up against me,
>the ruthless seek my life;
>they set not God before their eyes. ℟.

Behold, God is my helper;
>the Lord sustains my life.
Freely will I offer you sacrifice;
>I will praise your name, O Lord, for its goodness. ℟.

Reading II (James 3:16—4:3)
A reading from the Letter of Saint James

The fruit of righteousness is sown in peace for those who cultivate peace.

**Beloved:
Where jealousy and selfish ambition exist,
 there is disorder and every foul practice.
But the wisdom from above is first of all pure,
 then peaceable, gentle, compliant,
 full of mercy and good fruits,
 without inconstancy or insincerity.
And the fruit of righteousness is sown in peace
 for those who cultivate peace.

Where do the wars
 and where do the conflicts among you come from?
Is it not from your passions
 that make war within your members?
You covet but do not possess.
You kill and envy but you cannot obtain;
 you fight and wage war.
You do not possess because you do not ask.
You ask but do not receive,
 because you ask wrongly, to spend it on your passions.

The word of the Lord.** All: **Thanks be to God.**

Gospel (Mark 9:30-37)
Alleluia (See 2 Thessalonians 2:14)

℣. Alleluia, alleluia. ℟. **Alleluia, alleluia.**
℣. God has called us through the Gospel
 to possess the glory of our Lord Jesus Christ. ℟.

✢ **A reading from the holy Gospel according to Mark**

All: **Glory to you, O Lord.**

The Son of Man is to be handed over. . . . Whoever wishes to be first will be the servant of all.

**Jesus and his disciples left from there and began a
  journey through Galilee,
 but he did not wish anyone to know about it.
He was teaching his disciples and telling them,
 "The Son of Man is to be handed over to men
 and they will kill him,
 and three days after his death the Son of Man will rise."
But they did not understand the saying,
 and they were afraid to question him.**

**They came to Capernaum and, once inside the house,
 he began to ask them,
 "What were you arguing about on the way?"
But they remained silent.
They had been discussing among themselves on the way
 who was the greatest.
Then he sat down, called the Twelve, and said to them,
 "If anyone wishes to be first,
 he shall be the last of all and the servant of all."
Taking a child, he placed it in their midst,
 and putting his arms around it, he said to them,
 "Whoever receives one child such as this in my name,
  receives me;
 and whoever receives me,
 receives not me but the One who sent me."**

The Gospel of the Lord. All: **Praise to you, Lord Jesus Christ.**

Prayer over the Offerings
Receive with favor, O Lord, we pray,
the offerings of your people,
that what they profess with devotion and faith
may be theirs through these heavenly mysteries.
Through Christ our Lord. All: **Amen.**

Communion Antiphon (Psalm 119[118]:4-5)
You have laid down your precepts to be carefully kept;
may my ways be firm in keeping your statutes.

Or:

(John 10:14)
I am the Good Shepherd, says the Lord;
I know my sheep, and mine know me.

PRAYER AFTER COMMUNION
Graciously raise up, O Lord,
those you renew with this Sacrament,
that we may come to possess your redemption
both in mystery and in the manner of our life.
Through Christ our Lord. **All: Amen.**

Twenty-Sixth Sunday in Ordinary Time

September 27, 2015

Reflection on the Gospel

Focused completely on his saving mission to bring about the kingdom of God, Jesus directly confronts human pettiness and sinfulness. He uses graphic examples to demand that disciples turn from whatever is inconsistent with acting in his name, with continuing his mission. Any behavior which causes us to sin or to lead others into sin must be cut off. Being a disciple demands radical choices about how we live and relate to others. It means being as completely focused on Jesus' saving mission as he was.

- *The Kingdom of God demands that I . . .*

—Living Liturgy™, *Twenty-Sixth Sunday in Ordinary Time 2015*

ENTRANCE ANTIPHON (Daniel 3:31, 29, 30, 43, 42)
All that you have done to us, O Lord,
you have done with true judgment,
for we have sinned against you

and not obeyed your commandments.
But give glory to your name
and deal with us according to the bounty of your mercy.

Collect

O God, who manifest your almighty power
above all by pardoning and showing mercy,
bestow, we pray, your grace abundantly upon us
and make those hastening to attain your promises
heirs to the treasures of heaven.
Through our Lord Jesus Christ, your Son,
who lives and reigns with you in the unity of the Holy Spirit,
one God, for ever and ever. All: **Amen.**

Reading I (L 137-B) (Numbers 11:25-29)

A reading from the Book of Numbers

Are you jealous for my sake? Would that all the people of the Lord were prophets!

The Lord came down in the cloud and spoke to Moses.
Taking some of the spirit that was on Moses,
    the Lord bestowed it on the seventy elders;
    and as the spirit came to rest on them, they prophesied.

Now two men, one named Eldad and the other Medad,
    were not in the gathering but had been left in the camp.
They too had been on the list, but had not gone out to
    the tent;
    yet the spirit came to rest on them also,
    and they prophesied in the camp.
So, when a young man quickly told Moses,
    "Eldad and Medad are prophesying in the camp,"
    Joshua, son of Nun, who from his youth had been
        Moses' aide, said,
    "Moses, my lord, stop them."
But Moses answered him,
    "Are you jealous for my sake?
Would that all the people of the Lord were prophets!
Would that the Lord might bestow his spirit on them all!"

The word of the Lord. All: **Thanks be to God.**

Responsorial Psalm 19

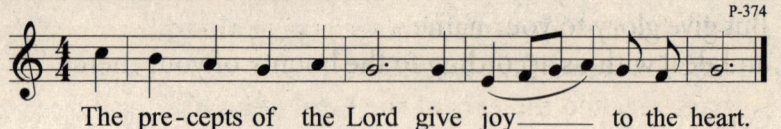

The precepts of the Lord give joy to the heart.

Music: Jay F. Hunstiger, © 1990, administered by Liturgical Press. All rights reserved.

Psalm 19:8, 10, 12-13, 14

℟. (9a) **The precepts of the Lord give joy to the heart.**

The law of the Lord is perfect,
 refreshing the soul;
the decree of the Lord is trustworthy,
 giving wisdom to the simple. ℟.

The fear of the Lord is pure,
 enduring forever;
the ordinances of the Lord are true,
 all of them just. ℟.

Though your servant is careful of them,
 very diligent in keeping them,
yet who can detect failings?
 Cleanse me from my unknown faults! ℟.

From wanton sin especially, restrain your servant;
 let it not rule over me.
Then shall I be blameless and innocent
 of serious sin. ℟.

Reading II (James 5:1-6)

A reading from the Letter of Saint James

Your wealth has rotted away.

**Come now, you rich, weep and wail over your impending miseries.
Your wealth has rotted away, your clothes have become moth-eaten,
 your gold and silver have corroded,
 and that corrosion will be a testimony against you;
 it will devour your flesh like a fire.
You have stored up treasure for the last days.**

Behold, the wages you withheld from the workers
> who harvested your fields are crying aloud;
> and the cries of the harvesters
> have reached the ears of the Lord of hosts.

You have lived on earth in luxury and pleasure;
> you have fattened your hearts for the day of slaughter.

You have condemned;
> you have murdered the righteous one;
> he offers you no resistance.

The word of the Lord. All: Thanks be to God.

Gospel (Mark 9:38-43, 45, 47-48)

Alleluia (See John 17:17b, 17a)

℣. Alleluia, alleluia. ℟. **Alleluia, alleluia.**
℣. Your word, O Lord, is truth;
> consecrate us in the truth. ℟.

✠ A reading from the holy Gospel according to Mark

All: **Glory to you, O Lord.**

Whoever is not against us is for us. If your hand causes you to sin, cut it off.

At that time, John said to Jesus,
> "Teacher, we saw someone driving out demons in
>> your name,
> and we tried to prevent him because he does not
>> follow us."

Jesus replied, "Do not prevent him.
There is no one who performs a mighty deed in my name
> who can at the same time speak ill of me.

For whoever is not against us is for us.
Anyone who gives you a cup of water to drink
> because you belong to Christ,
> amen, I say to you, will surely not lose his reward.

"Whoever causes one of these little ones who believe in
> me to sin,
> it would be better for him if a great millstone
> were put around his neck
> and he were thrown into the sea.

If your hand causes you to sin, cut it off.
It is better for you to enter into life maimed
    than with two hands to go into Gehenna,
    into the unquenchable fire.
And if your foot causes you to sin, cut if off.
It is better for you to enter into life crippled
    than with two feet to be thrown into Gehenna.
And if your eye causes you to sin, pluck it out.
Better for you to enter into the kingdom of God with
    one eye
    than with two eyes to be thrown into Gehenna,
    where 'their worm does not die, and the fire is not
    quenched.'"

The Gospel of the Lord. All: **Praise to you, Lord Jesus Christ.**

Prayer over the Offerings
Grant us, O merciful God,
that this our offering may find acceptance with you
and that through it the wellspring of all blessing
may be laid open before us.
Through Christ our Lord. All: **Amen.**

Communion Antiphon (Cf. Psalm 119[118]:49-50)
Remember your word to your servant, O Lord,
by which you have given me hope.
This is my comfort when I am brought low.

Or:

(1 John 3:16)
By this we came to know the love of God:
that Christ laid down his life for us;
so we ought to lay down our lives for one another.

Prayer after Communion
May this heavenly mystery, O Lord,
restore us in mind and body,
that we may be coheirs in glory with Christ,
to whose suffering we are united
whenever we proclaim his Death.
Who lives and reigns for ever and ever. All: **Amen.**

Twenty-Seventh Sunday in Ordinary Time

October 4, 2015

Reflection on the Gospel

The longer form of this Sunday's gospel unfolds in two interrelated situations. The Pharisees approach Jesus to test him about his stance concerning marriage and divorce; the disciples rebuke the people for bringing their children to Jesus. In both situations, Jesus upholds human relationships as fundamental to embracing the kingdom of God. In both situations, faithful ones are embraced and blessed by God. In this gospel Jesus exposes the hardness of the Pharisees' hearts. This challenges us to look deep within our own hearts.

- *The Kingdom of God challenges me to . . .*

—Living Liturgy™, *Twenty-Seventh Sunday in Ordinary Time 2015*

Entrance Antiphon (Cf. Esther 4:17)

Within your will, O Lord, all things are established,
and there is none that can resist your will.
For you have made all things, the heaven and the earth,
and all that is held within the circle of heaven;
you are the Lord of all.

Collect

Almighty ever-living God,
who in the abundance of your kindness
surpass the merits and the desires of those who entreat you,
pour out your mercy upon us
to pardon what conscience dreads
and to give what prayer does not dare to ask.
Through our Lord Jesus Christ, your Son,
who lives and reigns with you in the unity of the Holy Spirit,
one God, for ever and ever. **All: Amen.**

Reading I (L 140-B) (Genesis 2:18-24)

A reading from the Book of Genesis

The two of them become one flesh.

The Lord God said: "It is not good for the man to be alone.
I will make a suitable partner for him."
So the Lord God formed out of the ground
   various wild animals and various birds of the air,
     and he brought them to the man to see what he would call them;
     whatever the man called each of them would be its name.
The man gave names to all the cattle,
   all the birds of the air, and all wild animals;
   but none proved to be the suitable partner for the man.

So the Lord God cast a deep sleep on the man,
   and while he was asleep,
   he took out one of his ribs and closed up its place with flesh.
The Lord God then built up into a woman the rib
   that he had taken from the man.
When he brought her to the man, the man said:
   "This one, at last, is bone of my bones
     and flesh of my flesh;
   this one shall be called 'woman,'
     for out of 'her man' this one has been taken."
That is why a man leaves his father and mother
   and clings to his wife,
   and the two of them become one flesh.

The word of the Lord. **All:** Thanks be to God.

Responsorial Psalm 128

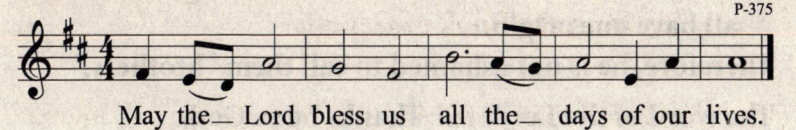

May the Lord bless us all the days of our lives.

<small>Music: Jay F. Hunstiger, © 1990, administered by Liturgical Press. All rights reserved.</small>

Psalm 128:1-2, 3, 4-5, 6

℟. (*See 5*) **May the Lord bless us all the days of our lives.**

> Blessed are you who fear the LORD,
> > who walk in his ways!
>
> For you shall eat the fruit of your handiwork;
> > blessed shall you be, and favored. ℟.
>
> Your wife shall be like a fruitful vine
> > in the recesses of your home;
>
> your children like olive plants
> > around your table. ℟.
>
> Behold, thus is the man blessed
> > who fears the LORD.
>
> The LORD bless you from Zion:
> > may you see the prosperity of Jerusalem
> > all the days of your life. ℟.
>
> May you see your children's children.
> > Peace be upon Israel! ℟.

Reading II (Hebrews 2:9-11)

A reading from the Letter to the Hebrews

He who consecrates and those who are being consecrated all have one origin.

Brothers and sisters:
He "for a little while" was made "lower than the angels,"
> that by the grace of God he might taste death for
> > everyone.

For it was fitting that he,
> for whom and through whom all things exist,
> in bringing many children to glory,
> should make the leader to their salvation perfect
> > through suffering.

He who consecrates and those who are being consecrated
 all have one origin.
Therefore, he is not ashamed to call them "brothers."

The word of the Lord. All: **Thanks be to God.**

GOSPEL (Mark 10:2-16) *or* Shorter Form [ ] (Mark 10:2-12)
ALLELUIA (1 John 4:12)

℣. Alleluia, alleluia. ℟. **Alleluia, alleluia.**
℣. If we love one another, God remains in us
 and his love is brought to perfection in us. ℟.

✠ **A reading from the holy Gospel according to Mark**

All: **Glory to you, O Lord.**

Therefore what God has joined together, let no human being separate.

[The Pharisees approached Jesus and asked,
 "Is it lawful for a husband to divorce his wife?"
They were testing him.
He said to them in reply, "What did Moses command you?"
They replied,
 "Moses permitted a husband to write a bill of divorce
 and dismiss her."
But Jesus told them,
 "Because of the hardness of your hearts
 he wrote you this commandment.
But from the beginning of creation, *God made them
 male and female.*
*For this reason a man shall leave his father and mother
 and be joined to his wife,*
 and the two shall become one flesh.
So they are no longer two but one flesh.
Therefore what God has joined together,
 no human being must separate."
In the house the disciples again questioned Jesus about
 this.

He said to them,
> "Whoever divorces his wife and marries another commits adultery against her;
> and if she divorces her husband and marries another, she commits adultery."]

And people were bringing children to him that he might touch them,
> but the disciples rebuked them.

When Jesus saw this he became indignant and said to them,
> "Let the children come to me;
> do not prevent them, for the kingdom of God belongs to such as these.

Amen, I say to you,
> whoever does not accept the kingdom of God like a child
> will not enter it."

Then he embraced them and blessed them,
> placing his hands on them.

The Gospel of the Lord. All: **Praise to you, Lord Jesus Christ.**

Prayer over the Offerings

Accept, O Lord, we pray,
the sacrifices instituted by your commands
and, through the sacred mysteries,
which we celebrate with dutiful service,
graciously complete the sanctifying work
by which you are pleased to redeem us.
Through Christ our Lord. All: **Amen.**

Communion Antiphon (Lamentations 3:25)

The Lord is good to those who hope in him,
to the soul that seeks him.

Or:

(Cf. 1 Corinthians 10:17)

Though many, we are one bread, one body,
for we all partake of the one Bread and one Chalice.

Prayer after Communion

Grant us, almighty God,
that we may be refreshed and nourished
by the Sacrament which we have received,
so as to be transformed into what we consume.
Through Christ our Lord. All: **Amen.**

Twenty-Eighth Sunday in Ordinary Time

October 11, 2015

Reflection on the Gospel

The man in the gospel must have had an inkling that keeping the commandments was not enough, or else he never would have approached Jesus with his question about how to inherit eternal Life. In spite of his faithfulness in keeping God's commandments and his being loved by Jesus, the man nevertheless had a divided heart: "he went away sad, for he had many possessions." The man needed to turn his focus from earthly life to eternal Life, from possessions to single-heartedly following Jesus. Where is our heart?

• I single-heartedly follow Jesus by . . .

—*Living Liturgy*™, *Twenty-Eighth Sunday in Ordinary Time 2015*

Entrance Antiphon (Psalm 130[129]:3-4)

If you, O Lord, should mark iniquities,
Lord, who could stand?
But with you is found forgiveness,
O God of Israel.

Collect

May your grace, O Lord, we pray,
at all times go before us and follow after
and make us always determined
to carry out good works.

Through our Lord Jesus Christ, your Son,
who lives and reigns with you in the unity of the Holy Spirit,
one God, for ever and ever. All: **Amen.**

READING I (L 143-B) (Wisdom 7:7-11)

A reading from the Book of Wisdom

I deemed riches nothing in comparison to wisdom.

> **I prayed, and prudence was given me;**
> **I pleaded, and the spirit of wisdom came to me.**
> **I preferred her to scepter and throne,**
> **and deemed riches nothing in comparison with her,**
> **nor did I liken any priceless gem to her;**
> **because all gold, in view of her, is a little sand,**
> **and before her, silver is to be accounted mire.**
> **Beyond health and comeliness I loved her,**
> **and I chose to have her rather than the light,**
> **because the splendor of her never yields to sleep.**
> **Yet all good things together came to me in her company,**
> **and countless riches at her hands.**

The word of the Lord. All: **Thanks be to God.**

RESPONSORIAL PSALM 90

Fill us with your love, O Lord, and we will sing for joy!

Music: Jay F. Hunstiger, © 1990, administered by Liturgical Press. All rights reserved.

Psalm 90:12-13, 14-15, 16-17

℟. (14) **Fill us with your love, O Lord, and we will sing for joy!**

> Teach us to number our days aright,
>   that we may gain wisdom of heart.
> Return, O LORD! How long?
>   Have pity on your servants! ℟.

(continued)

Fill us at daybreak with your kindness,
> that we may shout for joy and gladness all our days.
Make us glad, for the days when you afflicted us,
> for the years when we saw evil. ℟.

Let your work be seen by your servants
> and your glory by their children;
and may the gracious care of the Lord our God be ours;
> prosper the work of our hands for us!
> Prosper the work of our hands! ℟.

Reading II (Hebrews 4:12-13)

A reading from the Letter to the Hebrews

The word of God discerns reflections and thoughts of the heart.

**Brothers and sisters:
Indeed the word of God is living and effective,
> sharper than any two-edged sword,
> penetrating even between soul and spirit, joints and marrow,
> and able to discern reflections and thoughts of the heart.
No creature is concealed from him,
> but everything is naked and exposed to the eyes of him to whom we must render an account.

The word of the Lord. All: Thanks be to God.**

Gospel (Mark 10:17-30) *or* Shorter Form [ ] (Mark 10:17-27)

Alleluia (Matthew 5:3)
℣. Alleluia, alleluia. ℟. **Alleluia, alleluia.**
℣. Blessed are the poor in spirit,
> for theirs is the kingdom of heaven. ℟.

✠ **A reading from the holy Gospel according to Mark**

All: **Glory to you, O Lord.**

Sell what you have, and follow me.

**[As Jesus was setting out on a journey, a man ran up,
> knelt down before him, and asked him,
>> "Good teacher, what must I do to inherit eternal life?"**

Jesus answered him, "Why do you call me good?
No one is good but God alone.
You know the commandments: *You shall not kill;*
   you shall not commit adultery;
   you shall not steal;
   you shall not bear false witness;
   you shall not defraud;
   honor your father and your mother."
He replied and said to him,
   "Teacher, all of these I have observed from my youth."
Jesus, looking at him, loved him and said to him,
   "You are lacking in one thing.
Go, sell what you have, and give to the poor
   and you will have treasure in heaven; then come,
      follow me."
At that statement his face fell,
   and he went away sad, for he had many possessions.

Jesus looked around and said to his disciples,
   "How hard it is for those who have wealth
   to enter the kingdom of God!"
The disciples were amazed at his words.
So Jesus again said to them in reply,
   "Children, how hard it is to enter the kingdom of God!
It is easier for a camel to pass through the eye of a needle
   than for one who is rich to enter the kingdom of God."
They were exceedingly astonished and said among
      themselves,
   "Then who can be saved?"
Jesus looked at them and said,
   "For human beings it is impossible, but not for God.
All things are possible for God."]
Peter began to say to him,
   "We have given up everything and followed you."
Jesus said, "Amen, I say to you,
   there is no one who has given up house or brothers
      or sisters

or mother or father or children or lands
for my sake and for the sake of the gospel
who will not receive a hundred times more now in
   this present age:
houses and brothers and sisters
and mothers and children and lands,
with persecutions, and eternal life in the age to come."

The Gospel of the Lord. All: **Praise to you, Lord Jesus Christ.**

Prayer over the Offerings
Accept, O Lord, the prayers of your faithful
with the sacrificial offerings,
that, through these acts of devotedness,
we may pass over to the glory of heaven.
Through Christ our Lord. All: **Amen.**

Communion Antiphon (Cf. Psalm 34[33]:11)
The rich suffer want and go hungry,
but those who seek the Lord lack no blessing.

Or:

(1 John 3:2)
When the Lord appears, we shall be like him,
for we shall see him as he is.

Prayer after Communion
We entreat your majesty most humbly, O Lord,
that, as you feed us with the nourishment
which comes from the most holy Body and Blood of your Son,
so you may make us sharers of his divine nature.
Who lives and reigns for ever and ever. All: **Amen.**

Twenty-Ninth Sunday in Ordinary Time

October 18, 2015

(World Mission Sunday)

Reflection on the Gospel

Why did the apostles follow Jesus? This gospel suggests they had reward on their minds: the glory of sitting at the right and left of Jesus in positions of honor. It took the apostles a long time to learn that the real reward of following Jesus would be to "drink the cup" and "be baptized" with his baptism. His baptism was his lifelong choice to do the will of the Father no matter what the cost. As Jesus' followers, we can choose no less.

- *Following Jesus, to "drink the cup" and "be baptized" means I must . . .*

—Living Liturgy™, *Twenty-Ninth Sunday in Ordinary Time 2015*

ENTRANCE ANTIPHON (Cf. Psalm 17[16]:6, 8)

To you I call; for you will surely heed me, O God;
turn your ear to me; hear my words.
Guard me as the apple of your eye;
in the shadow of your wings protect me.

COLLECT

Almighty ever-living God,
grant that we may always conform our will to yours
and serve your majesty in sincerity of heart.
Through our Lord Jesus Christ, your Son,
who lives and reigns with you in the unity of the Holy Spirit,
one God, for ever and ever. All: **Amen.**

READING I (L 146-B) (Isaiah 53:10-11)

A reading from the Book of the Prophet Isaiah

If he gives his life as an offering for sin, he shall see his descendants in a long life.

The LORD was pleased
   to crush him in infirmity.

> If he gives his life as an offering for sin,
>> he shall see his descendants in a long life,
>> and the will of the LORD shall be accomplished
>>> through him.
>
> Because of his affliction
>> he shall see the light in fullness of days;
> through his suffering, my servant shall justify many,
>> and their guilt he shall bear.

The word of the Lord. All: **Thanks be to God.**

RESPONSORIAL PSALM 33

Lord, let your mer-cy be on us, as we place our trust in you.

Music: Jay F. Hunstiger, © 1991, administered by Liturgical Press. All rights reserved.

Psalm 33:4-5, 18-19, 20 and 22

℟. (22) **Lord, let your mercy be on us, as we place our trust in you.**

> Upright is the word of the LORD,
>> and all his works are trustworthy.
>
> He loves justice and right;
>> of the kindness of the LORD the earth is full. ℟.
>
> See, the eyes of the LORD are upon those who fear him,
>> upon those who hope for his kindness,
>
> to deliver them from death
>> and preserve them in spite of famine. ℟.
>
> Our soul waits for the LORD,
>> who is our help and our shield.
>
> May your kindness, O LORD, be upon us
>> who have put our hope in you. ℟.

October 18 397

Reading II (Hebrews 4:14-16)
A reading from the Letter to the Hebrews

Let us confidently approach the throne of grace.

**Brothers and sisters:
Since we have a great high priest who has passed through the heavens,
   Jesus, the Son of God,
   let us hold fast to our confession.
For we do not have a high priest
   who is unable to sympathize with our weaknesses,
   but one who has similarly been tested in every way,
   yet without sin.
So let us confidently approach the throne of grace
   to receive mercy and to find grace for timely help.

The word of the Lord.** All: **Thanks be to God.**

Gospel A Longer Form (Mark 10:35-45)
Alleluia (Mark 10:45)
℣. Alleluia, alleluia. ℟. **Alleluia, alleluia.**
℣. The Son of Man came to serve
and to give his life as a ransom for many. ℟.

✠ **A reading from the holy Gospel according to Mark**

All: **Glory to you, O Lord.**

The Son of Man came to give his life as a ransom for many.

**James and John, the sons of Zebedee, came to Jesus and said to him,
   "Teacher, we want you to do for us whatever we ask of you."
He replied, "What do you wish me to do for you?"
They answered him, "Grant that in your glory
   we may sit one at your right and the other at your left."
Jesus said to them, "You do not know what you are asking.
Can you drink the cup that I drink
   or be baptized with the baptism with which I am baptized?"**

They said to him, "We can."
Jesus said to them, "The cup that I drink, you will drink,
   and with the baptism with which I am baptized, you
      will be baptized;
   but to sit at my right or at my left is not mine to give
   but is for those for whom it has been prepared."
When the ten heard this, they became indignant at
   James and John.
Jesus summoned them and said to them,
   "You know that those who are recognized as rulers
      over the Gentiles
   lord it over them,
   and their great ones make their authority over them
      felt.
But it shall not be so among you.
Rather, whoever wishes to be great among you will be
   your servant;
   whoever wishes to be first among you will be the slave
      of all.
For the Son of Man did not come to be served
   but to serve and to give his life as a ransom for many."

The Gospel of the Lord. All: **Praise to you, Lord Jesus Christ.**

Or:

B Shorter Form (Mark 10:42-45)

✠ **A reading from the holy Gospel according to Mark**

All: **Glory to you, O Lord.**

The Son of Man came to give his life as a ransom for many.

Jesus summoned the twelve and said to them,
   "You know that those who are recognized as rulers
      over the Gentiles
   lord it over them,
   and their great ones make their authority over them
      felt.

But it shall not be so among you.
Rather, whoever wishes to be great among you will be
    your servant;
    whoever wishes to be first among you will be the slave
        of all.
For the Son of Man did not come to be served
    but to serve and to give his life as a ransom for many."

The Gospel of the Lord. All: Praise to you, Lord Jesus Christ.

Prayer over the Offerings
Grant us, Lord, we pray,
a sincere respect for your gifts,
that, through the purifying action of your grace,
we may be cleansed by the very mysteries we serve.
Through Christ our Lord. All: Amen.

Communion Antiphon (Cf. Psalm 33[32]:18-19)
Behold, the eyes of the Lord
are on those who fear him,
who hope in his merciful love,
to rescue their souls from death,
to keep them alive in famine.

Or:

(Mark 10:45)
The Son of Man has come
to give his life as a ranson for many.

Prayer after Communion
Grant, O Lord, we pray,
that, benefiting from participation in heavenly things,
we may be helped by what you give in this present age
and prepared for the gifts that are eternal.
Through Christ our Lord. All: Amen.

Thirtieth Sunday in Ordinary Time

October 25, 2015

Reflection on the Gospel

The verbs describing Bartimaeus's actions in this gospel say everything about faith, encountering Jesus, and choosing to follow him. He cried out, kept calling, threw aside his cloak, sprang up and came to Jesus, stated his request, received his sight, followed Jesus. Such need, such urgency, such conviction! These verbs describe Bartimaeus's faith-in-action, his deepening relationship with Jesus. Faith is the insight and cause of action. So must it be for us.

- *Faith in action, I . . .*

—Living Liturgy™, *Thirtieth Sunday in Ordinary Time 2015*

Entrance Antiphon (Cf. Psalm 105[104]:3-4)

Let the hearts that seek the Lord rejoice;
turn to the Lord and his strength;
constantly seek his face.

Collect

Almighty ever-living God,
increase our faith, hope and charity,
and make us love what you command,
so that we may merit what you promise.
Through our Lord Jesus Christ, your Son,
who lives and reigns with you in the unity of the Holy Spirit,
one God, for ever and ever. **All: Amen.**

Reading I (L 149-B) (Jeremiah 31:7-9)

A reading from the Book of the Prophet Jeremiah

The blind and the lame I will bring back: I will console them.

**Thus says the Lord:
Shout with joy for Jacob,
exult at the head of the nations;
proclaim your praise and say:**

The Lord has delivered his people,
   the remnant of Israel.
Behold, I will bring them back
   from the land of the north;
I will gather them from the ends of the world,
   with the blind and the lame in their midst,
the mothers and those with child;
   they shall return as an immense throng.
They departed in tears,
   but I will console them and guide them;
I will lead them to brooks of water,
   on a level road, so that none shall stumble.
For I am a father to Israel,
   Ephraim is my first-born.

The word of the Lord. **All: Thanks be to God.**

Responsorial Psalm 126

P-378

The Lord has done great things for us; we are filled with joy,____ we are filled with joy.

Music: Jay F. Hunstiger, © 1990, administered by Liturgical Press. All rights reserved.

Psalm 126:1-2ab, 2cd-3, 4-5, 6

℟. (3) **The Lord has done great things for us; we are filled with joy.**

When the Lord brought back the captives of Zion,
   we were like men dreaming.
Then our mouth was filled with laughter,
   and our tongue with rejoicing. ℟.

Then they said among the nations,
   "The Lord has done great things for them."
The Lord has done great things for us;
   we are glad indeed. ℟.

(continued)

Restore our fortunes, O LORD,
>   like the torrents in the southern desert.
Those that sow in tears
>   shall reap rejoicing. ℟.

Although they go forth weeping,
>   carrying the seed to be sown,
they shall come back rejoicing,
>   carrying their sheaves. ℟.

READING II (Hebrews 5:1-6)

A reading from the Letter to the Hebrews

You are a priest forever according to the order of Melchizedek.

Brothers and sisters:
Every high priest is taken from among men
>   **and made their representative before God,**
>   **to offer gifts and sacrifices for sins.**
He is able to deal patiently with the ignorant and erring,
>   **for he himself is beset by weakness**
>   **and so, for this reason, must make sin offerings for himself**
as well as for the people.
No one takes this honor upon himself
>   **but only when called by God,**
>   **just as Aaron was.**
In the same way,
>   **it was not Christ who glorified himself in becoming high priest,**
>   **but rather the one who said to him:**
>>   *You are my son:*
>>   *this day I have begotten you;*
>   **just as he says in another place:**
>>   *You are a priest forever*
>>   *according to the order of Melchizedek.*

The word of the Lord. All: **Thanks be to God.**

Gospel (Mark 10:46-52)
Alleluia (See 2 Timothy 1:10)

℣. Alleluia, alleluia. ℟. **Alleluia, alleluia.**
℣. Our Savior Jesus Christ destroyed death
and brought life to light through the Gospel. ℟.

✠ **A reading from the holy Gospel according to Mark.**

All: **Glory to you, O Lord.**

Master, I want to see.

**As Jesus was leaving Jericho with his disciples and a sizable crowd,
Bartimaeus, a blind man, the son of Timaeus,
sat by the roadside begging.
On hearing that it was Jesus of Nazareth,
he began to cry out and say,
"Jesus, son of David, have pity on me."
And many rebuked him, telling him to be silent.
But he kept calling out all the more,
"Son of David, have pity on me."
Jesus stopped and said, "Call him."
So they called the blind man, saying to him,
"Take courage; get up, Jesus is calling you."
He threw aside his cloak, sprang up,
and came to Jesus.
Jesus said to him in reply, "What do you want me to do for you?"
The blind man replied to him, "Master, I want to see."
Jesus told him, "Go your way; your faith has saved you."
Immediately he received his sight
and followed him on the way.**

The Gospel of the Lord. All: **Praise to you, Lord Jesus Christ.**

Prayer over the Offerings
Look, we pray, O Lord,
on the offerings we make to your majesty,
that whatever is done by us in your service
may be directed above all to your glory.
Through Christ our Lord. All: **Amen.**

COMMUNION ANTIPHON (Cf. Psalm 20[19]:6)
We will ring out our joy at your saving help
and exult in the name of our God.

Or:

(Ephesians 5:2)
Christ loved us and gave himself up for us,
as a fragrant offering to God.

PRAYER AFTER COMMUNION
May your Sacraments, O Lord, we pray,
perfect in us what lies within them,
that what we now celebrate in signs
we may one day possess in truth.
Through Christ our Lord. All: **Amen.**

All Saints

November 1, 2015

Reflection of the Gospel

It is no accident that the Gospel of Matthew has Jesus go "up the mountain," traditionally a place associated with divine encounter, to teach the Beatitudes to his disciples. The Beatitudes reveal the very Being of God ("Blessed," holy), God's care for God's beloved people ("poor in spirit," "those who mourn," etc.), God's intent for faithful ones ("theirs is the kingdom of heaven"). The Beatitudes reveal the mind and heart of God. Those who have encountered God and lived the Beatitudes have the same mind and heart. We call them "saints."

• *Encounter God, climb the mountain, be . . .*

—Living Liturgy™, *All Saints 2015*

ENTRANCE ANTIPHON
Let us all rejoice in the Lord,
as we celebrate the feast day in honor of all the Saints,
at whose festival the Angels rejoice
and praise the Son of God.

Collect

Almighty ever-living God,
by whose gift we venerate in one celebration
the merits of all the Saints,
bestow on us, we pray,
through the prayers of so many intercessors,
an abundance of the reconciliation with you
for which we earnestly long.
Through our Lord Jesus Christ, your Son,
who lives and reigns with you in the unity of the Holy Spirit,
one God, for ever and ever. All: **Amen.**

Reading I (L 667) (Revelation 7:2-4, 9-14)

A reading from the Book of Revelation

I had a vision of a great multitude, which no one could count, from every nation, race, people and tongue.

I, John, saw another angel come up from the East,
   holding the seal of the living God.
He cried out in a loud voice to the four angels
   who were given power to damage the land and the sea,
   "Do not damage the land or the sea or the trees
      until we put the seal on the foreheads of the servants
         of our God."
I heard the number of those who had been marked with
      the seal,
   one hundred and forty-four thousand marked
   from every tribe of the children of Israel.

After this I had a vision of a great multitude,
   which no one could count,
   from every nation, race, people, and tongue.
They stood before the throne and before the Lamb,
   wearing white robes and holding palm branches in
      their hands.
They cried out in a loud voice:

   "Salvation comes from our God, who is seated on the
      throne,
         and from the Lamb."

All the angels stood around the throne
   and around the elders and the four living creatures.
They prostrated themselves before the throne,
   worshiped God, and exclaimed:

   "Amen. Blessing and glory, wisdom and thanksgiving,
      honor, power, and might
   be to our God forever and ever. Amen."

Then one of the elders spoke up and said to me,
   "Who are these wearing white robes, and where did
      they come from?"
I said to him, "My lord, you are the one who knows."
He said to me,
   "These are the ones who have survived the time of
      great distress;
they have washed their robes
   and made them white in the Blood of the Lamb."

The word of the Lord. All: **Thanks be to God.**

Responsorial Psalm 24

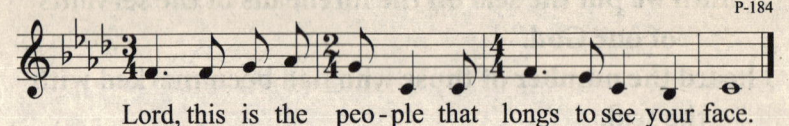

Lord, this is the peo-ple that longs to see your face.

Music: Jay F. Hunstiger, © 1990, administered by Liturgical Press. All rights reserved.

Psalm 24:1bc-2, 3-4ab, 5-6

℟. (*See* 6) **Lord, this is the people that longs to see your face.**

   The Lord's are the earth and its fullness;
      the world and those who dwell in it.
   For he founded it upon the seas
      and established it upon the rivers. ℟.

   Who can ascend the mountain of the Lord?
      or who may stand in his holy place?
   One whose hands are sinless, whose heart is clean,
      who desires not what is vain. ℟.

He shall receive a blessing from the Lord,
> a reward from God his savior.
Such is the race that seeks him,
> that seeks the face of the God of Jacob. ℟.

Reading II (1 John 3:1-3)
A reading from the first Letter of Saint John

We shall see God as he is.

Beloved:
See what love the Father has bestowed on us
> that we may be called the children of God.
Yet so we are.
The reason the world does not know us
> is that it did not know him.
Beloved, we are God's children now;
> what we shall be has not yet been revealed.
We do know that when it is revealed we shall be like him,
> for we shall see him as he is.
Everyone who has this hope based on him makes himself pure,
> as he is pure.

The word of the Lord. All: **Thanks be to God.**

Gospel (Matthew 5:1-12a)
Alleluia (Matthew 11:28)
℣. Alleluia, alleluia. ℟. **Alleluia, alleluia.**
℣. Come to me, all you who labor and are burdened,
> and I will give you rest, says the Lord. ℟.

✠ **A reading from the holy Gospel according to Matthew**

All: **Glory to you, O Lord.**

Rejoice and be glad, for your reward will be great in heaven.

When Jesus saw the crowds, he went up the mountain,
> and after he had sat down, his disciples came to him.
He began to teach them, saying:

> "Blessed are the poor in spirit,
> > for theirs is the Kingdom of heaven.

Blessed are they who mourn,
  for they will be comforted.
Blessed are the meek,
  for they will inherit the land.
Blessed are they who hunger and thirst for righteousness,
  for they will be satisfied.
Blessed are the merciful,
  for they will be shown mercy.
Blessed are the clean of heart,
  for they will see God.
Blessed are the peacemakers,
  for they will be called children of God.
Blessed are they who are persecuted for the sake of righteousness,
  for theirs is the Kingdom of heaven.
Blessed are you when they insult you and persecute you and utter every kind of evil against you falsely because of me.
Rejoice and be glad,
  for your reward will be great in heaven."

The Gospel of the Lord. All: **Praise to you, Lord Jesus Christ.**

Prayer over the Offerings

May these offerings we bring in honor of all the Saints
be pleasing to you, O Lord,
and grant that, just as we believe the Saints
to be already assured of immortality,
so we may experience their concern for our salvation.
Through Christ our Lord. All: **Amen.**

Communion Antiphon (Matthew 5:8-10)

Blessed are the clean of heart, for they shall see God.
Blessed are the peacemakers,
for they shall be called children of God.
Blessed are they who are persecuted for the sake of righteousness,
for theirs is the Kingdom of Heaven.

Prayer after Communion

As we adore you, O God, who alone are holy
and wonderful in all your Saints,
we implore your grace,
so that, coming to perfect holiness in the fullness of your love,
we may pass from this pilgrim table
to the banquet of our heavenly homeland.
Through Christ our Lord. **All: Amen.**

Thirty-Second Sunday in Ordinary Time

November 8, 2015

Reflection of the Gospel

Jesus teaches the crowds to beware of the hypocrisy of the scribes who know God's word and law, yet seek places of honor and hurt those whom the law demands they protect—the widows. Jesus condemns them severely. "Calling his disciples to himself," he teaches them that they are not to do like the scribes. They are instead to do like the widow in the temple who gives all she has. True disciples give all they have, their whole livelihood—not goods, but themselves.

- *Keep nothing back, give all to God . . .*

—Living Liturgy™, *Thirty-Second Sunday in Ordinary Time 2015*

Entrance Antiphon (Cf. Psalm 88[87]:3)

Let my prayer come into your presence.
Incline your ear to my cry for help, O Lord.

Collect

Almighty and merciful God,
graciously keep from us all adversity,
so that, unhindered in mind and body alike,
we may pursue in freedom of heart
the things that are yours.

Through our Lord Jesus Christ, your Son,
who lives and reigns with you in the unity of the Holy Spirit,
one God, for ever and ever. All: **Amen.**

READING I (L 155-B) (1 Kings 17:10-16)
A reading from the first Book of Kings

The widow made a little cake from her flour and gave it to Elijah.

**In those days, Elijah the prophet went to Zarephath.
As he arrived at the entrance of the city,
a widow was gathering sticks there; he called out to her,
"Please bring me a small cupful of water to drink."
She left to get it, and he called out after her,
"Please bring along a bit of bread."
She answered, "As the LORD, your God, lives,
I have nothing baked; there is only a handful of flour
in my jar
and a little oil in my jug.
Just now I was collecting a couple of sticks,
to go in and prepare something for myself and my son;
when we have eaten it, we shall die."
Elijah said to her, "Do not be afraid.
Go and do as you propose.
But first make me a little cake and bring it to me.
Then you can prepare something for yourself and your
son.
For the LORD, the God of Israel, says,
'The jar of flour shall not go empty,
nor the jug of oil run dry,
until the day when the LORD sends rain upon the earth.'"
She left and did as Elijah had said.
She was able to eat for a year, and he and her son as well;
the jar of flour did not go empty,
nor the jug of oil run dry,
as the LORD had foretold through Elijah.**

The word of the Lord. All: **Thanks be to God.**

Responsorial Psalm 146

Praise the Lord, my soul! Al-le-lu-ia.

Music: Jay F. Hunstiger, © 1990, administered by Liturgical Press. All rights reserved.

Psalm 146:7, 8-9, 9-10

℟. (1b) **Praise the Lord, my soul!** *or:* ℟. **Alleluia.**

> The LORD keeps faith forever,
>> secures justice for the oppressed,
>> gives food to the hungry.
> The LORD sets captives free. ℟.

> The LORD gives sight to the blind;
>> the LORD raises up those who were bowed down.
> The LORD loves the just;
>> the LORD protects strangers. ℟.

> The fatherless and the widow he sustains,
>> but the way of the wicked he thwarts.
> The LORD shall reign forever;
>> your God, O Zion, through all generations. Alleluia. ℟.

Reading II (Hebrews 9:24-28)

A reading from the Letter to the Hebrews

Christ was offered once to take away the sins of many.

**Christ did not enter into a sanctuary made by hands,
a copy of the true one, but heaven itself,
that he might now appear before God on our behalf.
Not that he might offer himself repeatedly,
as the high priest enters each year into the sanctuary
with blood that is not his own;
if that were so, he would have had to suffer repeatedly
from the foundation of the world.
But now once for all he has appeared at the end of the ages
to take away sin by his sacrifice.**

Just as it is appointed that human beings die once,
   and after this the judgment, so also Christ,
   offered once to take away the sins of many,
   will appear a second time, not to take away sin
   but to bring salvation to those who eagerly await him.

The word of the Lord. All: Thanks be to God.

GOSPEL *A* Longer Form (Mark 12:38-44)
ALLELUIA (Matthew 5:3)

℣. Alleluia, alleluia. ℟. **Alleluia, alleluia.**
℣. Blessed are the poor in spirit,
   for theirs is the kingdom of heaven. ℟.

✛ A reading from the holy Gospel according to Mark

All: **Glory to you, O Lord.**

This poor widow put in more than all the others.

In the course of his teaching Jesus said to the crowds,
   "Beware of the scribes, who like to go around in long robes
   and accept greetings in the marketplaces,
   seats of honor in synagogues,
   and places of honor at banquets.
They devour the houses of widows and, as a pretext
   recite lengthy prayers.
They will receive a very severe condemnation."

He sat down opposite the treasury
   and observed how the crowd put money into the treasury.
Many rich people put in large sums.
A poor widow also came and put in two small coins
   worth a few cents.
Calling his disciples to himself, he said to them,
   "Amen, I say to you, this poor widow put in more
   than all the other contributors to the treasury.

For they have all contributed from their surplus wealth,
> but she, from her poverty, has contributed all she had,
> her whole livelihood."

The Gospel of the Lord. All: **Praise to you, Lord Jesus Christ.**

Or:

B Shorter Form (Mark 12:41-44)

☩ A reading from the holy Gospel according to Mark

All: **Glory to you, O Lord.**

This poor widow put in more than all the others.

Jesus sat down opposite the treasury
> and observed how the crowd put money into the treasury.

Many rich people put in large sums.
A poor widow also came and put in two small coins
> worth a few cents.

Calling his disciples to himself, he said to them,
> "Amen, I say to you, this poor widow put in more
> than all the other contributors to the treasury.

For they have all contributed from their surplus wealth,
> but she, from her poverty, has contributed all she had,
> her whole livelihood."

The Gospel of the Lord. All: **Praise to you, Lord Jesus Christ.**

Prayer over the Offerings

Look with favor, we pray, O Lord,
upon the sacrificial gifts offered here,
that, celebrating in mystery the Passion of your Son,
we may honor it with loving devotion.
Through Christ our Lord. All: **Amen.**

Communion Antiphon (Cf. Psalm 23[22]:1-2)

The Lord is my shepherd; there is nothing I shall want.
Fresh and green are the pastures where he gives me repose,
near restful waters he leads me.

Or:

(Cf. Luke 24:35)
The disciples recognized the Lord Jesus in the breaking of bread.

PRAYER AFTER COMMUNION
Nourished by this sacred gift, O Lord,
we give you thanks and beseech your mercy,
that, by the pouring forth of your Spirit,
the grace of integrity may endure
in those your heavenly power has entered.
Through Christ our Lord. All: **Amen.**

Thirty-Third Sunday in Ordinary Time

November 15, 2015

Reflection on the Gospel

In this gospel Jesus teaches about the future; his words deal with cosmic events, his final coming in power to overcome darkness, and his drawing the elect into the light of his final glory. Jesus uses the image of the greening of "the fig tree" when summer is near as a sign that "he is near." Those who hear and heed his words are in the greening of their lives. For them, the future is now.

• *See the signs, hear the words, the future is now . . .*

—Living Liturgy™, *Thirty-Third Sunday in Ordinary Time 2015*

ENTRANCE ANTIPHON (Jeremiah 29:11, 12, 14)
The Lord said: I think thoughts of peace and not of affliction.
You will call upon me, and I will answer you,
and I will lead back your captives from every place.

COLLECT
Grant us, we pray, O Lord our God,
the constant gladness of being devoted to you,
for it is full and lasting happiness
to serve with constancy
the author of all that is good.
Through our Lord Jesus Christ, your Son,

who lives and reigns with you in the unity of the Holy Spirit, one God, for ever and ever. All: **Amen.**

Reading I (L 158-B) (Daniel 12:1-3)
A reading from the Book of the prophet Daniel
At that time your people shall escape.

In those days, I, Daniel,
   heard this word of the Lord:
"At that time there shall arise
   Michael, the great prince,
   guardian of your people;
it shall be a time unsurpassed in distress
   since nations began until that time.
At that time your people shall escape,
   everyone who is found written in the book.

"Many of those who sleep in the dust of the earth shall awake;
   some shall live forever,
   others shall be an everlasting horror and disgrace.

"But the wise shall shine brightly
   like the splendor of the firmament,
and those who lead the many to justice
   shall be like the stars forever."

The word of the Lord. All: **Thanks be to God.**

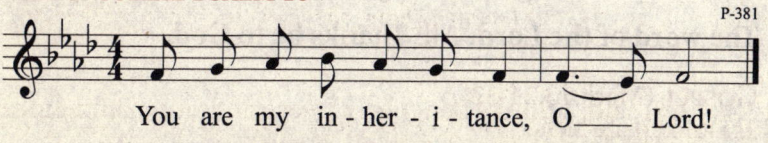

Responsorial Psalm 16

You are my in-her-i-tance, O ___ Lord!

Music: Jay F. Hunstiger, © 1990, administered by Liturgical Press. All rights reserved.

Psalm 16:5, 8, 9-10, 11

℟. (1) **You are my inheritance, O Lord!**
   O Lord, my allotted portion and my cup,
     you it is who hold fast my lot.
   I set the Lord ever before me;
     with him at my right hand I shall not be disturbed. ℟.

(continued)

Therefore my heart is glad and my soul rejoices,
> my body, too, abides in confidence;
because you will not abandon my soul to the netherworld,
> nor will you suffer your faithful one to undergo corruption. ℟.

You will show me the path to life,
> fullness of joys in your presence,
> the delights at your right hand forever. ℟.

Reading II (Hebrews 10:11-14, 18)
A reading from the Letter to the Hebrews

By one offering he has made perfect forever those who are being consecrated.

Brothers and sisters:
Every priest stands daily at his ministry,
> **offering frequently those same sacrifices**
> **that can never take away sins.**
But this one offered one sacrifice for sins,
> **and took his seat forever at the right hand of God;**
> **now he waits until his enemies are made his footstool.**
For by one offering
> **he has made perfect forever those who are being consecrated.**

Where there is forgiveness of these,
> **there is no longer offering for sin.**

The word of the Lord. All: **Thanks be to God.**

Gospel (Mark 13:24-32)
Alleluia (Luke 21:36)
℣. Alleluia, alleluia. ℟. **Alleluia, alleluia.**
℣. Be vigilant at all times
> and pray that you have the strength to stand before the Son of Man. ℟.

✠ **A reading from the holy Gospel according to Mark**

All: **Glory to you, O Lord.**

He will gather his elect from the four winds.

Jesus said to his disciples:
"In those days after that tribulation
>   the sun will be darkened,
>   and the moon will not give its light,
>   and the stars will be falling from the sky,
>   and the powers in the heavens will be shaken.

"And then they will see 'the Son of Man coming in the clouds'
>   with great power and glory,
>   and then he will send out the angels
>   and gather his elect from the four winds,
>   from the end of the earth to the end of the sky.

"Learn a lesson from the fig tree.
When its branch becomes tender and sprouts leaves,
>   you know that summer is near.
In the same way, when you see these things happening,
>   know that he is near, at the gates.
Amen, I say to you,
>   this generation will not pass away
>   until all these things have taken place.
Heaven and earth will pass away,
>   but my words will not pass away.

"But of that day or hour, no one knows,
>   neither the angels in heaven, nor the Son, but only the Father."

The Gospel of the Lord. **All: Praise to you, Lord Jesus Christ.**

Prayer over the Offerings
Grant, O Lord, we pray,
that what we offer in the sight of your majesty
may obtain for us the grace of being devoted to you
and gain us the prize of everlasting happiness.
Through Christ our Lord. **All: Amen.**

Communion Antiphon (Psalm 73[72]:28)
To be near God is my happiness,
to place my hope in God the Lord.

Or:

(Mark 11:23-24)
Amen, I say to you, whatever you ask in prayer,
believe that you will receive,
and it shall be given to you, says the Lord.

PRAYER AFTER COMMUNION
We have partaken of the gifts of this sacred mystery,
humbly imploring, O Lord,
that what your Son commanded us to do
in memory of him
may bring us growth in charity.
Through Christ our Lord. All: **Amen.**

Our Lord Jesus Christ, King of the Universe

November 22, 2015

Reflection on the Gospel

In this conversation Pilate questions Jesus about his identity ("Are you the King of the Jews?") and about why he is on trial ("What have you done?"). What unfolds is a conversation about two very different worlds. That of Pilate and the chief priests, in which fighting, falsehood, and obstinacy predominate. That of Jesus, in which life, truth, and openness prevail. Yes, Jesus is a King—but of a kingdom different from Herod's. To which kingdom do we choose to belong?

- *What kind of a king is Jesus?...*

—Living Liturgy™, *Christ the King 2015*

ENTRANCE ANTIPHON (Revelation 5:12; 1:6)
How worthy is the Lamb who was slain,
to receive power and divinity,
and wisdom and strength and honor.
To him belong glory and power for ever and ever.

Collect

Almighty ever-living God,
whose will is to restore all things
in your beloved Son, the King of the universe,
grant, we pray,
that the whole creation, set free from slavery,
may render your majesty service
and ceaselessly proclaim your praise.
Through our Lord Jesus Christ, your Son,
who lives and reigns with you in the unity of the Holy Spirit,
one God, for ever and ever. All: **Amen.**

Reading I (L 161-B) (Daniel 7:13-14)

A reading from the Book of the Prophet Daniel

His dominion is an everlasting dominion.

**As the visions during the night continued, I saw
one like a Son of man coming,
on the clouds of heaven;
when he reached the Ancient One
and was presented before him,
the one like a Son of man received dominion, glory,
and kingship;
all peoples, nations, and languages serve him.
His dominion is an everlasting dominion
that shall not be taken away,
his kingship shall not be destroyed.**

The word of the Lord. All: **Thanks be to God.**

Responsorial Psalm 93

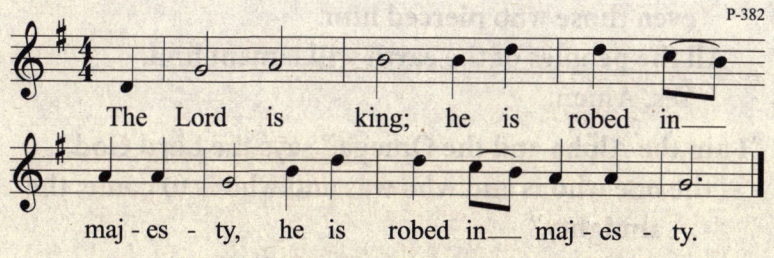

The Lord is king; he is robed in maj-es-ty, he is robed in maj-es-ty.

Music: Jay F. Hunstiger, © 1990, administered by Liturgical Press. All rights reserved.

Psalm 93:1, 1-2, 5

℟. (1a) **The Lord is king; he is robed in majesty.**

The L<small>ORD</small> is king, in splendor robed;
 robed is the L<small>ORD</small> and girt about with strength. ℟.

And he has made the world firm,
 not to be moved.
Your throne stands firm from of old;
 from everlasting you are, O L<small>ORD</small>. ℟.

Your decrees are worthy of trust indeed;
 holiness befits your house,
 O L<small>ORD</small>, for length of days. ℟.

R<small>EADING</small> II (Revelation 1:5-8)
A reading from the Book of Revelation

The ruler of the kings of the earth has made us into a kingdom, priests for his God and Father.

**Jesus Christ is the faithful witness,
 the firstborn of the dead and ruler of the kings of the earth.
To him who loves us and has freed us from our sins by his blood,
 who has made us into a kingdom, priests for his God and Father,
to him be glory and power forever and ever. Amen.**

Behold, he is coming amid the clouds,
 and every eye will see him,
 even those who pierced him.
All the peoples of the earth will lament him.
 Yes. Amen.

"I am the Alpha and the Omega," says the Lord God,
 "the one who is and who was and who is to come, the almighty."

The word of the Lord. All: Thanks be to God.

Gospel (John 18:33b-37)
Alleluia (Mark 11:9, 10)

℣. Alleluia, alleluia. ℟. **Alleluia, alleluia.**
℣. Blessed is he who comes in the name of the Lord!
   Blessed is the kingdom of our father David that is to come! ℟.

✠ A reading from the holy Gospel according to John

All: **Glory to you, O Lord.**

You say I am a king.

Pilate said to Jesus,
   "Are you the King of the Jews?"
Jesus answered, "Do you say this on your own
   or have others told you about me?"
Pilate answered, "I am not a Jew, am I?
Your own nation and the chief priests handed you over
   to me.
What have you done?"
Jesus answered, "My kingdom does not belong to this
   world.
If my kingdom did belong to this world,
   my attendants would be fighting
   to keep me from being handed over to the Jews.
But as it is, my kingdom is not here."
So Pilate said to him, "Then you are a king?"
Jesus answered, "You say I am a king.
For this I was born and for this I came into the world,
   to testify to the truth.
Everyone who belongs to the truth listens to my voice."

The Gospel of the Lord. All: **Praise to you, Lord Jesus Christ.**

Prayer over the Offerings
As we offer you, O Lord, the sacrifice
by which the human race is reconciled to you,
we humbly pray,
that your Son himself may bestow on all nations
the gifts of unity and peace.
Through Christ our Lord. All: **Amen.**

COMMUNION ANTIPHON (Psalm 29[28]:10-11)
The Lord sits as King for ever.
The Lord will bless his people with peace.

PRAYER AFTER COMMUNION
Having received the food of immortality,
we ask, O Lord,
that, glorying in obedience
to the commands of Christ, the King of the universe,
we may live with him eternally in his heavenly Kingdom.
Who lives and reigns for ever and ever. All: **Amen.**

Eucharistic Prayer for Reconciliation I

Preface

It is truly right and just
that we should always give you thanks,
Lord, holy Father, almighty and eternal God.

For you do not cease to spur us on
to possess a more abundant life
and, being rich in mercy,
you constantly offer pardon
and call on sinners
to trust in your forgiveness alone.

Never did you turn away from us,
and, though time and again we have broken your covenant,
you have bound the human family to yourself
through Jesus your Son, our Redeemer,
with a new bond of love so tight
that it can never be undone.

Even now you set before your people
a time of grace and reconciliation,
and, as they turn back to you in spirit,
you grant them hope in Christ Jesus
and a desire to be of service to all,
while they entrust themselves
more fully to the Holy Spirit.

And so, filled with wonder,
we extol the power of your love,
and, proclaiming our joy
at the salvation that comes from you,
we join in the heavenly hymn of countless hosts,
as without end we acclaim:

Holy, Holy, Holy Lord God of hosts.
Heaven and earth are full of your glory.
Hosanna in the highest.
Blessed is he who comes in the name of the Lord.
Hosanna in the highest.

Priest:
You are indeed Holy, O Lord,
and from the world's beginning
are ceaselessly at work,
so that the human race may become holy,
just as you yourself are holy.
Look, we pray, upon your people's offerings
and pour out on them the power of your Spirit,

Eucharistic Prayer for Reconciliation I

that they may become the Body and ✜ Blood
of your beloved Son, Jesus Christ,
in whom we, too, are your sons and daughters.
Indeed, though we once were lost
and could not approach you,
you loved us with the greatest love:
for your Son, who alone is just,
handed himself over to death,
and did not disdain to be nailed for our sake
to the wood of the Cross.

But before his arms were outstretched between heaven and earth,
to become the lasting sign of your covenant,
he desired to celebrate the Passover with his disciples.

As he ate with them,
he took bread
and, giving you thanks, he said the blessing,
broke the bread and gave it to them, saying:

Take this, all of you, and eat of it,
for this is my Body,
which will be given up for you.

In a similar way, when supper was ended,
knowing that he was about to reconcile all things in himself
through his Blood to be shed on the Cross,
he took the chalice, filled with the fruit of the vine,
and once more giving you thanks,
handed the chalice to his disciples, saying:

Take this, all of you, and drink from it,
for this is the chalice of my Blood,
the Blood of the new and eternal covenant,
which will be poured out for you and for many
for the forgiveness of sins.

Do this in memory of me.

The mystery of faith.

People:

A **We proclaim your Death, O Lord,**
and profess your Resurrection
until you come again.

B **When we eat this Bread and drink this Cup,**
we proclaim your Death, O Lord,
until you come again.

Eucharistic Prayer for Reconciliation I

C Save us, Savior of the world,
for by your Cross and Resurrection
you have set us free.

Priest:
Therefore, as we celebrate
the memorial of your Son Jesus Christ,
who is our Passover and our surest peace,
we celebrate his Death and Resurrection from the dead,
and looking forward to his blessed Coming,
we offer you, who are our faithful and merciful God,
this sacrificial Victim
who reconciles to you the human race.

Look kindly, most compassionate Father,
on those you unite to yourself
by the Sacrifice of your Son,
and grant that, by the power of the Holy Spirit,
as they partake of this one Bread and one Chalice,
they may be gathered into one Body in Christ,
who heals every division.

Be pleased to keep us always
in communion of mind and heart,
together with N. our Pope and N. our Bishop.*
Help us to work together
for the coming of your Kingdom,
until the hour when we stand before you,
Saints among the Saints in the halls of heaven,
with the Blessed Virgin Mary, Mother of God,
the blessed Apostles and all the Saints,
and with our deceased brothers and sisters,
whom we humbly commend to your mercy.

Then, freed at last from the wound of corruption
and made fully into a new creation,
we shall sing to you with gladness
the thanksgiving of Christ,
who lives for all eternity.

Through him, and with him, and in him,
O God, almighty Father,
in the unity of the Holy Spirit,
all glory and honor is yours,
for ever and ever.

---

* Mention may be made here of the Coadjutor Bishop, or Auxiliary Bishops,
as noted in the *General Instruction of the Roman Missal*, no. 149.

Personal Prayers

Thy Holy Name
Blessed be God. Blessed be his Holy Name. Blessed be Jesus Christ true God and true man. Blessed be the name of Jesus. I believe, O Jesus that thou art the Christ the Son of the Living God. I proclaim my love for the Vicar of Christ on earth. I believe all the sacred truths which the Holy Catholic Church believes and teaches. I promise to give good example by the regular practice of my faith. In honor of his divine Name—I pledge myself against perjury, blasphemy, profanity, and obscene speech. I pledge my loyalty to the flag of my country and to the God-given principles of freedom, justice and happiness for which it stands. I pledge my support to all lawful authority both civil and religious. I dedicate myself to the honor of the sacred name of Jesus Christ and beg that he will keep me faithful to these pledges until death. Amen.

Memorare
Remember, O most gracious Virgin Mary that never was it known that anyone who fled to your protection, implored your help, or sought your intercession was left unaided. Inspired with this confidence, we fly to you, O Virgin of virgins, our Mother. To you we come; before you we stand, sinful and sorrowful. O Mother of the word incarnate, despise not our petitions, but in your mercy, hear and answer us. Amen.

A Prayer for Families
Heavenly Father, you have provided us with a magnificent example in the Holy Family of Jesus, Mary, and Joseph. Give us the grace to follow that ideal through the practice of family virtues in the bond of charity and thereby assure ourselves of living happily forever in your heavenly home. This we ask of you.

Prayer for Life

Lord Jesus Christ, Son of God, in you we adore the eternal origin of all life. Born of the Father before all time, you were born of the Virgin Mary in time. In your humanity and person you sanctified motherhood from the first instant of conception through all stages, for our salvation. Recall all people to these divine blessings, to appreciate the unborn as persons and to enlighten every human being coming into this world. In your mercy avert your just anger from the enemies of life, to allow God's infants to give him glory and to be crowned with the heavenly life of grace. From the cross you called, "Behold your Mother." Amen.

Anima Christi

Soul of Christ, sanctify me.
Body of Christ, save me.
Blood of Christ, inebriate me.
Water from the side of Christ, wash me.
Passion of Christ, strengthen me.
O good Jesus, hear me.
Within thy wounds hide me.
Suffer me not to be separated from thee.
From the malicious enemy defend me.
In the hour of my death call me and bid me come unto thee
That with thy saints I may praise thee forever and ever.
    Amen.

Prayer of St. Teresa of Jesus

O my hope and Father and my creator and my true Lord and brother! When I remember how you said that your delights are to be with your children, my soul rejoices greatly. What words are these, O Lord of heaven and earth, to prevent any sinner from losing trust in you. At the time of your son's baptism, the voice which was heard said that your delight was in him. Can it be then Lord that you delight equally in us? Oh, what great mercy and what favor far beyond our deserving! Remember our great misery, O God, and look kindly upon our weakness, since you know all things.

GUIDELINES FOR RECEIVING COMMUNION

For Catholics

As Catholics, we fully participate in the celebration of the Eucharist when we receive Holy Communion. We are encouraged to receive Communion devoutly and frequently. In order to be properly disposed to receive Communion, participants should not be conscious of grave sin and normally should have fasted for one hour. A person who is conscious of grave sin is not to receive the Body and Blood of the Lord without prior sacramental confession except for a grave reason where there is no opportunity for confession. In this case, the person is to be mindful of the obligation to make an act of perfect contrition, including the intention of confessing as soon as possible (Code of Canon Law, canon 916). A frequent reception of the Sacrament of Penance is encouraged for all.

For our fellow Christians

We welcome our fellow Christians to this celebration of the Eucharist as our brothers and sisters. We pray that our common baptism and the action of the Holy Spirit in this Eucharist will draw us closer to one another and begin to dispel the sad divisions which separate us. We pray that these will lessen and finally disappear, in keeping with Christ's prayer for us "that they may all be one" (Jn 17:21).

Because Catholics believe that the celebration of the Eucharist is a sign of the reality of the oneness of faith, life, and worship, members of those churches with whom we are not yet fully united are ordinarily not admitted to Holy Communion. Eucharistic sharing in exceptional circumstances by other Christians requires permission according to the directives of the diocesan bishop and the provisions of canon law (canon 844 § 4). Members of the Orthodox Churches, the Assyrian Church of the East, and the Polish National Catholic Church are urged to respect the discipline of their own Churches. According to Roman Catholic discipline, the Code of Canon Law does not object to the reception of Communion by Christians of these Churches (canon 844 § 3).

For those not receiving Holy Communion

All who are not receiving Holy Communion are encouraged to express in their hearts a prayerful desire for unity with the Lord Jesus and with one another.

For non-Christians

We also welcome to this celebration those who do not share our faith in Jesus Christ. While we cannot admit them to Holy Communion, we ask them to offer their prayers for the peace and unity of the human family.

Copyright © 1997 United States Conference of Catholic Bishops. All rights reserved.